Early Reviews

Neighbourhoods in Urban India is a brilliant exploration of urbanism between the concept city and the lived city. With a multidisciplinary approach, the volume focuses on urban life lived between home and the world, institutions and experiences, representations and affects. While the theoretically sharp introduction alone is worth the price of the book, its fascinating range of empirically rich and analytically sophisticated excavations of neighbourhoods make the volume a must-have in the bookshelf on South Asian urban studies.

— **Gyan Prakash,** Professor of History, Princeton University, and the author of *Mumbai Fables* (2010)

A welcome addition to the literature of urban studies, this book on neighbourhoods opens up a new dimension to comprehend urban India. A must-read for those who wish to study the micro aspects of contemporary urbanity.

— **Sujata Patel**, Distinguished Professor, Department of Sociology, Savitribai Phule Pune University, Maharashtra

The neighbourhood has been a much referenced but significantly understudied component of Indian urbanism. This important collection by a new generation of scholars thankfully fills this gap, bringing together philosophical debates, ethnographic enquiries and histories of planning. We enter the debates on memory and history, time and space, regional, national and global movements of planning. The arguments flow from research conducted in cities and towns across India—Ahmedabad, Delhi, Banaras, Lucknow, Kolkata, Darbhanga—and much more. This book is a powerful addition to the study of Indian urbanism.

— **Ravi Sundaram**, Senior Fellow, Centre for the Study of Developing Societies (CSDS), Delhi

Neighbourhoods in Urban India

Neighbourhoods in Urban India

In between Home and the City

Edited by

Sadan Jha

Dev Nath Pathak

Amiya Kumar Das

BLOOMSBURY

NEW DELHI • LONDON • OXFORD • NEW YORK • SYDNEY

BLOOMSBURY INDIA
Bloomsbury Publishing India Pvt. Ltd
Second Floor, LSC Building No. 4, DDA Complex, Pocket C – 6 & 7,
Vasant Kunj, New Delhi, 110070

BLOOMSBURY, BLOOMSBURY ACADEMIC INDIA and the Diana logo
are trademarks of Bloomsbury Publishing Plc

First published in India 2021
This edition published 2021

ISBN: HB: 978-93-90252-62-6; eBook: 978-93-90252-64-0
2 4 6 8 10 9 7 5 3 1

Typeset in Manipal Technologies Limited

Printed and bound in India by Replika Press Pvt. Ltd.

Contents

Part III: Engendering Neighbourhood: Female Neighbours and Contested Subjectivities

Part IV: A House in a Neighbourhood: Planning, History and Aspirations of Housing

List of Figures and Maps

Acknowledgements

The making of this book entails various levels of preparation and participation. Connecting three temporally separated levels was, perhaps, one of the foregone conclusions: the advent of a research idea vis-à-vis neighbourhood, a formal meeting as part of manifold activities and the diverse possibility in future. While we can't confidently acknowledge the activities in future, we shall try to briefly name everything that has passed by.

The engagement with the idea of neighbourhoods in contemporary urban India began as an intellectual journey with emotional investment. Some of us from various disciplinary backgrounds from across India came along to start a collaborative research project. This involved scholars such as Sonal Mithal (architect, curator and faculty member at CEPT University, Ahmedabad), Gauri Bharat (Faculty of Architecture and Urban Planning, CEPT University, Ahmedabad), Aparajita De (Department of Geography, University of Delhi), Garima Dhabhai (Department of Political Science, Presidency University, Kolkata, West Bengal), Himadri Chatterjee (Department of Political Science, KNU, Asansol, West Bengal), Amiya Kumar Das (sociologist, Tezpur Central University, Assam), Dev Nath Pathak (sociologist, South Asian University, Delhi) and Sadan Jha (historian, Centre for Social Studies, Surat). We all came from different directions, are located at different places and have had different disciplinary groundings. Yet, we all shared common interests as far as the intrigue of the neighbourhood is concerned. In one way or another, we all are passionate about discussing city life in order to explore the relatively less explored in the context of India. Originally a research plan, the endeavour received another imperative: to formally meet and discuss. We were indeed contemplating meeting at various destinations at various stages of our engagement with the neighbourhood question, and we thought the first meeting could be a stepping stone in that direction.

Amiya Kumar Das undertook the ordeal of organising the seminar under the aegis of the Department of Sociology, Tezpur Central

University, Assam. Sadan Jha and Dev Nath Pathak were co-conveners of the seminar. There was an agreement that this should not be yet another seminar that merely adds to similar events proliferating around us. We all agreed to return to the fundamental purpose of the meeting: intensive engagement with one another without the usual constraints and vested interests that allegedly impair the deliberative and interrogative spirit of a seminar. The seminar 'Locating Neighbourhoods in the Global South' was held on 25–26 September 2019. Interestingly enough, many scholars participated in the seminar, in addition to the core group that had agreed to be part of the research project. We are grateful to Aparajita De, Brian Gomes, Camila Pierobon, Dhiraj Kumar Borkotoky, Garima Dhabai, Himadri Chatterjee, Jyotiraj Pathak, Kaushik Paul, Nirmali Goswami, Naorem Pushparani Chanu, Neha Gupta, Nishpriha Thakur, Praveen Priyadarshi, Ratan Kumar Roy, Samprati Pani, Sarmistha Das, Sreya Sen, Surojit Sen Gupta, Upashana Khanikar, Prafulla Kr. Nath, Smita Yadav and others for making the seminar a truly academic experience in which paper ideas were put through the rigour of earnest discussion. We extend our gratitude to Tezpur University for providing the necessary support to organise the seminar. We appreciate the help and support rendered by UNICEF Assam in organising a special panel on the vulnerability of women and children in the urbanscape. Our gratitude is also due to the colleagues at the Department of Sociology, Tezpur University, who contributed significantly in enlivening the intellectual energy of the discussions in the seminar; the senior colleagues—Chandan Kumar Sharma, Rabin Deka, Kedilezo Kikhi, P.K. Das—were instrumental in the process. Subhadeepta Ray, Sumeh S.S., Pamidi Hagjer and A.S. Shimreiwurng graciously added to the symposium. We are also grateful to Mithilesh Kumar Jha, IIT Gauhati, for accepting our invitation to be an observer of the seminar and offering a critical overview.

We especially acknowledge the guiding presence of AbdouMaliq Simone, who patiently heard all the papers, made his intervention and enthusiastically interacted with participants during the seminar. We would like to thank him for graciously agreeing to write the afterword of this book—he was forthright in accepting our request. We are more than sure that our association will continue in the future, too.

This book, unfortunately, is unable to accommodate all the papers presented in the seminar. A good number of papers were dropped after two rounds of blind reviews and extensive comments. The making of the book, thereby, included a prolonged process of editorial discussion between the editors and the authors during and after the seminar. Many of the authors in this volume had to revise their drafts four times in the light of comments from anonymous reviewers, editors and, finally, the anonymous referee commissioned by the publisher. We thank the authors for having undertaken an arduous journey with us without procedural ado or dissatisfaction. Many of the scholars, who participated in the seminar but could not take the time out to work on their papers to become part of this volume, also deserve our gratitude. We are confident that we will come together in other activities, meetings and books in the future.

We are grateful to Gyan Prakash, Ravi Sundaram and Sujata Patel. They read the manuscript and generously offered us advance praise. Such words have indeed pleasantly surprised us, given us a sense of achievement and motivated us in this collaborative exercise.

Last but not the least, we would like to thank the Bloomsbury team for their unstinting editorial support: Chandra Sekhar, the publisher, for taking a keen interest in the book and helping create, in consultation with the design team, an uplifting cover design; and Shreya Chakraborti and Thanglenhao Haokip, for being sensitive to the integrity of the text while editing the manuscript.

Sadan Jha
Dev Nath Pathak
Amiya Kumar Das

1

Introducing Neighbourhood: Reading the Urban Backward and Forward

Sadan Jha, Dev Nath Pathak and Amiya Kumar Das

From *gali* Qasim Jan of Ballimaran, the iconic address of the poet Mirza Ghalib, to innumerable Valmiki and Adarsh Nagars, from Lahurabir in Banaras to Barabazar of Kolkata and Dhanmondi of Dhaka, the landscape called 'city' in South Asia is inconceivable without their neighbourhoods. Outside the confines of social sciences, cities circulate in the memory of their neighbourhoods. The *wādās* of Maharashtra, the *pols* of Ahmedabad, the *pārās* of Bengal, the medieval *mohallās* and those *bastis* at the edge of colonial *urbs* are not merely addresses on postcards and in worn-out ration cards of urban dwellers;[1] these are their dwellings. Outside the cartographic imagination, these are where people breathe with their experiences and subjectivities. These are not non-descriptive dots or amoeba-shaped spatial puzzles on the map on a town planner's drawing board. These neighbourhoods make possible the very act of living in a city. Yet, in social sciences, we happily forgot to pay attention to these neighbourhoods and the life they breathe. This book, in a nutshell, is an attempt to listen to the lives of neighbourhoods—their subjectivities and experiences—in India. In such an endeavour, this introductory chapter curates a discursive framework to facilitate the act of listening to and seeing, engaging with and understanding neighbourhoods in India. The introduction entails constant backward and forward movements, which means perpetually thrashing out the basic term with reference to the predecessors and

1 Words and phrases that are not in common circulation in English are italicised when they occur first or while appearing after a considerable gap. However, in cases of repeated appearance or in short intervals, they are not in italics. The use of diacritical marks is kept minimum and only one long vowel ā is used.

the details from the various chapters in this book. The emergent discursive framework in this introductory chapter that underpins the book shall bring about a coherent—to be optimistic—fusion of history, geography, anthropology, sociology and political economy. Such a fusion duly determines the nature of the book on the whole. The idea is not only to develop an understanding of the nature and scope of the term neighbourhood but also show the way this book is fulfilling various other prerequisites, namely, the socio-spatial detailing of the neighbourhood with reference to specific cases in each chapter. And by implication, the book invites us to rethink the idea of a city in contemporary India.

South Asia is home to 23 per cent of the world's population and at least 14 per cent of its urban population. India, with a lion's share in this statistical profile, has more than 377 million people or 31.16 per cent of the country's population living in cities (Census of India 2011). With this one-third share in the total population, the urban landscape, as well as the idea of the urban, is the crucial source and a key site of dreams, material aspirations and harsh social realities for citizens and leaders across the board. Compared to the statistical share, the influence that cities exert upon the social life is far greater as they are initiating and controlling centres of economic, political and cultural life (Wirth 1938). This is also crucial as Louis Wirth, among others, has identified the urban as synonymous with the modern. The question, as Wirth himself poses, is how potent cities are in moulding the character of social life? In many ways, this has been the defining concern among scholars looking at cities and urban life for nearly 100 years. To engage with the question at a very fundamental level, we can safely go with Louis Wirth's schema in which he identifies urbanism at three levels: (a) as a physical structure comprising a population base, a technology and an ecological order; (b) as a system of social organisation involving a characteristic social structure, a series of social institutions and a typical pattern of social relationships and (c) as a set of attitudes and ideas and a set of constellations of personalities (Wirth 1938: 18–19).

In the Indian milieu, with the urban turn in social sciences witnessing 'a noticeable surge in the attention paid by scholars to the city life in India', the 'city as society' has acquired a sharpened focus (Prakash 2002). However, this scholarship, predating as well as cohabiting the urban turn, has remained focused upon either the first set of the aforementioned concerns of Wirth (i.e., pertaining to physical structure) or the third rubric (related to a set of attitudes and ideas, broadly speaking, of cultural dimensions of the urban), largely ignoring the question of the social (institutions, structures and relationships) in relation to the urban. Harping upon this relationship between the urban and the social, this book focuses upon an essential yet highly ignored element of the urban social life—the neighbourhood.

A neighbourhood occupies a unique location in the life of a city. It is located *in between* the home on one side of a social axis and the anonymous and alienated city on the other. It's an in-between space as has also been put forward by H. Donner and G. de Neve (Donner and De Neve 2006: 11). We build upon this idea, albeit differently, emphasising not so much upon the processes and linkages made possible by globalisation as offered by Donner and De Neve. Instead, we harp upon the fluidity of practices, contested subjectivities and experiential dynamics. Therefore, the idea of a neighbourhood not merely mediates and connects the interiority of homes with the anonymous city, but due to this unique spatial function, it is also endowed with its *own spatial agency and subjectivity*. The in-between-ness is then less and less about a passage or a bridge between home and the city and more and more about spatially immersed social lives in an urban landscape. Thus, for the chapters presented in this volume, a neighbourhood is not about a little bit of warmth that a home longs for and a little share of violence that the urban unleashes. It is about a space of dwelling for both—the home and the city. Without this space of neighbourhood, one can neither get an entry into home nor access to the city. Therefore, we argue for this in-between space as the one that is not about being a threshold, some kind of spatial *rite de passage*, but as one that has its own interiorities, complex practices and convoluted histories.

Conceptualising neighbourhoods as social-spatial constellations, the core idea behind the volume is to emphasise and problematise a unique coming together of social realities and spatial dynamics. The cities of contemporary India provide a broader canvas, both feeding in and drawing resources for our understanding of neighbourhoods.

We cannot conceive social life in a city without its neighbourhoods. The idea of the neighbourhood precedes the city. Yet, ironical though this may sound, there is little that reflects upon a critical understanding of this key building block of urban India called neighbourhoods. A systematic glance at this building block is relatively less explored—as shown later in this introductory chapter—in the larger body of scholarship in sociology, anthropology, urban studies, planning, policymaking and urban governance in India. Filling in the lacunae, the eleven chapters in this book excavate neighbourhoods both as a space and as a social institution and not merely as administrative units bereft of their neighbourliness. Therefore, neighbourhoods in their spatial locations are perceived as embedded in social and historical specificities. Together, these spatial, social and historical characteristics of neighbourhoods determine the form of the urban, another neglected domain of scholarship. To achieve this objective of attending to these neglected dimensions, the volume adopts a multidisciplinary framework, mobilising disciplines to explore neighbourhoods and their relationship to the social life of cities in India.

Conceiving the idea of neighbourhoods as an entangled concept—as socio-spatial in nature—then makes it imperative to explore them in terms of their locations and as concepts embedded in social and historical specificities. Together, these characteristics—spatial, social and historical—of neighbourhoods determine the form of the urban society. A focus on neighbourhoods in a theoretically informed and empirically layered manner, thereby, enables us a richer and grounded understanding of the urban social life in India. With this objective in mind, the core question asked in all these chapters is how to make sense of this intertwining of the social and the spatial in the making of a neighbourhood in a non-Western urban landscape like that of India.

Building upon insights from Martin Heidegger that 'space is neither an external object nor an inner experience' (Heidegger 1971: 154) and phenomenological explorations of the later decades of the 20th century, the chapters in this book make a case for subjectivities located in the space called neighbourhood and spatial experiences embedded in the social and the historical. Together, these twining allow us access to what we may call spatial subjectivities. In such an overarching frame of the spatial-social, these chapters are oriented towards exploring four core rubrics of spatial subjectivities, namely (a) value regimes, (b) inequalities and exclusionary dimensions of space rooted in the logic of caste and community, (c) gendered forms of spatial relationships and (d) the politics of planning and housing in and through which dwelling in space takes its material manifestation. Together, an account of these allows us to reconstruct a wider picture of neighbourhood subjectivities. These explorations are less premised upon how these social contingencies normatively aspire to engage with the spatial. Instead, we privilege how these social contingencies in terms of their experiential dynamics—in terms of practices—are enmeshed in a space called the neighbourhood. With these orientations and thematic focus, this book approaches practices, processes and experiences, instead of merely institutions and structures, in the formation of neighbourhoods and neighbourliness.

Idea of Neighbourhood: History and Geography of the Social as Spatial

The meanings and usages of the term neighbourhood come before us as historically dynamic and not static in terms of its form. In the context of American cities—a landscape that has functioned as having a paradigmatic influence on the subject—the dominant discourse informs us that neighbourhoods as identifiable units came into being with the transition of pedestrian cities of the 18th and 19th centuries to complex, large and differentiated structures in the early decades of the 20th century (Melvin 1985). This widely held view was itself rooted in the belief that in the 18th and 19th centuries, American cities were characterised more by the mixture than by the separation of land uses (Abbott 1974). However, 'residential neighborhoods were in fact differentiated according to wealth and occupational status' even in the late 18th and 19th centuries. Records from this period from Boston and Philadelphia, among others, suggest,

> [It] is not merely that the abjectly poor were exiled to the outskirts of town. Rather, there appears to have been a pattern of concentric zones

> focused on the urban center. Merchants and successful professional men lived in the core of the city, surrounded first by a belt of prosperous artisans and then by the laboring poor. (Abbott 1974: 35–36)

Abbott writes,

> City life in preindustrial Europe and the Mediterranean revolved around central squares where cathedrals, guild houses, city halls, and palaces overlooked market days, religious celebrations, itinerant merchants, and gossiping grandees. In cities where everyone moved on foot, the homes of the rich crowded the center, while craftspeople, traders, and workers arrayed themselves in surrounding neighborhoods. The ubiquitous urban form was portable. (Abbott 2008: 25)

With the growth of industrial cities and its complexities, the concentric zones and segregation of residential spaces led to enhanced attention on neighbourhoods. For example, the relation between neighbourhoods, the city and the nation attracted Robert A. Woods and Wilbur C. Phillips. In the essays by Woods titled 'The City and the Local Community' (1923) and 'The Neighborhood in Social Reconstruction' (1914), the city came to be seen as a cluster of interlacing communities (or neighbourhoods), each with its own vital ways of expression but all together creating the municipality to render the fullest service through the participation of its residents (Melvin 1985: 358). For them, the neighbourhood as a discrete entity operated in a complementary manner with other neighbourhoods to form the larger metropolis (Ibid.). From the mid-1920s, this paradigm of complementarity gave way to the community-centric logic. Scholars working on the urban issues at the University of Chicago like Ernest Burgess, Harvey W. Zorbaugh, Louis Wirth, Robert E. Park and Roderick D. McKenzie heavily relied upon the segregated units of neighbourhoods in terms of common experiences and the sense of territorial linkages.

Another key moment in the history of the idea of the neighbourhood came in the 1960s with the 'neighbourhood revolution' when 'a score of neighbourhoods began to argue vigorously for their own versions of local revitalisation in the later 1960s'. This was not a singular problem or an issue of a single neighbourhood. The phrases like 'neighbourhood movement' and 'neighbourhood groups' were part of a deep transformation of community life. This coincided with the emergence of scores of grassroots, issue-based organisations with inveterate civic participants (Abbott 2008: 208).

At a broader level, the neighbourhood came to be

> usually thought of more in geographical terms as a distinct part of a town or city, which may be distinct by virtue of certain boundaries (e.g. made by roads, railways, rivers, parks etc.) and marked out from other neighbourhoods by a certain homogeneity of housing within the area. As a corollary of the similarity of housing, there can be expected a certain homogeneity of social class within the given neighbourhood. The geographical, or physical, elements and the social ones do not always go together, and indeed the above definition would not always result in two observers delimiting neighbourhoods in any given town being an agreement. (Mann 1970: 569)

Also, for Ruth Glass, a neighbourhood becomes 'a territorial group, the members of which meet on common ground within their own area for primary social activities and organised and spontaneous social contacts' (Mann 1970: 569). For Carpenter, the key became 'primary group spirit which is the fulcrum of neighbourhood life' (Ibid.: 579). However, such a definition exposed the inherent contradiction between conceiving a neighbourhood and its larger location in the city: 'If all the forces of urbanism are "hostile" to the preservation of neighbourhood life, then how can the neighbourhood be an urban phenomenon?' (Ibid.).

In all these approaches and definitions, the neighbourhood units remain key to town planning for the well-being of the social life in large cities. Within this broad perspective, the idea of homogeneity, distinct territory and harmonious social life continued to attract certain utopian energy both for town planners and social scientists. The utopia was in conceiving smaller units of the neighbourhood as retaining certain essential human characteristics in the larger field of metropolitan life characterised by alienation, regimentation and violence. Therefore, for Jane Jacobs, '[A] successful city neighbourhood is a place that keeps sufficiently abreast of its problems so it is not destroyed by them. An unsuccessful neighbourhood is a place that is overwhelmed by its defects and problems and is progressively more helpless before them' (Jacobs 1992: 112). An influential critique of the discourse on neighbourhood planning, Jacobs offers us to look at neighbourhoods at three levels: at the level of streets, at the district level and, finally, thinking of the city itself (made up of hop- and skip-relationships) as a neighbourhood. Jacobs writes that we need

> to abandon conventional planning ideas about city neighborhoods. The 'ideal' neighborhood of planning and zoning theory, too large in scale to possess any competence or meaning as a street neighbourhood, is at the same time too small in scale to operate as a district. It is unfit for anything. It will not serve as even a point of departure. (Jacobs 1961: 118–119)

However, while the dominant practices of urban planning were attacked, the hope bestowed upon the affective potentials of neighbourhoods in fostering social bonding and in neighbourliness towards creating a harmonious city lingered on.

Turning streets as units—to conceive neighbourliness and the space of the neighbourhood, as Jacobs did—opened up new vistas, particularly for anthropologists (Duneier 1999), the full potentialities of which are yet to be actualised by scholars, particularly in the Global South. Along with the hope and positive energies of neighbourliness, an important dimension inviting the attention of scholars and planners alike was the question of inequality embroiled in the circuits of ethnicity, public health, crime and informality. It was acknowledged that neighbourliness and spatial solidarities operate differently in middle- and working-class neighbourhoods. Many times, such working-class or Afro-American settlement—or other immigrant settlements like 'Cornerville', a slum district inhabited by Italian immigrants in Boston, USA (studied by William Foote Whyte in 1940s)—posed as 'problem area' to the rest of the city: 'a mysterious, dangerous and depressing area' (Whyte 1943: XV). These studies on treating slums as neighbourhoods not merely emphasised upon the 'dark corners' of the urban landscape but also enables us to see the complex social and political structures that go into the making up of the 'darkness'. With the passage of time, alongside these inequalities that go into the making of slums and their stereotypes, and with a shift in scholarship from Euro-American urban landscape to a landscape that increasingly came to be known as that of the Global South (i.e., Sao Paulo in Brazil, Dharavi in Mumbai, Johannesburg in South Africa etc.), we also come face-to-face with the fact that 'the city brutally undermines the resourcefulness of slums' (Caldeira 2000; Sharma 2000; Simone 2019). Parallel to this stream of scholarship, which focused on slums as neighbourhoods, we also find writings on other forms of spatial segregation in the scholarship on Muslim neighbourhoods (Jamil 2014, 2017; Khan 2015; Kirmani 2008; Menon 2015; Patil 2017) and in ghettoes emerging in the aftermath of communal violence (De 2016; Jaffrelot and Thomas 2012: 43–80).

Recapitulating this discourse from a bird's eye view, we find that anxieties pertaining to zoning, segregation, spatial proximity, territoriality and the location of communities in urban landscape emerge as some crucial coordinates in thinking about the neighbourhood and its relationship with the urban. In the last few decades, while these concerns continued in one or other forms, the discourse on the urban itself has undergone a massive transformation and it is obvious to expect its impact upon the ways of looking at neighbourhoods, too.

If an overarching factor shaping the earlier discourse was urban governance and its episteme, the urban planning discourse in the recent five decades has tilted considerably towards understanding the dynamics of space. A large share of these studies (since the 1980s) owe directly or indirectly to the works like Henry Lefebvre's (1991) *The Production of Space*, Manuel Castells's Marxist frame of analysing the urban question and to David Harvey's theorisation wherein the history of the capital and the history of the city overlap. Here, two key epistemic trajectories need to be underlined: (a) an unprecedented influence of social geographers on social sciences and (b) the overall milieu of the enhanced global flow of capital, goods and ideas, a phenomenon often referred to as globalisation. The amplified intervention of geography led to spatial turn (and vice versa), and the global flow of spaces and the role of new technologies (Castells 1996) complicated our existing understanding of studying neighbourhoods as units.

This was also the time (1980 onwards) when gated communities as exclusionary zones, structured around economic inequality and the idea of keeping dissimilar social groups away from its precincts began drawing the attention of scholars (Low 2001). While we do have a long history of urban segregation along racial lines, as has been pointed out earlier in this introduction too, since the 1980s, there has been a pattern of hyper-segregation leading to the coming up of these fortress cities (Davis 1990, 1994) and the City of Walls (Caldeira 2001). These gated communities, in the words of Mollenkopf and Castells (1991), emerge out of structural readjustments to late capitalism. Keeping aside these gated communities and moving beyond the frames of inequality and fear, neighbourhoods seem to disappear from the agenda of urban scholars in the milieu of globalisation. If we take recourse to a cliché that goes back to an often-quoted theorisation by Arjun Appadurai (1997), in scholarly engagements, the locality as a relational concept devoured the situatedness of the neighbourhood in an age of globalisation.

Largely in and through the coordinates of this binary between locality and neighbourhood, in this contemporary milieu, scholars have conceptualised the social dynamics *in* neighbourhoods from the perspective of placemaking (Donner and De Neve 2006). Therefore, the emphasis has been upon how global linkages restructuring new spatial relationships 'shape contemporary cultural forms and the experience of social relationships in unprecedented ways' and 'the role that place plays in the relationship between culture and power' (Ibid.). Engaging with the fundamental concern of whatever has happened to place in an age of globalisation, scholars like Donner and De Neve capitalised upon insights provided by geographers like Massey who asks, '[C]an we rethink [the] absence of place that is adequate to this era of time-space compression?' (Massey 1994: 147). Massey proposes alternative interpretations of place, in which place is no longer associated with essential identities, communities or past and tradition. She suggests instead that 'what gives [a] place its specificity is not some long internalised history but the fact that it is constructed out of a particular constellation of social relations, meeting and weaving together at a particular locus' (Ibid.: 154, as cited in Donner and De Neve 2006: 4). With this frame—'by taking the neighbourhood itself as a point of departure'—they try to unpack 'the ways in which neighbourhoods are made into meaningful places and are fundamental to an understanding of urban life more generally' (Donner and De Neve 2006: 7). In their own words, '[M]uch of this is concerned with the impact of global communication and information technologies on urban life, or with the nature of urban restructuring in the wake of liberalisation policies' (Donner and De Neeve 2006).

Our aim is neither to foreground nor ignore the contemporaneity of global flows and structures with the dynamics of placemaking at local levels. Our object of analysis is not globalisation. Instead, our focus is on unpacking the social life in neighbourhoods. In an interrogative sense, the book operates with probing questions such as 'how does the social and the spatial come together to shape an understanding of the sociality that is quite distinct from the givenness of some dominant rubrics like caste, community ties or religion in Indian society?' A focus on the neighbourhood allows us this opportunity. Therefore, the question before us is less about explaining the social life of neighbourhoods by privileging the global linkages. We are, to a great extent, oblivious—in fact, opposed—to the local/global binary. Instead, the primary task before us is about how to look at this social life of the neighbourhood itself. Does it mean being ignorant of the external linkages or treating neighbourhoods as an insular category or romanticising them as isolated islands? Far from these analytical entrapments, we are less concerned about the boundedness of our object of study—neighbourhoods. The chapters in this book exhibit an epistemological openness. However, this does not mean abandoning the unit-centric idea of neighbourhood altogether.

Is it a carelessness to the boundary-making and its role in neighbourhood formation? Does it make our methods and approaches towards treating neighbourhoods as units, precarious? Perhaps, yes. However, let us reiterate that we precisely aim at unpacking neighbourhoods as units of social reality. These units, we believe, are crucial building blocks for understanding life in cities. Here, we encounter a number of difficulties and challenges. Let us identify at least four of them. First is the question of the neighbourhood as a unit of study, flagged earlier in this essay, too; we ought to be returning to it often. Second, what does it mean to study neighbourhoods in contemporary milieu without falling into the binary trap of local as opposed to global? Third, how not to treat neighbourhoods merely as passive locations, backgrounds or mere settings for understanding community dynamics or other forms of social complexities. Fourth, a broad challenge that we face in this endeavour is to engage with the specificities of neighbourhoods in a non-Western, urban landscape like that of India. Keeping in mind these challenges, let us now turn to the synoptic view of the various chapters in this book to take note of reconciliation and implicit departures. And hence, while doing so we keep an eye on the ways our predecessors have engaged with some key categories discussed in this book.

The Socio-Spatial Intertwining in the Idea of the Neighbourhood

The core concern in this book is to acknowledge plural ways in which neighbourhood gets conceived and experienced in the urban landscape of India. Therefore, for Gauri Bharat, who has focused upon Jain neighbourhoods of Ahmedabad in this book, the key axis in the formation of a neighbourhood is less in terms of an administrative boundary; it is, instead, the institutions of *derāsar* and *upāshray*, which go into the making of the space of a neighbourhood. Jain families residing in a neighbourhood constitute a *sangh* (community), the locus of which is a *derāsar* and an *upāshray*. Membership in a *sangh* is registered through a record held by a *derāsar*, while it is performed through participation in ritual activities and collective practices such as sermons or festival feasts. What is particularly interesting is that the bonds between *sangh* members, and between *sangh* members and a *derāsar* or an *upāshray*, are not spatially delineated. Yet, the institutions engender a range of practices that spatially permeate the neighbourhood, influencing both ritual and everyday activities. In this way, the sacred space of the institutions become an important anchor for the neighbourhood. In this chapter, Gauri traces how families within a neighbourhood engage with Jain religious institutions. Further, by chronicling the shifts in *sangh* membership on account of migration within the city over time, she explores the dynamic relationship between these sacred institutions and the processes of neighbourhood formation. Using primarily ethnographic accounts and oral history narratives coming from families of worshippers, this study offers some preliminary yet highly insightful building blocks for what will hopefully develop into a framework for locating the sacred within the processes of contemporary city formation.

While Gauri has explored Jain religiosity and its investment in the space and built environment of Ahmedabad, Anakshi Pal in her ethnographic account explores the idea of neighbourhood among *Kāshivāsis*, residents of Kāshi (the modern city of Varanasi) residing in an *āshram* in Banaras, by looking at the everyday lives and emotional experiences of those who come to the city of Banaras (Varanasi) to die with the hope of attaining *moksha* or salvation. (But *vāsi* in the term *Kāshivāsis* is laden with certain temporality and transitoriness.) The aim is to demonstrate—by reflecting upon their daily interactions or non-interaction—the peculiarities of a 'neighbourhood' within the setup of an *āshram* inhabited primarily by *mumukshus* (seekers of *moksha* or salvation). Her primary contention lies in the fact that the philosophical underpinnings of *Kāshivās* negate the idea of a 'neighbourhood' as primarily a *social* unit, as is generally understood. (*Kāshivās*, literally 'this stay in Kāshi', constitutes the governing philosophy in the lives of the *mumukshus*.) The 'neighbourhood' as a spatial unit, in this case, does not espouse the norms of sociality or spontaneous social interactions, as might be found in other ordinary set-ups. Despite this absence of sociality, this chapter traces the dynamics and complexities of everyday life within the *āshram* to understand how neighbourhoods emerge as a negotiated space that is both geographical and social. This everydayness and the nature of the interaction, or the lack thereof, in the *āshram* is crucial for an understanding of the unique social character of this space and of the community of *Kāshivāsis*. By comprehending the unique interpersonal politics among the *āshram* residents and the emotional dynamics at play, this chapter contributes towards understanding the nature of *āshram* as a 'neighbourhood' and the behaviours of the *mumukshus*. The study further seeks to highlight different ways in which the particularities of this space of *āshram* comes before us as a heterotopic space between life and death.

A *derāsar* and an *āshram* both have a strong presence in society. Both are embedded in certain religiosity or, broadly speaking, in certain value regimes. The latter aspect, value regime, needs to be kept in mind, as we know from the history of Gandhian experiments that the space of an *āshram* was neither confined to religiosity nor was it ignorant of politics. Yet, ironically we have not paid sufficient attention to these *āshram* spaces (Skaria 2002; Thomson 1993). In Anakshi Pal's treatment, these *āshrams* reveal heterotopic characteristics too, pushing us to think about the transitory and intermediary nature of neighbourhoods, in between this world and the other world, or freedom from the cycle of birth and death (*moksha*). Though coming from two very different religious traditions, the *derāsar* and the Kāshi *āshram* force us to shift our focus away from the Euro-American scholarship on neighbourhoods to new sites to make room for asking different sets of questions and to look at the city from hitherto untouched locations.

To that end, we need to first address the question of the neighbourhood as a unit of study, flagged earlier in this Introduction too, and we ought to be returning to it often. At a conceptual level, this translates into ways of not merely problematising the givenness or the fixity of its territorial nature but also ways of going beyond the concerns of territory- and boundary-making, which are otherwise so central to the approaches to neighbourhoods. Therefore, if a neighbourhood is not merely about the physical space or a container of the social relationship, or about administrative wards (or such units) from government files, and if a neighbourhood has to be understood as a coming together of the spatial and the social, where the social is itself fraught with pluralities, ambiguities, fluid practices and contested circuits of power, then how can one treat it as a singular unit of analysis?

Responding to these challenges, at one level, our approach has been to replace administrative units of neighbourhoods with that of a conceptualisation of the neighbourhood space from the perspectives and experiences of people who inhabit that space. It is here we find a different logic of boundary-making at place. For example, Abhijit Dasgupta in his study of a Christian *pārā* in Kolkata observes specific kinds of behavioural-moral alertness among girls when they are inside the *pārā* space, which restrained them from entering into a conversation with a stranger—in this case, the researcher—compared to their conversational willingness outside the *pārā* space. With an investment in the world of oral tradition and gossips of the street, Abhijit shows us that neighbourhoods in South Asia display distinct characteristics and informal connectivity, which are determined by physical proximities, kinship ties and everyday familiarities. He tunes his ears to this archive of gossip to understand the nature of power dynamics in a predominantly Christian neighbourhood. The objective is to pay close attention to contestations, belongingness and social control, which go into the making up of urban space. Through an ethnographic engagement in a Christian lower-middle-class neighbourhood (*pārā*) in the district of North 24 Parganas, West Bengal, Abhijit probes into the processes of internal 'schism' (Handman 2014) in one of the Protestant churches and the emergence of smaller prayer units. The chapter analyses how schism happens through the practices of 'gossip' and 'ridicule', which are used as cultural weapons to construct a narrative of domination and hegemony in the *pārā*. He seeks to explore the way schism intermingles with kinship and family disputes, subsequently leading to conflict over the 'social' and 'spiritual' capital in the neighbourhood. He argues that such processes legitimise the *act* of gossip and indicate its *impact* as a noteworthy event to explicate new relationships. While engaging with some of these concerns, Abhijit attempts to capture how Christianity and *pārā* politics at the local level intersect each other, thus shaping and forming the contours of neighbourhood relations and faith practices, and in turn enable us the story of how faith and place-making are embedded into each other.

While the *āshram* mediates between material life and *moksha* in a world view that is deeply ingrained in specific religious trajectory, refugee camps offer us another example of such an in-betweenness (or other spaces). Akanksha Kumar looks at Dalit refugee resettlement colonies in post-Partition Delhi. The partition of India in 1947 and its aftermath had a significant impact on the social profile of Delhi as the rapid influx of half a million refugees played a vital role in the making of a 'new city' in post-Independence India. In subsequent decades, a large section of these refugees unleashed a vision to expand commercially across the city. Some of these groups succeeded in moving upwards in business, which gave them a sense of connectedness to Delhi. This also led to the transformation of a small segment of these refugees into a middle class. In contrast, Akanksha focuses her attention to Jhilmil, a Dalit refugee colony in East Delhi. She mobilises both archival and oral narratives from the field to complicate the processes of transformation of refugee personhood at the spatial level. This is a story of neglect and apathy given to neighbourhoods that do not match middle-class norms and points towards a differentiated history of refugee neighbourhoods in Delhi.

While the story narrated by Akanksha is of a refugee colony that has a history of planning attached to it, another and more frequent examples of lower-caste (Scheduled-Caste) settlements often come with the label *basti* attached to them. In an urban discourse in India, *busti* or *basti* is a typology that has definite rural connotations. *Bastis* are residential clusters in an urban landscape but demonstrate features that are stigmatised as rural. In the first Master Plan of Delhi, a *basti* is defined as 'a cluster of sub-standard and temporary structures made of scrap material like straw, mud, bamboo, wooden planks, thatched roof etc.' (Delhi Development Authority 1962: 94). These *bastis* were quintessentially a cause for grave concern among planners and governments. Awadhendra Sharan writes, '[T]o be in [a] city and inhabit its numerous *bastis* was to be always under the injunction to mutate into one another, the violence of the policing of colonial difference yielding to the burden of the nationalist/modernist desire for assimilation' (2006: 4908).

How do these Dalit refugee colonies or *bastis* fight systemised discrimination and resist stigmas imposed upon them? Continuing our engagement with Dalit neighbourhoods as sites of discrimination along socio-spatial lines, Vijay Kumar narrates about these urban *bastis* as sites of resistance as we travel with him further north and east of Delhi to Uttar Pradesh. Vijay Kumar weaves a complex history of these *bastis* as sites of everyday resistance, discrimination and negotiations. He studies the colonial history of Khatik (a Scheduled-Caste community) *bastis* and points towards the dangers of conceiving the politics of urban spaces in universal terms and vocabularies. The chapter pushes us to think about Dalit specificities that go into the making of a space of neighbourhood in North India. Drawing upon the historical trajectory of this space, the essay points towards different layers of contestation and claims-making that have shaped the contours of these neighbourhoods. Vijay argues that Dalit *bastis* were sites of silent protests; they reveal layers of transgressive politics and subversive strategies, unleashing transformative energy. He argues that this transformation of the neighbourhood space can only be documented by paying attention to everyday forms of resistance or subversive strategies deployed by people living in these *bastis*. In this struggle, inhabitants used meagre resources and mobilised whatever means available to them.

While scholars have written about Scheduled-Caste colonies and untouchable neighbourhoods in the past (Jaoul 2012; Lynch 1969; Prashad 2001), chapters by Akanksha and Vijay in this volume bring out the spatial transformation of Scheduled-Caste neighbourhoods in a forceful manner. In many ways, in these chapters, the spaces have acquired certain historical and social agency, which open up possibilities of focusing on looking at community histories in spatial terms for future scholars.

Talking about the agency of the space and its transformation in the course of history, as highlighted in the chapters by Vijay and Akanksha, on the one hand, and the spatial embeddedness in religious values and institutions, in the chapters by Gauri, Anakshi and Abhijit, on the other hand, lead us to ask our second broad question (as listed earlier): what does it mean to study neighbourhoods in a contemporary milieu without falling into the binary trap of conflating local and global as opposites? Binaries are not only unavoidable but also suffocating. Once we abandon the binary frame of local versus global, we open up fresh ways of locating neighbourhood and neighbourly practices in their contemporaneity. Thus, while the contemporaneity of the social-spatial approach has been privileged across the chapters presented here, neither globalisation nor a pregiven idea of neighbourhood finds analytic centre stage in our treatment. Yet, such a move must not be seen as apathy towards the significance of globalisation or other metanarratives of the time we live in. This is also not about an attitude to ignore these dominant signages. The idea is to go beyond analytically saturated vantage points and nodes of looking at the urban. Therefore, while being well aware of the global nature of the contemporary, while not abandoning the importance of looking at neighbourhoods in terms of units and while acknowledging the need to relate empirical ground realities to larger questions of structures and institutions of urban social life, these studies, which follow this introduction, aim to harp upon practices and experiences instead of ideologies, economic categories and processes. In many ways, this is quite close to Ajay Gandhi and Lotte Hoek's approach in which they argue that '[t]he open-endedness of the living city in South Asia requires an open and exploratory ethnographic approach unburdened by inflexible terminology' (Gandhi and Hoek 2012: 3).

This contemporaneity looms large in so many ways in these chapters. For example, in the study of conversations among women neighbours in a town called Golakgunj in Dhubri District, Assam, bordering Bangladesh, Joyashree Sarma looks at a neighbourhood through the widespread anxieties around identity politics. Here, in this border town, where the neighbourhood as space is located at the geographical margins of the nation state that is fenced and guarded by soldiers, spatial intimacies or neighbourliness, too, are entrenched in the political debate of who belongs to the nation state. The political debates and apprehensions of 'illegal immigration', contestations and documentation of citizenship in Assam as implied in the National Register of Citizens (NRC) or the Citizenship (Amendment) Bill, 2016, or CAB, also extend to the border town and its inhabitants. These two political processes question each individual's existence as a citizen and mark out differences in terms of her/his religious affiliation. Yet, these nationalist scribblings do not wipe out the localised politics of placemaking. Instead, we come face-to-face with a scenario in which the local and the national are closely enmeshed into each other in such a way that it is not possible to think about one without the other.

The neighbourhoods in the borderland have stories of migration, separation, memories and heterogeneous population due to a shared past: the partition of British India into India and Pakistan in 1947 and the formation of a new nation state when Bangladesh attained Independence from Pakistan in 1971. Drawing on ethnographic fieldwork, the chapter asks, 'How does the political situation impinge on the neighbourhood and its people?' The chapter addresses the micro-social elements of everyday life like gossips among women, prevailing stereotypes, tactics of secret-keeping and trust-building in the lanes of the neighbourhoods. It is in the lanes of the neighbourhoods where the experiences of the families, households, nation state are discussed, articulated and mediated to constitute not just intimate spaces of belonging but also distant and segregated spaces of othering. In the backdrop of identity creation, the chapter spells out the strategies of political participation and everyday peacekeeping that happen within the neighbourhoods.

In the case of Delhi's urban villages, contemporaneity comes in the form of conflict of value regimes between single female migrant tenants and their landlords and between the former and their neighbours. Rashi Bhargava and Richa Chilana explore the interactional dynamics between 'single' tenants and numerous entities within their residential environments. The neighbourhood in this chapters emerges as a constant mediation between multiple value regimes that are coordinated through tenancy, migration, gender and singlehood of the tenants. The study looks at the social organisation of urban spaces through the category of marital status where accessing and establishing 'home' is contingent upon societal perceptions of being in a society. The processes of accessing a home, establishing homeliness and homemaking are then extremely gendered processes where their attempt/s to overcome societal biases and prejudices are not only fraught with many challenges but often reinstate the same biases and perceptions. The experiences of single men and women also underline their unique perception of neighbourliness or it's lack thereof. Hence, the study is interested in looking at the everyday lived realities, spatial regimes, representational practices and ways of operating (De Certeau 1984) that these single men and women experience, engage and negotiate with. In the study, 'singlehood' emerges as a significant variable affecting one's chances of accessing certain kinds of rental housing; it also affects the negotiations that follow after having established access. The study also seeks to interrogate the idea of urban itself, given that 'urban village' has emerged as an important variable when looking at access to rental housing vis-à-vis single working men and women.

The figure of these single female tenants living in a neighbourhood gets another dimension when Sadan Jha deliberates upon the figures of *parosi* and *parosan* as crucial to any understanding of a neighbourhood. Scholars working at the intersection of gender politics and geography have alerted us that spaces are not ignorant of their claims over bodies. Drawing insights from this scholarship, Sadan locates the affectivity of *paros* in the problematique of urban experience as it comes down through its specific genealogy. This figure of the *paros* and its phenomenological grounding in the conceptualisation of urban experience allow him to pay attention to people who inhabit the *paros*, namely *parosi* and *parosan*, male and female neighbours, respectively. These figures, particularly the analytically privileged *parosan*, then allow us to engender the space of the neighbourhood; they also lead to the specificities in which feminisation of space allows us new facets of what he terms as spatial affectivity in South Asian urban landscapes.

Our third major challenge has been to engage with neighbourhoods not merely as backdrops or settings. In other words, the question we ask is how not to treat neighbourhoods merely as passive locations—as backgrounds—for understanding community dynamics or other forms of social complexities. The pervasive practice among social scientists has been to approach neighbourhoods merely in a geographical context or as administrative units. At another level, the spatial dynamics of neighbourhoods push us to ask if we can engage with issues like proximity, intimacy, shared everydayness without ignoring the microphysics of power—of claims and counter-claims exercised on and by bodies that form the social space of neighbourhoods. Thus, instead of harping upon pregiven homogeneity and shared vocabulary in the making of a neighbourhood, we tend to keep ourselves open to practices that construct the idea of neighbourhood and neighbourliness.

In many ways, imbuing neighbourhoods with certain socio-spatial dynamics directly leads us to the fourth broad challenge in this endeavour: how to engage with the specificities of neighbourhoods in a non-Western urban landscape like that of India?

It must be emphasised here that many of these chapters speak to each other in more ways than one. Thus, while the chapters by Gauri, Anakshi and Abhijit share a common analytical concern of religiosity and space, another set of chapters allow us to engage with engendering of neighbourhoods and neighbourliness in and through their engagement with conversational space of women (Joyashree), circulating bodies of *parosan* (Sadan) or scribbled codes of values on the bodies of single female tenants (Rashi and Richa). Similarly, we have another set of chapters on Dalit lived experience of spaces (Vijay) and on housing of Dalit refugees (Akanksha). Therefore, the question of a rented home, which is at the centre of Rashi and Richa's study, allows us to pay close attention to home and living as core constituents in the conceptualisation of neighbourhoods.

One cannot imagine a neighbourhood without its homes. The chapters by Sonal Mithal, Yugank Goyal and Sheema Fatima squarely deal with the knowledge economy, financial logic and politics, respectively, of housing and neighbourhood-making. Sonal digs into architectural history and an idea of modular aspiration for the home. Both Sonal and Yugank bring together the idea of home and aspiration, two highly ignored themes in Indian social sciences. In both these studies, the modular modernity and its multiple manifestations in South Asian milieu loom large.

Yugank enters into this linkage between home and aspiration by raising a sharp question: why do we buy a house as opposed to renting one? He claims that this question, in its simplistic formulation, captures some of the most fundamental emotions of human values that often appear in various senses of accomplishments as much as in varying degrees of misery. Yet, the question has attracted little scholarly scrutiny. The chapter by Yugank excavates the silences of the assumptions buried in the cacophony of emotions that manifestly shape the aspirations of buying a house. In doing so, it relies on understanding humans as temporally plural beings and investigates the role of socio-legal frameworks to assert and reify structures of modernity that dilute the temporal self-view of humans when they make their choices, one of which is the choice to buy a house. Yugank looks at the financial logic of buying and renting a house and quite innovatively combines this economics with the idea of time. Tracking this connection, he goes into the notions of time and its modernity to ask how our views about the temporal plurality of today's times in a fast-growing 'urban' world (of India) justifies an idiosyncratic investment on houses. What are the contours of modernity that underlie these decisions and build claims of rationality in them? The question takes Yugank in the direction of alternative conceptions of ethics to reimagine a social order. He seeks to examine the role of economic and legal architecture—for instance, the insurance industry—to foster the cultivation of alternative realities of rationality that push a particular way of imagining temporal transitions and homogenising those imaginations.

One such homogenising institution for imagination is the architectural model of modular homes. Sonal dexterously traces the lineage of this model, which has influenced several generations of urban dwellers in terms of shaping their aspirations for a home. This is about making an ideal type—a model home. Focusing on Lucknow, Sonal shows that this idea of modular home comes before us closely tied with the spatial history of urban planning and concerns towards the formation of specific constellations of urban neighbourhoods. After independence, Lucknow saw the establishment of public institutions on a large scale to cater to the new agenda of progress as laid down under the First Five-Year Plan. The plan warranted setting up of research facilities for agriculture (Sugarcane Research Institute), medicine (Central Drug Research Institute), aviation (Hindustan Aeronautics Limited), waterworks (Hydelworks) and the establishment of a Housing Board to provide housing solutions for the new India. The employees of these public sector projects live in precincts exclusively designed for their needs. These precincts are closer to the workplace, are low in human density and the housing units are designed in accordance with the hierarchy of the employees. The quality of construction is good and amenities are well laid out.

The presence of such precincts forms a large component of the urban landscape of Lucknow. Until the neoliberal policies started to govern the urban landscape policies, these precincts tended to marginalise the residential precincts of non-public sector employees. Sonal considers these precincts as a neighbourhood typology and discusses the dynamics of exclusivity and gentrification formalised by the State and the market (in pre-neoliberal phase) through architectural designs, town planning parameters and land policy frameworks.

She particularly asks why architectural design practices in India consider active occupational and economic segregation as a normalised practice of creating neighbourhoods. In pursuit of an answer, the chapter addresses the following questions: How did government officers' housing precincts continue the European ideals of organisation, hierarchy and segregation? What was the desirable urban lifestyle that the architectural designs emulated? To what extent were these precincts conceived as self-sustainable units and functioned as isolated microcosms?

The concerns towards urban planning and the question of housing are addressed by Sheema Fatima through her study of a social housing programme in post-independent Patna. She argues that though the Patna Improvement Trust and the Bihar State Housing Board failed to provide housing for the urban poor, an important component of the social housing programme of the government both at the Centre and the state since the 1950s, the social housing programme continuously facilitated formation and construction of housing cooperatives for the middle class and the higher income groups in the city. This chapter, through a historical reading of housing programmes and policies formulated by the trust and the board since the early 1950s, probes the question of neighbourhood formation in a provincial capital town of North India. Did these institutions encourage the formation and consolidation of neighbourhoods in the city in a particular pattern deliberately for the middle class at the expense of the urban poor? What insight does the historical spatial mapping provide today when poor urban neighbourhoods are recognised as encroachment while middle-class residential areas are being regularised. Located in Patna, Sheema's study develops hitherto untouched narratives of the vast, varied processes of urban transformation situated in the larger context of the newly emerging urban centres of India. Capturing the essence of the volume, she argues that it is important to identify these complexities of engagement and historical shifts rather than reducing the messy dynamics to a singular analytical category or a singular act of worlding factors (Roy and Ong 2011). And, thus, this book joins the larger corpus of scholarship in which a rethinking on the neighbourhood from the locations of the Global South is pertinent.

Another View from the Global South: Moving from Economic to Social Frames of the Spatial

In the contemporary Global South, Ananya Roy and Aihwa Ong have analysed the aspirational urbanisation through the idiom of 'worlding' (Roy and Ong 2011), where each city becomes a site of 'experimentation' in relation to capital and technologies. There is a robust scholarship on the nature of this linkage between capital and a city, with contributions from scholars like David Harvey, Neil Brenner, Manuel Castells and Saskia Sassen, to name a few. In this discourse, there is a certain emphasis upon the transnational network of capital, the flow of ideas and knowledge that provide the contemporary its specific urban form. Yet, as AbdouMaliq Simone forcefully argues, the creative potential in these processes remain alive. In the context of Africa, Simone (2019) talks about it in terms of 'people as infrastructure'. Elsewhere, scholars have harped upon informality (Roy 2004) to emphasise the specific characteristics of urbanisation in the Global South. This scholarship, however, underplays the ever-shifting social contours of urban spaces as affective spaces and as one that generates different forms of sociability. It is important then to shift our attention away from economic frames, categories and linkages to social processes, practices and experiences. The key question we need to ask here is about the peculiarity of social relationship in neighbourhoods, which can lead to a richer understanding of the social life of cities in India.

In this regard, Rajnarayan Chandavarkar in his exploration of mill districts and the working class in Mumbai insightfully refers to neighbourhoods as a 'social institution' (Chandavarkar 2009: 76). He writes that the daughters of mill workers 'brought up in Bombay would never willingly marry an agriculturalist in Ratnagiri' and their marriages were mainly arranged with 'men who work in the same or adjoining mills and reside in the same neighbourhood' (Ibid.). Chandavarkar points out that terms like 'neighbourhood' or 'community' have often nudged historians and social scientists towards an assumption of homogeneity or even of an inherent social harmony. However, collectivity, shared values and a sense of mutuality are not necessarily predicated upon proximate living. Indeed, to a large extent, close connections are forged in the neighbourhood most extensively in conditions in which the survival strategies of its residents force them to draw heavily upon their friends and relatives. Yet, it is precisely in these conditions that social relations are most explicitly characterised by competition and conflict. It is by recognising how far the social relations of a neighbourhood are constituted by antagonism and conflicts, rather than by assuming a natural harmony, that it might be possible to discern and delineate more accurately the bonds of community that are forged within them (Chandavarkar 2009: 124). He writes that the making of Girnigaon, a mill district in Mumbai, was in a fundamental sense an explicitly political process (Ibid.). This political process then makes it imperative that

> the social organization of the urban neighbourhood cannot simply be studied in terms of patronage or power relations which flow in one direction. There were several locations of power and influence in the neighbourhood, some of them deriving from patterns of association within them and all of them operating under constraints. (Ibid.: 230)

Neighbourhoods are predominantly studied with concerns towards deprivation (studies on slums) or to emphasise the segregated urban landscape (harping on gated communities, ghettos and neighbourhoods along ethnic lines). These studies of neighbourhoods and community initiatives are geared towards neighbourhood improvement. They rely upon simplified assumptions about boundaries, defining neighbourhoods primarily as administrative units. In architecture, urban design and planning, the neighbourhood is often assumed to have specific form and boundary, clearly identifiable residents and usages, and definite associations and identity. However, cities, neighbourhoods, dwellings and people are not so unproblematically bound. Thus, the complexities of social life often get erased, leaving no space for in-betweenness—ambiguous value systems and cultural and community dynamics—that urban planning must engage with for cohesive urban governance.

The core concerns running across the chapters in this book are twofold: first, to excavate social practices and flows by using ethnographic fieldwork; second, to look into the production of knowledge that shapes different discourses and disciplinary frames of the neighbourhood and its ties with the urban. In the book, while Gauri, Anakshi and Sadan engage with one or more aspects of spatial connotations of value regimes, enabling us to understand the vividness of neighbourhoods in a South Asian milieu; there are also examples where a certain amount of transitoriness—certain temporariness—has gone into the making of spaces and relationships, be it the case of the travelling Jain monks in Gauri's discussion or the *āshram* residents aspiring for *moksha* in Anakshi's or the linguistic concepts of *paros* and *parosan* (*padosan*) in Sadan's study. Within this overall ambit, different disciplinary perspectives have been mobilised to address ethnographic practices of creating neighbourhoods. In these practices, we come face-to-face with ambiguities, the richness of social life and community dynamics, which create local and varied meanings of neighbourhoods in varied contexts within specific regional moorings.

The endeavour undertaken in this book holds relevance in an age when words and concepts no longer carry any universal singular meaning and when contexts delineate concepts; the neighbourhood also comes before us as a historically dynamic and shifting term (Melvin 1985) with meanings accrued to it by processes that are regionally specific, fluid, unstable and plural. This poses a serious methodological challenge in studying neighbourhoods as social units or study sites.

Neighbourhood as a term has strong spatial connotations attached to it. In this sense, the term floats, having ramifications on territory and territoriality, boundary-making and as a physical landscape. Aspects of proximity functions as a key determinant in these usages. These implications of the neighbourhood remain central to the discourses of international relations and politics of boundary-making. This is just one example in the vast geographies of scholarship dotted with fields like epidemiology, animal behaviour, floral pollination in ecology and botany etc. The term neighbourhood circulates in these vast disciplinary geographies. We must immediately place a disclaimer upfront that in our engagement with the term neighbourhood, our focus remains confined to locating neighbourhoods in the social life of cities in northern India, which is geographically and culturally often referred to as North India, to emphasise its contrast with the 'other' India—South India. In North India, there are several terms for the neighbourhood: *mohallā*, *pol*, *wādā*, *basti*, *paros*, *pārā*, *jawaar* etc.[2]

In the absence of a robust discourse on the urban social life in India, we know little about the history and etymological trajectories or even the contemporary dynamics of how these terms intersect with society. Due to this scholarly neglect, we often end up framing these vernacular terms as synonyms for traditional neighbourhoods or as atavistic, pre-industrial and pre-modern reminiscences of the past. As a corollary, these terms also become susceptible to be perceived as organic, unplanned and imprecise spatial units. In usages, these units also circulate with overlapping connotations in which streets, bylanes and neighbourhoods are used interchangeably. Arjun Appadurai (1987) differentiates between streets and narrow lanes and associates the latter with the neighbourhood when he writes, '[T]iny lanes and streets ... characterize the *mohullas* of the north, the *agraharams* of the Tamil south, the *wadas* of Maharashtra, and the other semi-insulated zones of rural and small town India ....' Here, one may wonder whether it is the degree or the scale that differentiates a narrow lane from a street. If a street is characterised by certain anonymity and a narrow lane, in this scheme, embodies certain familiarity in its social geography, then what do such narrow lanes tell us about neighbourhoods? Unfortunately, while the street as a theatre of the 'outside' has attracted certain conceptual focus (Chakrabarty 1992; Kaviraj 1997), neighbourhoods have remained less privileged in attaining such scholarly energy. Thus, while streets can become ambiguous outside in Kaviraj's deliberation, a Bengali *pārā* or residential neighbourhood remains conceptually a taken-for-granted site and becomes a space 'characterised by sociability in which the relation between people was not the transient reciprocity of interests but of more stable common pursuits, temperaments, social bonding' (Kaviraj 1997: 102). We argue that there is a certain

2 By North India, we mean non-peninsular India consisting of western, eastern and northern parts of India. While we were keen to have essays reflecting on neighbourhoods in southern parts of the country, the term North India sets geo-social limitations of this volume.

conceptual blind spot, a certain taken for granted-ness, with which the neighbourhood comes before us in the discourse on urban society in India. Our attempt to privilege the neighbourhood is fundamentally oriented against such treatments. For example, Sadan tries to move beyond the bounded and segregated ideas of the neighbourhood or the unbounded-ness of the *mohallā* as a contrast to Western concepts. This is to critique the dominant discursive trajectory, largely coming from post-industrial town planning, that remains tied to the frames of territoriality in engaging with neighbourhoods. Instead, Sadan proposes another term, *paros*, for consideration in the lived experience of South Asian cityscapes. He argues that *paros* can be translated as 'in the neighbourhood'. It is a spatial term. However, *paros*, unlike neighbourhood, is not scalar. He argues that a focus on *paros* allows us to engage with the subjectivities—the experiential dynamics—of social-spatial relationship that a unit-based understanding of neighbourhood doesn't allow.

When we hear the colloquial term *gali-mohallā*, we can neither conceptually afford to leave aside the *mohallā* in the spatial complex these two (*gali* and *mohallā*) constitute together nor can we uncritically accept *mohallā* as a harmonious space made out of stable, common social bonding. If the street, the bazaar and the fair (*mela*) have formed the spatial complex in India (Chakrabarty 1992), we need to factor in the neighbourhood in conceptualising the ambiguous outside.

The conceptualisation of neighbourhood, therefore, often begins in a landscape of decolonised society trying to address the methodological crisis of anthropology. Thus, we almost instinctively invoke Arjun Appadurai's dictum of contrasting the scalar or spatial neighbourhood with that of the locality as 'primarily relational' (Appadurai 1997: 178). Appadurai directly confronts the question of the relationship between anthropology and locality in a decolonised world. But his dictum has acquired much wider circulation, and it has been serving almost contradictory purposes simultaneously: opening up scholarly attention towards neighbourhoods and also closing the possibilities of offering ethnographically grounded research on the subject. Therefore, it is crucial to be reminded of the dilemma that Appadurai centrally locates while thinking of the neighbourhood. He writes, 'The central dilemma is that neighbourhoods both are contexts and at the same time require and produce contexts.' While in the first sense, the neighbourhood provides the 'frame or setting', in the latter, it is 'a set of contexts, within which meaningful social action can be both generated and interpreted.... A neighbourhood is a multiplex interpretative site' (Appadurai 1997: 184). An insightful opening would be to remain attentive towards possibilities and challenges that neighbourhood as a concept throws up before us as researchers of urban social life in India.

Historically speaking, when grappling with vernacular constellations like *mohallā*, *pārā*, *wādā* etc., the question we need to ask is whether the imprecise nature of these terms simply suggests lack of town planning in precolonial India. Or, in other words, when we are oriented towards studying neighbourhoods in non-Western societies like India, are we trying to study these vernacular forms of urban socio-spatial units, or are we trying to judge *mohallā* lives through an imposed prism of the 'neighbourhood'? There has been strong opposition to impose Western terms on Indian landscapes. For Soraswati (Saraswati) Raju, 'The mohallā not only carries a narrow spatial connotation, but it also encompasses the entire gamut of familial and sociocultural relationships among its individual residents. In this sense it is one large extended family' (Raju 1980: 281). According to her, '[N]eighborhood units owe their origin to urban planners' overreliance ... to generate and maintain cohesion and fellow-feeling among socioeconomically diverse communities.' For her, a *mohallā* is an

> evolved reality that resembles the jati or endogamous caste enclaves of rural communities, and, like those enclaves, relates to the occupational, religious or geographical origin of the mohallā dwellers.... The degree and nature of involvement of residents of a mohallā are altogether different from those inherent in the concept of a neighborhood.... In Indian mohallā, the persons or families who live together there have mutually meaningful social relationships of a primary character. (Raju 1980)

She emphasises upon the closely interwoven, smooth and inconspicuous form of sociality having a humane—almost 'rural'—environment and associated with very intense personal interaction. Given the homogeneity of the milieu and the intense interaction of a primary order within it, 'everybody knows everybody' in a given *mohallā*. Incidentally, this 'know-ing' involves much more than the English word suggests; no cause for concern is implied in the word 'know-ing'. *Mohallā* residents thus have few opportunities for exposure to values and norms other than the ones they learned in childhood (Raju 1980).

From a contemporary perspective with obsessive concern towards contestation, conflict and power dynamic, it is easier to reject such a romantic idea of the neighbourhood as an abode of harmony and organic ties between its members. Yet, the memory of this harmony and the neighbourhood as a safe place often circulate almost as ubiquitous templates in the aftermath of communal violence in recent decades. For example, during his long conversations with victims of the Partition violence, a member of this editorial collective was repeatedly told that their perpetrators came from outside. They were not their neighbours; their neighbours, who were from other religious communities, remained committed to safeguarding them.

The outsider–neighbour binary, however, got complicated in the recent communal riots in Delhi in February 2020 when Afreen, a victim, narrated, 'The mobs were from outside, but there were also locals there. The locals told them where we lived—this is a Hindu house, this is a Muslim house' (Barton and Srivastava 2020).

One may disapprove of such a romanticisation of the harmonious ideas of the *mohallā*, but she/he will not necessarily reject the centrality of these *mohallās* in terms of their larger roles in the making of the city. For example, Narayani Gupta tells us,

> Indian towns were loose federations with each locality ('mohulla') populated by members of an extended family, a caste or an occupational group, and with gates to shut off one *mohulla* (mohallā) from the others. The leaders of *mohulla* organisations were on a level of equality which ignored the social hierarchy of castes. These leaders were intermediaries between the townsfolk and the officials, whose role was thus a limited one. (Gupta 1981)

Historian S. Nurul Hasan in his study of the urban morphology of medieval Delhi argues,

> [The] number of streets and mohallās which have continued to exist under the same name is remarkably large. Some of these have retained their traditional features, while many other cases though the names have survived the type of activity and the character of the population has undergone a complete change. For example, in Paiwalan near Jama masjid, one can still buy fireworks; similarly, in Chawri Bazar, shops selling copper or brass utensils are still found. (Hasan 1994: 88)

In this scenario, we are left with a number of unanswered questions. For example, are vernacular forms of neighbourhood merely illustrations of change and continuity of urban social landscape? Are these mere socio-spatial and linguistic traces from the past? If these questions about vernacular units can be linked to the earlier raised issues of imprecise spatial meaning, unsegregated nature of these *mohallās* and the mythic lack of town planning in precolonial India, we do find examples of historians testifying to both segregated as well as unsegregated neighbourhoods in precolonial periods. For example, in the context of ancient India, Shonaleeka Kaul writes that Sanskrit *kavya* texts, a primary source of her study,

> display a notion of quarters (*catvaara*), localities, or neighbourhoods (*vaata*) by which residential areas in the city are denoted. However, perhaps in keeping with the principle of Sringaara rasa, the only localities the Kaavyas dwell on are those of courtesans (*vesavavaasah, vesavaata, vesa-sannivesa*) and much less, those of affluent merchants (*sresthicatvaarah*). (Kaul 2010: 101–102)

We find that in ancient India, *sannivesa* was a generic Sanskrit term for both settlement—even towns and cities (Rai 1965: 15–25, 274–294)—and a neighbourhood or a residential unit like *vesa-sannivesa* mentioned earlier. These *sannivesa* and *vaata* were premised upon various types of social segregations such as separate residential quarters for spate guilds, state officials, *varna* orders etc. On the other hand, in medieval cities, for example in Shahjahanabad, Nurul Hasan writes,

> The most commonly used term for a locality is mohallā. It could be named after an individual, such as mohallā Hakim Muhsin Khan or mohallā Muhammad Ali Khan, but the commonest are those named after artisan, such as mohallā chungaran, mohallā *dhobiwala*

> (quarters of washermen) or mohallā *kashtibalan* (boatmen). Some of the mohallās bear the name of some characteristic features of the place, such as mohallā *imli* (tamarind) or mohallāh chah-i-rahat (well with a Persian wheel). In the case of Matia Mahal, mohallā changes its form. Two interesting names are *chhatta* and *katra. Chhatta* literally means a covered lane or bazar, but it frequently refers to the locality where artisans practising a particular craft lived and/or worked, such as *chhatta mimaran* (masons), or *chhatta momgaran* (wax makers). In many cases, a *chhatta* would be named after the person who built it, or with a place with which it may otherwise have been associated, such as Chhatta Lala Tansukh Rai or Chhatta Jan Nisar Khan, or Chhatta Nigambodh Ghat or Chhatta Lahori darwaza. *Katra* literally means a small square bazar, but quite often it refers to a wholesale market or where stocks were kept. There is a *nishan* of Nur Jahan Begum ordering officers not to interfere with the merchants stocking their merchandise in a *katra*. Some of these were named after merchants of a particular commodity, such as *katra bazzazan* (cloth merchants) *katra Roghan Zard* or *ghi ka katra* (clarified butter), *katra nil* (indigo) but quite often it was named after the builder or the owner, such as *katra Adina Beg Khan*, or *katra Munshi Kanwal. Tripolia* (lit. three gates) was also used as a term denoting a locality. In *Tripolia* were the makan of Shagunchand Sahu, *mandvi gul faro shan*, a *sharab-khana* (pub; wine-house) Mumtazganj, the habitation of *garihanan* (cart owners or drivers) later the royal artillery, going up to Kauriapul (bridge over Faiz canal). (Hasan 1982)

Hasan also writes that in Shahjahanabad there was no segregation of houses between the rich and the poor or between residential and commercial parts—a feature that developed under the British (Hasan 1994: 89).

With a reference to Franklin, a traveller who visited the city in 1793, another historian Ataullah mentions thirty-six *mohallās* in the city of Delhi in the 18th century. Each of these was named either after the Omrah who resided there or because of some local circumstances linked to the place. In the early 19th century, Mirza Sangin Beg in his *Sair-ul Manazil* mentions that there were twenty-nine *mohallās* within the walls of Shahajahanabad and thirty-seven *mohallās* or *bastis* (suburban settlements) outside the city walls (Ataullah 2006–2007). Alongside this description of unsegregated Shahjahanabad, we have *pols* of Ahmedabad with a fair amount of segregation inbuilt into their spatial structures (Doshi 1974).

Whatever the case of segregation and imprecision in the boundary between residential and commercial units, these examples at least make the link between segregation and town planning futile. These also suggest that the history of neighbourhoods cannot be the ground to suggest whether towns were planned or grew in an unplanned manner in precolonial periods in India.[3]

Having outlined this history, let us clarify that we are not interested in the neighbourhoods of precolonial periods. A brief foray in history has been offered here only to unpack the politics in the conceptual lineage of the *mohallā* or neighbourhood in a non-Western milieu like India. This history is crucial as the concept of the neighbourhood comes down to us with historically shifting meanings, as we saw earlier in the Euro-American contexts. The question we need to ask at this stage is this: what kinds of insights and provocations the history of these vernacular, spatial constellations offer us for a richer understanding of neighbourhoods in India or to a great extent in South Asia?

Among scholars who have treated neighbourhoods and neighbourly social relations beyond mere passive locations, Sylvia Vatuk's 'fictive kinship' exhibits certain uniqueness in her usage of the term to describe the social relationship in a neighbourhood. She argues, '[T]his use of kin terms does not normally reflect the presence of a ritual kin tie between neighbors or of any other institutionalised form of fictive kin relationship.' Kinship here is not to be understood in genealogical terms. She notes that in this setting

> children may call the elders of a neighboring family *mausi* and *mausa*, but address the younger cousins of the latter as *bhai sāhab* and *jiji*. A man may refer to a male friend as 'elder brother,' but to the latter's wife as 'elder sister' rather than 'elder brother's wife. (Vatuk 1969)

3 While one source of this myth of absence of town planning in India goes to colonial prejudices, the other strand goes back to Bernier, the French traveller who noted that Indian cities were merely military camps (Chandra 1994). Historians have also written on urban planning in ancient India and the corpus of texts dealing with building, planning and other organisational dimensions of urban life (Rai 1965; Kaul 2010).

In the same breath, it is worth recalling Janaki Abraham's work that draws on her fieldwork in the Indian cities of Bikaner and Thalassery to study neighbours as guardians of local norms and rules, exercising considerable social control. Moving away from a focus on social problems and poverty, she explores the implications of proximity that allow various kinds of face-to-face and sensorial interactions. She analyses everyday practices that make up the web of relations that constitutes the neighbourhood—social control, social approval, legitimacy and support—with a focus on how gender relations are produced in everyday neighbourhood life (Abraham 2018). Abraham argues that 'neighbourhood spaces and relationships within them have the potential of exercising tremendous social and cultural influence' that 'emerges precisely from [the] proximity of living and the everyday sensorial interactions between people—the sights, sounds and smells' (Ibid.: 106). For her, this is a space

> in which identities are produced in everyday life. In this context, neighbourhoods may not be commensurate with class/caste/religion—categories that are reproduced by marriage and kinship patterns. However, neighbourhoods are simultaneously shaped by kinship practices, whether in terms of the relationship a woman has with those in the neighbourhood ... or as a result of residence and inheritance regimes.... Neighbourhoods attain their quality from these relationships, as also from the shared sensorial space of everyday life. (Ibid.: 107)

Conclusion: An Outline for the Way Forward

Urban transformations shape subjectivities and experiences of people who live there. By placing these subjectivities and perceptions in their specific contextual frames, we hope to get a rich tapestry of the broader field of urban life and the idea of urban social. This edited volume is conceptualised to focus on neighbourhoods, their particularities and role in shaping our understanding of the urban in India. The chapters in this volume disclose the linkages and disjuncture between the social practices of neighbourhoods and the language, logic and experience of dwelling, housing, urban planning and governance. In sum, the book brings about an understanding of the particularities and heterogeneities of neighbourhoods and neighbourliness.

With these objectives, we sum up the implications of this book by making the following sets of arguments as we engage with the vast corpus of knowledge on the theme of enquiry. First, there is a presence of religious institutions and religiosity in the making of neighbourhoods, which needs to be recognised and factored in our understanding of space. While scholars have studied linkages between religion and space at sites of pilgrimage towns and towards a spatial understanding of communalism, we have seldom paid attention to how religiosity is an overt or hidden presence of the sacred in our everyday life and its role in the making of a neighbourhood.

Second, Just as no discussion on the social in South Asia can afford to ignore the dimension of caste in general and untouchability in particular, neighbourhood studies ought to pay attention to how caste and untouchability have shaped the hitherto ignored domain of the spatial history of urban landscape. This history needs to be written by attending to spatial segregation both along caste lines and through the lived experiences of Dalit neighbourhoods. These together make a case for spatial subjectivities.

Third, an anthropology of the spatial-social concept of neighbourhood has to capitalise upon oral archives of the everyday to engage with the contestations and micro-physics of politics. In the everyday-ness of conversations and through the mundane, we get to understand how processes of community and neighbourhood formations get intermeshed with each other.

Fourth, at the axes of both community and neighbourhood formations, the spatial subjectivities come into being in and through contestations and subversions. These processes than make it imminent for us to foreground figures of neighbours and their circulating bodies scribbled with gendered codes of different types. Without paying attention to these bodies and without engendering neighbourhoods, there can neither be any spatial subjectivities nor can there be any discourse on spatial affectivity in South Asia.

Fifth, in scholarly engagements, neighbourhoods need to be populated by people and their subjectivities to resist any singular and universally circulating templates of the urban. Thus, while we acknowledge the dominance of planning concerns in the discourse on the neighbourhood and try to move away from a planning-centric approach, we cannot and must not ignore these concerns. However, we argue that these concerns have to be recalibrated to address how neighbourhoods are formed by their responses to dominant planning templates and by rearticulating aspirations of housing. It is only through these responses emanating from the ground that we would be able to venture outside the confinements of the megacity-saturated discourse of the South Asian urban and be able to grasp urban social life in its regional vividness and experiential ambiguities.

Finally, this book is a modest attempt to respond to the aforementioned issues. Needless to say, there is an enormous possibility of additions to make a more holistic view of the neighbourhood and our attempts to understand this socio-spatial term. And hence, it would not be out of place to underline in the body of this book the under-represented aspects of the neighbourhood or the components of cultural expressions. After all, any attempt to make an exploration exhaustive meets with a spatial-temporal limit! So is the case with the present book. And yet, we admit the imperative of exploring the neighbourhood with reference to a large body of literary and popular cultural materials, domains of mediated communications and a larger trope of sensorium in which one can concretely smell, touch, hear, see and feel neighbourhood. A project of another kind—where the authors and editors would be assured of the basics, and they would venture towards unearthing deeply concealed mythologies of urban folk—is something we save for the future.

References

Abbott, Carl. 1974. 'The Neighborhoods of New York, 1760–1775'. *New York History*, Vol. 55, No. 1 (January), pp. 35–54.

———. 2008. *How Cities Won the West: Four Centuries of Urban Change in Western North America*. Albuquerque: University of New Mexico Press.

Appadurai, Arjun. 1987. 'Street Culture'. *The India Magazine*, Vol. 8, No. 1 (December), pp. 2–23.

Appadurai, Arjun. 1997. 'The Production of Locality'. In *Modernity at Large: Cultural Dimensions of Globalization*. Delhi: Oxford University Press, pp. 178–200.

Ataullah. 2006–2007. 'Mapping 18th-century Delhi: The Cityscape of a Pre-Modern Sovereign City'. *Proceedings of the Indian History Congress*, Vol. 67, pp. 1042–1057.

Ballhatchet, Kenneth and John Harrison (eds). 1980. *The City in South Asia: Premodern and Modern*. London: Curzon.

Banga, Indu (ed.). 1991. *The City in Indian History: Urban Demography, Society, and Politics*. New Delhi: South Asia Publications.

Barton, Naomi and Srishti Srivastava. 2020. 'They Took Down Their Pants, Pointed Their Genitals at Us, and Said, "Yeh Lo Azaadi"', *The Wire*. Available at https://thewire.in/women/delhi-riots-women-sexual-harassment (accessed on 5 March 2020).

Bates, Crispin and Minoru Mio. 2015. *Cities in South Asia*. New York: Routledge.

Bharathi, Naveen, Deepak Malghan and Andaleeb Rahman. 2018. 'Isolated by Caste: Neighbourhood-Scale Residential Segregation in Indian Metros'. Working Paper 572. Indian Institute of Management, Bangalore.

Caldeira, Teresa P.R. 2001. *City of Walls: Crime, Segregation, and Citizenship in Sao Paulo*. Berkeley: University of California Press.

Castells, Manuel. 1996. *The Information Age: Economy, Society and Culture*, Vol. I: The Rise of the Network Society. Cambridge, MA: Blackwell Publishers.

Chakrabarti, Indranil. 2006. 'Local Governance: Politics and Neighbourhood Activism in Calcutta'. In *The Meaning of the Local: Politics of Place in Urban India*, edited by Geert De Neve and Henrik Donner, pp. 68–89. London: Routledge.

Chakrabarty, Dipesh. 1992. 'Of Garbage, Modernity and the Citizen's Gaze'. *Economic and Political Weekly*, Vol. 27 (10/11), pp. 541–547.

Chandavarkar, Rajnarayan. 2009. *History, Culture and the Indian City*. Cambridge: Cambridge University Press.

Chandra, Satish. 1994. 'Some Aspects of Urbanisation in Medieval India'. In *The City in Indian History: Urban Demography, Society, and Politics*, edited by Indu Banga, pp. 81–86. Delhi: Manohar and Urban History Association of India.

Dasgupta, Keya. 2003. 'Genesis of a Neighbourhood: The Mapping of Bhabanipur'. Occasional Paper 175. Centre for Studies in Social Sciences, Kolkata.

De Neve, Geert and Henrik Donner (eds). 2006. *The Meaning of the Local: Politics of Place in Urban India*. London: Routledge.

De, Aparajita. 2016. 'Spatialisation of Selves: Religion and Liveable Spaces among Hindus and Muslims in the Walled City of Ahmedabad, India'. *City, Culture and Society*, Vol. 7, pp. 149–154.

Delhi Development Authority. 1962. Master Plan of Delhi. Delhi.

Dirlik, Arif. 2001 'Place-based Imagination: Globalism and the Politics of Place'. In *Places and Politics in an Age of Globalization,* edited by Roxanne Praznaik and Arif Dirlik. Lanham: Rowman and Littlefield.

Donner, Henrike and Geert de Neve. 2006. 'Space, Place and Globalization: Revisiting the Urban Neighbourhood in India'. In *The Meaning of the Local: Politics of Place in Urban India,* edited by Geert de Neve and Henrike Donner, pp. 1–20. New York: Routledge.

Doshi, Harish. 1974. *Traditional Neighbourhood in a Modern City.* Delhi: Abhinav Publication.

Duneier, Mitchell. 1999. *Sidewalk.* New York: Farrar, Straus and Giroux.

Dupont, Veronique, Emma Tarlo and Denis Vidal (eds). 2000. *Delhi: Urban Space and Human Destinies.* Delhi: Manohar.

Foote Whyte, William. 1955. *Street Corner Society: The Social Structure of an Italian Slum.* Chicago and London: University of Chicago Press.

Gandhi, Ajay and Lotte Hoek. 2012. 'Introduction to Crowds and Conviviality: Ethnographies of South Asian City'. *Ethnography,* Vol. 13, No. 1, pp. 3–11.

Gayer, Laurent and Christophe Jaffrelot (eds). 2012. *Muslims in Indian Cities: Trajectories of Marginalisation.* London: Hurst and Company.

Jamil, Ghazala. 2014. 'The Capitalist Logic of Spatial Segregation: A Study of Muslims in Delhi'. *Economic and Political Weekly*, Vol. 49, No. 3, pp. 52–58.

———. 2017. *Accumulation by Segregation: Muslim Localities in Delhi.* Delhi: Oxford University Press.

Gupta, Narayani. 1981. 'Twelve Years On: Urban History in India'. *Urban History Yearbook*, Vol. 8, pp. 76–79.

Gupta, Radhika. 2015. 'There Must Be Some Way Out of Here: Beyond a Spatial Conception of Muslim Ghettoization in Mumbai?' *Ethnography*, Vol. 16, No. 3, pp. 352–370.

Hasan, Nurul S. 1982. 'The Morphology of a Mediaeval Indian City: A Case Study of Shahjahanabad in the 18th and Early 19th Century'. *Proceedings of the Indian History Congress*, Vol. 43, pp. 307–317.

———. 1991/1994. 'The Morphology of a Medieval Indian City: A Case Study of Shahjahanabad'. In *The City in Indian History* edited by Indu Banga, pp. 87–98. Delhi: Manohar and Urban History Association of India.

Holston, James. 1998. *Cities and Citizenship.* Durham: Duke University Press.

Hull, Matthew S. 2011. 'Communities of Place, Not Kind: American Technologies of Neighborhood in Postcolonial Delhi'. *Comparative Studies in Society and History*, Vol. 53, No. 4, pp. 757–790.

Jacobs, Jane. 1961. *The Death and Life of Great American Cities*. New York: Vintage Books.

Jaffrelot, Christophe and Charlotte Thomas. 2012. 'Facing Ghettoisation in "Riot-City": Old Ahmedabad and Juhapura between Victimisation and Self-help'. In *Muslims in Indian Cities: Trajectories of Marginalisation*, edited by Laurent Gayer and Christophe Jaffrelot, pp. 43–80. Delhi: HarperCollins.

Jaoul, Nicolas. 2012. 'The Making of a Political Stronghold: A Dalit Neighbourhood's Exit from the Hindu Nationalist Riot System'. *Ethnography*, Vol. 13, No. 1, Special Issue: Crowds and Conviviality: Ethnographies of the South Asian City, pp. 102–116.

Kaul, Shonaleeka. 2010. *Imagining the Urban: Sanskrit and the City in Early India*. Ranikhet: Permanent Black.

Kaviraj, Sudipta. 1997. 'Filth and the Public Sphere: Concepts and Practices about Space in Calcutta., *Public Culture*, Vol. 10, No. 1, pp. 83–113.

Khan, Sameera. 2007. 'Negotiating the Mohallā: Exclusion, Identity and Muslim Women in Mumbai'. *Economic and Political Weekly*, Vol. 42, No. 17, pp. 1527–1533.

Khan, Tabassum Ruhi. 2015. *Beyond Hybridity and Fundamentalism: Emerging Muslim Identity in Globalized India*. Delhi: Oxford University Press.

Kirmani, Nida. 2008. 'Competing Constructions of "Muslimness" in the South Delhi Neighborhood of Zakir Nagar'. *Journal of Muslim Minority Affairs*, Vol. 28, No. 3, pp. 355–369.

Low, S.M. 2001. 'The Edge and the Center: Gated Communities and the Discourse of the Urban Fear'. *American Anthropologist*, Vol. 103, No. 1 (March), pp. 45–58.

Lynch, Owen. 1969. *The Politics of Untouchability: Social Mobility and Social Change in a City of India*. New York: Columbia University Press.

Mann, Peter H. 1970. 'The Neighborhood'. In *Neighbourhood, City, and Metropolis: An Integrated Reader in Urban Sociology*, edited by Robert Gutman and David Popenoe, pp. 568–583. New York: Random House.

Masselos, Jim. 2007. 'Power in the Bombay "mohallā", 1904–15: An Initial Exploration into the World of Indian Urban Muslim'. In *The City in Action: Bombay Struggle for Power*. Delhi: Oxford University Press, pp. 15–45.

Massey, Doreen. 1994. *Space, Place and Gender*. Cambridge: Polity Press.

Melvin, Mooney Patricia. 1985. 'Changing Contexts: Neighborhood Definition and Urban Organization'. *American Quarterly*, Vol. 37, No. 3, pp. 357–367.

Menon, Devaki Kalyani. 2015. '"Security", Home, and Belonging in Contemporary India: Old Delhi as a Muslim Place'. *Etnofoor*, Vol. 27, No. 2, pp. 113–131.

Mines, Mattison. 2006. 'Temples and Charity: The Neighbourhood Styles of the Komati and Beeri Chettiar Merchants of Madras City'. In *The Meaning of the Local: Politics of Place in Urban India,* edited by Geert De Neve and Henrik Donner, pp. 89–115. London: Routledge.

Patel, Sujata and Kushal Deb (eds). 2006. *Urban Studies*. Delhi: Oxford University Press.

Prakash, Gyan. 2002. 'The Urban Turn'. *Sarai Reader 02: The Cities of Everyday Life*. Sarai, CSDS and Society for Old and New Media, Amsterdam, February, pp. 2–7.

Prashad, Vijay. 2001. *Untouchable Freedom: A Social History of a Community*, Delhi: Oxford University Press.

Rai, Udaynarayan. 1965. *Prachin Bharat me Nagar aur Nagar Jeevan*. Allahabad: Hindustani Akademy.

Raju, Soraswati. 1980. 'The Social Meaning of "Urban Neighborhood" in India'. *Ekistics* (Issue: Neighborhoods: Their Physical and Social Attributes), Vol. 47, No. 283, pp. 286–289.

Ray, C.N. 2008. 'Changing Pattern of Traditional Neighbourhood in the Walled City of Ahmedabad: Case of Vad Vali Pol and Navi Pol'. Working paper 44. CEPT University, Ahmedabad.

Roy, A. 2004. 'Transnational Trespassings: The Geopolitics of Urban Informality'. In *Urban Informality: Transnational Perspectives from the Middle East, South Asia and Latin America*, edited by A. Roy and N. AlSayyad, pp. 289–317. Lanham, MD: Lexington Books.

Roy, Ananya and Aihwa Ong (eds). 2011. *Worlding Cities: Asian Experiments and the Art of Being Global.* Sussex: Wiley Blackwell.

Ruef, Martin and Seok-Woo Kwon. 2016. 'Neighborhood Associations and Social Capital'. *Social Forces*, Vol. 95, No. 1, pp. 159–189.

Sharan, Awadhendra. 2006. 'In the City, Out of Place: Environment and Modernity, Delhi 1860s to 1960s'. *Economic and Political Weekly*, Vol. 41, No. 47 (25 November–1 December), pp. 4905–4911.

Sharma, Kalpana. 2000. *Rediscovering Dharavi: Stories from Asia's Largest Slum*. Delhi: Penguin.

Simone, AbdouMalick. 2019. 'Something Else Besides: Reconsidering the Sociality of the Urban Life'. Paper presented at the International Seminar on Locating Neighbourhoods in the Global South, Tezpur University, Tezpur, 25–26 September.

Shraddha, Navalli Patil. 2017. Building and Dwelling in Muslim Neighborhoods: Living Together, Albeit, Separately in Globalizing Delhi, Unpublished PhD. Dissertation in Architecture, University of California, Berkeley.

Skaria, Ajai. 2002. 'Gandhi's Politics: Liberalism and the Question of the Ashram'. *The South Atlantic Quarterly*, Vol. 101, No. 4, pp. 955–986.

Sobti, Manu P. 1996. 'Migration and Cultural Identity: Pathan mohallās in Bhopal, India'. *Traditional Dwellings and Settlements Review*, Vol. 8, No. 1 (Identity, Tradition and Built Form: The Role of Culture in Development and Planning, Fifth International Conference, 14–17 December 1996, Berkeley, California), pp. 49–50.

Soja, Edward W. 1989. *Postmodern Geographies: The Reassertion of Space in Critical Social Theory*. London: Verso.

Srivastava, Sanjay. 2015. *Entangled Urbanism: Slum, Gated Community, and Shopping Mall in Delhi and Gurgaon*. Delhi: Oxford University Press.

Tarlo, Emma. 2003. *Unsettling Memories: Narratives of the Emergency in Delhi*. London: Hurst.

Thakkar, Usha. 2004. 'Mohallā Committees of Mumbai: Candles in Ominous Darkness'. *Economic and Political Weekly*, Vol. 39, No. 6, pp. 580–586.

Thomson, Mark. 1993. *Gandhi and His Ashramas*. Bombay: Popular Prakashan.

Varshney, Ashutosh. 2002. *Ethnic Conflict and Civic Life: Hindu and Muslims in India*. Delhi: Oxford University Press.

Vatuk, Sylvia. 1969. 'Reference, Address, and Fictive Kinship in Urban North India'. *Ethnology*, Vol. 8, No. 3, pp. 255–272.

Vidyarthi, Sanjeev. 2010. 'Inappropriately Appropriated or Innovatively Indigenized?: Neighborhood Unit Concept in Post-independence India'. *Journal of Planning History* Vol. 9, No. 4, pp. 260–276.

Wirth, Louis. 1938. 'Urbanism as a Way of Life'. *The American Journal of Sociology*, Vol. 44, No. 1, pp. 1–24.

Part I

Spatial Religiosity and the Making of Neighbourhoods

2

Sacred Anchors in Contemporary Neighbourhoods: The Case of Jain Religious Institutions in Ahmedabad

Gauri Bharat*

This chapter explores the relationship between Jain religious institutions in Ahmedabad and Jain families who live in their vicinities to discuss how religious practices anchored in these institutions are important formative forces for the neighbourhoods. Before delving into the chapter, there are three points I would like to offer by way of background. The first is the question of disciplinary location. I'm an architectural historian by training; therefore, my reading of neighbourhoods follows primarily the spatial logic of both religious practices and neighbourhood. Social relations are explored primarily through their embedding in spatial relationships. The focus on religious institutions and their enmeshing with neighbourhoods is also in many ways a departure from the dominant tropes in neighbourhood studies that resonate in the editorial introduction of this book. Within built-environment related discourses, the planning or formation of a neighbourhood, and indeed the city itself, is largely imagined as agnostic.

What is extensively theorised is the economic logic of urban development or its politics. Religiosity on the other hand usually features as a source of conflict or contestation, more so in contemporary times with the rise of fundamentalism across the globe. In Ahmedabad, scholars have advanced a number of perspectives on the relationship between Hindutva politics and urban development (Desai 2011; Ghassem-Fachandi 2015; Mahadevia 2007). Jain religiosity and its

* The author would like to thank Vaidehi Shah, Arun Dalal, Navnit Thakershy, Nalini Thakershy, Pankaj Shah, Mayuri Shah, Jigish Shah, Maitriratna Shreeji Maharaj Saheb and Nandi Bhushakji Maharaj Saheb for consenting to be interviewed for the study.

role in urban neighbourhood formation do not quite fall within these tropes, and its spatial analysis has remained muted.

The second point, in a sense following from the first, is of position and method. The observations in this chapter are rooted partly in the experiences and religious identity of my husband's family. They identify themselves as Jains, although the levels of religious practices vary from negligible (in my husband's case) to nominal (in my parents-in-law's) to elaborate (among various members of the extended family). Much of the fieldwork for this chapter was carried out among family members and close acquaintances, and most of the inferences regarding how families engage with religious institutions and neighbourhoods are based on these interactions. The perusal of family networks also allowed intimate insights into past connections and memories of earlier institutions and places of living, particularly the circumstances in which changes took place over time. However, this is not just a question of the family being a site of enquiry. Being located at the largely 'non-practising' end of the religious spectrum is instrumental in my understanding of how moderately religious Jains engage with religious institutions; this also allows me access to the shifts in associations and practices that occur over time and across generations.

The third point is about the specific Jain sect I focus on. Jains today are broadly divided into four groups: Swetambar, Digambar, Sthanakvasi and Terapanthi. In this chapter, I engage with Swetambar Murtipujak Jains, the largest of the four divisions with a significant concentration in Ahmedabad, and more widely in North Gujarat.[1] A key difference between Murtipujaks and other sects—in addition to theological differences and ritual practices of ascetics—is the emphasis on idol worship (the other sects are relatively iconoclastic). Given the historic geographical distribution of the Murtipujak Jain community in North Gujarat, there is a high concentration of Jain temples in the area. The community in Ahmedabad is particularly

1 Cort suggests that historically Jains were divided into two main sects, viz. Digambar and Swetambar (2001: 41–42). Sthanakvasi separated from Swetambar between mid-15th and 17th centuries, while Terapanthis split in the mid-18th century.

influential since they have historically formed the mercantile class of the city. Within the medieval walled city of Ahmedabad alone, there are 115 Jain temples.[2]

Jain religious institutions in Ahmedabad are broadly of three kinds: (a) *derasar*, a temple where Jain deities are worshipped, (b) *upashray*, a place of temporary residence for Jain *sadhumaharaja* (monks) and *sadhvimaharaja* (nuns) and (c) community kitchens, where cooked foods are served according to ritual dietary requirements. Community kitchens are also of different types: *bhojanshala*, *ambayilshala* and *vayyavachshala*. *Bhojanshala* is open to most people and serves food broadly according to Jain dietary laws; *ambayilshala* caters specifically to Jains observing special fasts and *vayyavachsala* caters to ascetics alone. There are other institutions in Ahmedabad such as *bhata ghar*, located near places of worship where snacks and tea are provided to worshippers, and *panjrapole*, where sick and abandoned animals are supported through charity. In this chapter, I focus particularly on the first three and explore the relationship between these institutions and the everyday life and space of the neighbourhoods in which they are located. Jain lay worshippers form communities known as *sanghs*, the locus of which is usually a *derasar* and an *upashray*. There is no restriction on offering prayers in any *derasar*, but members of a *sangh* usually offer daily and other ritual prayers at the *derasar* where they belong and also participate in collective events like sermons, feasts and social events. In this chapter, I explore some of the ways in which these practices produce the idea of a Jain neighbourhood. I also trace some of the shifts in the institutions and neighbourhoods to suggest that the relationships between them are neither fixed nor constant but are contingent on wider processes of urban transformation.

2 The World Heritage City nomination dossier of Ahmedabad mentions ninety-seven *derasar* while a booklet published by a senior and a reputed ascetic identifies 115 *derasars*. The difference in number could be on account of the *ghar derasar*, which families build inside their houses for personal worship.

The *Sangh* and the Neighbourhood

The idea of a 'Jain neighbourhood' as a place densely populated by Jain families alone is a fact in Ahmedabad and possibly other cities with significant Jain population. The Paldi area of Ahmedabad, for instance, has a large number of Jain families. The density is particularly palpable in the traffic jams during the festival of Paryushan, the period of most-intense religiosity and festivity for Jains. During the festival, Jains will gather in large numbers to listen to sermons, observe fasts, have collective feasts and visit one another to seek forgiveness for the past year. It is a common practice to avoid Jain neighbourhoods or plan travels carefully since the roads are choked with vehicular traffic and parking space impossible to find during Paryushan. What is of interest for this chapter, however, are the relationship ties that function beyond physical proximity. The idea of a Jain neighbourhood is not just a matter of Jain families living together in one place, nor is it only the social ties that bind them. Jain neighbourhoods become sites in and through which imaginations and bonds of being a collective are enacted and located, which in turn offer a new reading of the processes that shape contemporary neighbourhoods in Ahmedabad.

Jain families who live in a particular neighbourhood and offer worship in a particular *derasar* constitute a *sangh* or community. Unlike in other religious groups where communities may temporally aggregate in places of worship, the Jain *sangh* appears institutionalised to a greater extent. Each member family is registered through a directory known as *vastipatra* maintained by the *derasar*. Families pay a nominal fee, almost like membership fees. Any additions to a family through marriage and birth are registered in the record; for instance, my name and those of my children's were included in our *sangh* record as we became part of the family. The theological roots of a *sangh* lie in the preachings of Lord Mahavir, who is believed to have systematised this grouping and structure. A *sangh* comprises of male ascetics (*sadhu maharaj*), female ascetics (*sadhviji maharaj*), male lay worshippers (*shravak*) and female lay worshippers (*shravika*).[3] While lay worshippers are families that live in the neighbourhood, monks and nuns do not usually permanently reside in any one place.[4] They travel through the year, moving from one location to another and sustaining themselves with food gathered from Jain families. They do not cook themselves nor do they have any worldly possessions. They take up temporary residence in *upashrays* usually located in the vicinity of Jain families. The presence of monks and nuns complete a *sangh*; it offers a theological anchor to lay members of the community through sermons—even informal conversations—on religious belief and practices.

While each *sangh* is anchored in a *derasar*, the same specificity does not apply to an *upashray*. One *upashray* may be supported by, and thus connected to, various *sanghs* in a neighbourhood. Another difference between a *derasar* and an *upashray* is in the architecture of the two institutions. While *derasars* were built and renovated according to treatises and advice from the learned *gurus* who are typically senior ascetics, *upashrays* are vastly varied structures. In a few cases, *upashrays* were custom-built, but in most other cases, they are houses donated to *sanghs* by their benefactors, which are subsequently used as *upashrays*. These, therefore, vary widely from new buildings and apartments, even

---

3 While this is a broadly accepted description of the *sangh*, Cort suggests that this term has three different connotations within Jain society (2001: 48). As the *caturvidh* (fourfold) or *sakal* (complete) *sangh*, it refers to the congregation of *sadhus*, *sadhvis*, *sravaks*, and *sravikas*, that is, the totality of Jain society consisting of male and female mendicants and male and female laity. As the *sadhu sangh* or *sadhu-sadhvi sangh*, it refers to the totality of the mendicant community. Third, it refers to neighborhood or city-wide lay congregations. Although such lay congregations are often affiliated with one particular mendicant *gacch* or *samudday*, they function largely as autonomous units. Under the religious charity laws of contemporary India, most neighborhood *sanghs* are legally constituted bodies with a board of trustees.

4 I say usually because under some circumstances, ascetics choose to or are compelled to become *sthayis* or residents. This happens when ascetics become too old to regularly travel or fall ill. In order to permanently reside in one *upashray*, an ascetic must seek permission from the *sangh* under whose auspices the *upashray* operates. Alternatively, *sangh* members may invite ascetics to take up residence for a specific reason.

bungalows, in western Ahmedabad, to older and renovated houses within the walled city. Considering the difference between the continued historical-canonical basis for the developments of *derasars*, the lack of any such underpinnings for *upashrays* points to the difference in the architectural histories of these two institutions. Spatially, *derasars* were a historically significant anchor, while *upashrays* may be of more recent vintage, or at least more varied and ambiguous in terms of their relationship with *sanghs*.

Most contemporary *upashrays* are established through donations or contributions by *sangh* members or other benefactors such as the trusts that oversee the management of these institutions. *Sangh* members offer financial contributions in various ways for the sustenance of *derasars*, *upashrays* and other *sangh* activities.[5] They do this under the guidance and patronage of a Maharaj Saheb who extends what may be considered as a religious sanction to the offerings. This equation between wealthy patrons and a Maharaj Saheb is an important formative force in establishing and sustaining *upashrays* within Jain neighbourhoods. Religious philanthropy is an important part of Jain culture and registers in many different ways, but at the level of the neighbourhood, an *upashray* is one of the more visible markers of how Jain lay devotees' religious practices intersect with the movements of Jain ascetics into concrete institutional forms.

The making of an *upashraya* may also be read as a process of spatialising a *sangh*. The idea of *sangh* is, as discussed earlier, traced back to Mahavir Swami. It is believed that he systematised the idea of *sangh*; all contemporary *sangh* formations can be traced back to these roots. During interviews with ascetics, they suggested that *upashrays* as a built institution is a relatively recent development since, in earlier times, ascetics took shelter in forests or any other places they found one. The relationship between ascetics and lay-worshipper communities has a long and complex history, and it is marked by persistent tension. Jain ascetics are forest dwellers, which allowed them greater isolation

---

5 These range from personal donations, contributions dedicated to the memory of a family members, or even funds raised through ritual auctions at the *derasar*, which I discuss later in the chapter.

from society, more in keeping with the ideals of ascetic life. However, when they engage with society and reside temporarily in temples, it naturally leads to reduced isolation and personal reflection but helps spread Jainism through patronage and further construction of temples (Dundas 2002 [1992]: 136–138). While the beliefs and practices of Jain ascetics have shifted over time, they continue to have minimal needs, which are reflected in the *upashray* buildings. Most *upashrays* have big halls for sermon and gathering or a smaller space if it is a retrofitted house. They also have individual space for ascetics to reflect and meditate in seclusion. Even today, many ascetics, particularly from the more orthodox sects, do not bathe or use the toilet and eschew the use of electricity even when available. *Upashrays* are then accordingly designed or retrofitted to the specific requirements of the monks.

Religious Activities in *Derasars* and *Upashrays*

There are three different kinds of ritual practices that constitute Jain worship. First is the *puja* that a worshipper offers in a *derasar*. A devout Jain will visit a *derasar* each morning before eating or drinking anything. This is similar to worship practised by other Hindu communities. However, there are other components to Jain belief: the practices of *samayik* and *pratikraman*. *Samayik* is a form of meditation practised by both lay worshippers and ascetics. Usually performed for forty-eight minutes known as one *muhurt*, this is a form of meditation and internal reflection. During this time, a worshipper attempts to refrain from thinking about temporal affairs. To aid in this focus, many worshippers chant *mantras* or may even listen to sermons by ascetics. This is usually done in the seclusion of a house, or an *upashray* if accompanied by a sermon. *Pratikraman* is the ritual that involves seeking atonement for any sins that a worshipper may have committed knowingly or unknowingly (Cort 2001: 124). This is done by chanting hymns related to the theme of atonement. More orthodox lay worshippers may perform *pratikraman* every day first thing in the morning and later in the evening; they also perform slightly different forms of *pratikraman* rituals every fortnight, every four months and during the annual Samvatsari festival.[6] Most other worshippers usually join in the Samvatsari *pratikraman* and also during *chaturmas* or four months of monsoon when Jain monks and nuns are in residence in *upashrays*. Considering the number of chants that are recited, *pratikraman* in many neighbourhoods in Ahmedabad is performed collectively and often takes place in an *upashraya*. Devotees gather at sunrise and sunset and take turns chanting *mantras*. This, in turn, affects the spatial form of an *upashray*, which today typically includes a hall where these gatherings may be held.

If we consider *samayik*, *pratikraman* and the *puja* as a three-part practice of worship, they are performed in a house, an *upashray* and a *derasar*, respectively. For a devout Jain, these three sites are bound by the geography of worship. *Pratikraman* does not necessarily have to be performed collectively, but it is usually done so, possibly because of the long duration required for it (approximately three hours). In places where devotees are unable to reach an *upashray* or do not have an *upashray* nearby, they may get together in groups and perform *pratikraman*. In housing tenements within the old city, for instance, families identify an open area where they would gather for *pratikraman* (particularly) and also for other activities. During *chaturmas* or when a large number of Jains gather to perform *pratikraman*, an *upashray* becomes a busy node in the neighbourhood. The collective nature of this practice of *pratikraman* is often emphasised in conversations with Jains, partly as a matter of facility where a number of people take turns in chanting under the guidance of a Maharaj Saheb. So, though not mandated, the conduct of *pratikraman* in an *upashray* adds a dimension of importance to the institution beyond its role as a place of residence for Jain ascetics.

In addition to providing spiritual guidance, Jain ascetics have a crucial relationship with a *sangh* since they depend on its members for daily sustenance. When ascetics take up temporary residence in an *upashray* and during longer stays in the monsoon months, they

6 Samvatsari is the last of Paryushan, which is the most important festival for Jains. For Swetambar Jains, Paryushan involves eight days of fasting and attending sermons, and it is at this time that most Jains perform *pratikraman*. Samvatsari is the day of asking friends and family for forgiveness.

visit Jain households in the neighbourhood and gather food for their meals (Dundas 1992: 174–176). Food must come from Jain families alone since their ritual dietary laws are extremely strict; they include principles such as not consuming food from the previous day, root vegetables and, even, leafy vegetables on certain days of the month. Most importantly, the ascetics must consume every morsel of food they collect, be it chillies or spices such as cloves and cinnamon. Jain families are usually aware of this; therefore, they usually ensure that Jain ascetics are offered food as per their beliefs, although they may not themselves follow these rules. Meals in my house, for instance, do not follow restrictions or dietary prescriptions of particulars days of the lunar cycle, but we usually, at the least, have food such as freshly made *rotli* (Gujarati flatbread) and rice, *khakra* (*rotli* that we dry roast at home until it becomes crisp and can be stored longer), milk, sugar or bananas, which we offer to the ascetics.[7]

As the ascetics regularly visit a family and become familiar with its members, they occasionally make other requests as well. One ascetic, for instance, needed a new pair of glasses; she handed me the prescription and asked me to take a look. It was an indirect suggestion that I should get the glasses made. Such requests are usually indirect because they fall in the realm of temporal matters, which the ascetics must strictly avoid. In another instance, a Maharaj Saheb said she requested someone to make a phone call to her family to inform them about her whereabouts.

One ascetic, who was also considered a spiritual leader by several *sanghs*, worked on a number of community and outreach activities with a temple trust and *yuvak mandal* or youth groups. The youths started disseminating information about his movements, sermons and advice on Facebook, Instagram and WhatsApp among various Jain groups both within and beyond Ahmedabad. When, during an interview, a group of pilgrimage from Mumbai was asked what brought them to the *derasar* (they were travelling beyond), they said they received information on WhatsApp about the day's activities in the *derasar* and decided to stop

7 *Khakra* is one of the foods that is offered to the ascetics in spite of it not being freshly made. However, the ascetics who visit our home usually agree to accept *khakra* only because it is home made.

by to seek the ascetic's blessings. In this and other cases, the ascetics themselves did not use any technology, but they had lay assistants who could use smartphones and computers on their behalf when required. These kinds of interactions indicate how the ascetics negotiated a range of 'worldly matters' in indirect ways through the *sanghs*. Members of the *sanghs* become a channel and an important support system for the ascetics.

Migrating Families, Shifting *Sanghs* and Changing Religious Landscape

Ahmedabad, as with most other cities, has undergone tremendous expansion in the past few decades. In the early 20th century, the city was concentrated within the medieval fortified area popularly known as the walled city, which lies to the east of the Sabarmati river. Since then, the city expanded westwards, such that the western side of the city is almost entirely new development. The residential neighbourhoods in the walled city are known as *pols*. Each *pol* would typically have families from the same caste or occupation.[8] Historically, there were many *pols* dominated by Jain families where even today the houses continue to be owned by them. Correspondingly, there is a high concentration of Jain *derasars* within or around these neighbourhoods. In Zaveri Vad—which has nine *pols*/*khadkis*/neighbourhood units—for instance, there are fifteen *derasars*. Waghan Pol in Zaveri Vad has three *derasars* next to each other on a short stretch of the street. According to a local ascetic, the large number of *derasars* became necessary on account of the high density of Jain families living in these neighbourhoods. Since each family member was required to perform daily *puja*, many *derasars* came to be built. The insistence on daily *puja* was quite common a few decades ago. An elderly Jain remembers that her grandmother would not permit anyone in the house to consume even a morsel of food until

---

8 According to Yagnik and Sheth (2011: 83–99), it is not historically recorded or known how and when the caste- or community-based divisions of the *pols* emerged as practised in the urban residential landscape. However, there is evidence to suggest that this was already the case as early as the 16th century.

they had performed the *snatra puja*, which is the ritual bathing of the *idol* of the deity in the *derasar* every morning (Cort 2001: 151).[9] As such, the walled city has many *derasars* and historically has had *sanghs* of varying sizes and strengths associated with each *derasar*.

With the westwards expansion that began in the 1930s, families gradually began moving out to other parts of the city. The new neighbourhoods continued to be organised around caste, and Jain neighbourhoods emerged alongside those of Patel, Brahman and Muslim neighbourhoods (Yagnik and Sheth 2011: 289–306). Following the spatial template of the walled city *pols*, the new neighbourhoods too were anchored in the idea of the *sangh*. Elderly family members, however, continued to maintain some degree of contact with the previous *sanghs*. They continued to pay membership charges and periodically visit the *derasars* to offer *puja*. The elderly people were particularly invested in ensuring the continuity of these networks since their social lives were often enmeshed within the *sanghs* and their activities. However, considering the distance that needed to be travelled and the fact that families eventually formed another *sanghs* around their new residences, this was a symbolic, almost nostalgic, connect rather than an active one based on regular religious practices. This pattern has continued until today. Some members of my extended family still visit the *derasar* of their childhood *pol* every year, if not more frequently, on key events such as the anniversary of its establishment or during the congregational feast known as *vatsalya*. In some cases, some individuals, usually men, join the temple trusts or participate informally in organising activities on behalf of the temple trusts and, in this way, maintain a more substantial association with the *derasars* and the *sanghs* despite living away from the neighbourhoods.

On the whole, however, the walled city of Ahmedabad has seen a consistent reduction in the number of Jain families and a gradual emptying of the *pols*, leading to the dissolution of, or at least greatly reduced, membership in many *sanghs* and similar reduction of ritual activities in the *derasars*. The moving of families and the dissolving of *sanghs* have

9 Each *derasar* has a *mul nayak* or primary deity, who is one of the twenty-four *tirthankars* worshipped by Jains. Most *derasars* usually have additional idols of other *tirthankars* as well.

impacted the network of movement and residence of the ascetics as well. With fewer families to provide sustenance, it's no longer tenable today for the ascetics to even temporarily reside in one of the many *upashrays*. Many *upashray*, therefore, lie vacant, and in a few cases, idols have been removed from the *derasars*, effectively abandoning the sites. In some cases, the trusts that administer *derasar*-related activities have become defunct, which further makes it difficult for the ascetics to engage with the few remaining lay worshippers in the region. One trustee stated that he continues to work for a *derasar* and its neighbourhood *upashray* since he has been associated with the place all his life, but he was certain that his children do not share the same affinity or commitment. In most cases, the trusts responsible for the *derasars* usually appoint caretakers and have basic facilities maintained for some ascetics who have chosen to reside permanently in a particular *upashray* on account of old age or poor health. However, compared to the vibrant activity that is usually found around other active places of worship, most of the smaller *derasars* in the walled city are extremely quiet. This is quite evidently the impact of out-migration of Jain families but, more significantly, signals the strong dependency of the religious institutions on the immediate neighbourhoods.

As discussed earlier, Jain families in new neighbourhoods have established *derasars* and *upashrays* in the vicinity of their homes. This followed two trajectories of development over time. The first case is illustrated by the Ambawadi *sangh*, which today has a very large membership of over 2500 members.[10] In recent times, smaller groups separated from the *sangh* to form another *sangh*. This became possible when a group of families living in one area approached and sought the patronage of a senior Maharaj Saheb to establish a new *derasar* in their immediate neighbourhood. The families found a plot, mobilised capital required for the project and built both a *derasar* and, when possible, an *upashray*. The Maharaj Saheb who consecrated the *derasar* is still closely associated with the *sangh* and ensures that monks and nuns regularly take up residence in the new *upashray*, offer sermons and supervise *pratikraman*. In this way, the foundations of new *sanghs* are laid. What is particularly interesting here is that most of these families were members

10 Sourced from the website of Jain International Trade Organisation (www.jitoahmedabad.org), accessed on 2 February 2020.

of another *sangh* not very far from where they live. Yet, they felt it essential to form another *sangh* and build the institutions required to anchor it. At a pragmatic level, issues of traffic and the inconvenience of commuting within Ahmedabad may well have been the factors that triggered the desire in Jain families to build *derasars* as close to their residences as possible. There are, however, religious motivations as well. Jain scholars note that since medieval times lay Jains have built temples and consecrated idols as a way of accruing religious merit (Cort 2001: 48–49). It is also common for wealthy Jain families to build a second, third or more temples in a neighbourhood for the same reason. It is arguably this belief that more significantly underpins the motivation to break away from a well-established *sangh* and form a new one.

The second trajectory of *sangh* formation is the making of *derasars* a part of the development of apartment complexes or housing societies to attract Jain families. Here, the presence of *derasar* holds the promise of *sangh* formation when families buy residences and come to live in the area. It also offers an already established connection with a group of ascetics who will have been involved in the consecration of temples in the developed properties. The fact that *derasars* are built before *sanghs* are established in the newly developed neighbourhoods may appear contradictory to the earlier discussion about reduced engagement with old-city *derasars* on account of out-migration of families. A key difference between these two situations lies in the patronage extended by senior ascetics to these newer developments. The ascetics usually have previously established networks in other localities, and when they consecrate a temple without a community living around, they effectively create conditions for the formation of a new community that they can engage with in the future. Within the context of growing real estate markets that target upwardly mobile urban families and are confident of eventually selling the properties, ascetics are reasonably certain of the possibility of *sanghs* developing in the future.[11] For the

11 One of the monks I interviewed described his involvement in the consecration of a few *derasars* as part of apartment housing developments. The monk and his followers usually resided in the Paldi area of Ahmedabad, which has a large number of *derasars* and *upashrays*. These new temples were clearly part of the process of reaching out to communities rather than a necessity for their everyday sustenance.

community leaders and financiers of such developments, it provides social traction since such projects become an opportunity to be seen as engaged in religious activity.

These shifts in *sangh* membership are not a new development that occurred in the wake of the expansion of the city beyond the medieval limits. Considering the sheer numbers and density of *derasars* in the walled city of Ahmedabad, it is likely that the *sanghs* associated with these institutions emerged similarly in the past as well. What adds further substance to this idea is the link between the history of migration and the coming together of *sangh* members (Yagnik and Sheth 2011: 83–99). Ahmedabad has historically been a mercantile city, with traders from neighbouring regions such as Rajasthan migrating into the city at various points in the past. Successive groups of Jain migrants came to live together in the *pols* and also join the same *sangh*s. Alternately, like we see today, if a group of migrants became prosperous enough to establish their own *sangh*, they would do so. These micro-histories of migrant clustering and *sangh* formation are evident in the names of the *sanghs*. Names such as Kachcchi Visa Oswal Jain Samaj and Deesa Shrimali Jain Mitra Mandal are *sanghs* in Ahmedabad, but the references to Kutch and Deesa are evidently the groups' place of origins. So the formation of a *sangh*, while anchored in shared practices and religious belief, is also intersected by regional identities and migration, both within and, historically, without Ahmedabad.

Derasars and Social Institutions

The rituals and practices taking place in the *derasars* and *upashrays* are in many instances collective and have resulted in the formation of *mandalis* (small groups or circles of membership). Two kinds of *mandalis* have sustained over at least the past century: *samayik mandalis* and *yuvak mandals*. The *samayik mandalis* comprise of women who get together in the afternoon to perform *samayik*.[12] In

12 The morning *samayik* is typically performed within the house, especially for younger women who shoulder the responsibility of domestic chores, while the afternoon *samayik* is sometimes performed together with the *mandalis*.

many cases, this gradually develops into social groups and the *mandalis* may engage in other activities of mutual interest of the groups. The *samayik mandali* in my neighbourhood *sangh,* for instance, plans visits to other religious places, organises collective religious instruction and even conducts exams for its members to assess their learning. While these activities remain religious in nature, for the women, the bonding becomes a social tie that binds them to the neighbourhood. And as they grow older, the *mandali* often becomes the only site of their social life and thus intrinsic to their sense of belonging to the neighbourhood. One elderly Jain woman in my neighbourhood lives with her married children who are now planning to move out to another residential area in the western periphery of the city. She has decided to stay on in her house, primarily on account of her *mandali* network. The *yuvak mandals* are important parallel networks comprising of young men from the *sanghs.* They organise activities on behalf of, and for, the *sangh* and become active organisational wings of the *sanghs.* They would, for instance, organise *jatra* or visits to religious places, which other members of the *sangh* would participate in. They may also organise special visits to religious places for old people and the *samayik mandalis,* thus making travel possible for those Jains who may otherwise be unable to do so themselves. Most such *mandals* remain focused on activities that are closely allied to religious practice, but in recent times, some *yuvak mandals* have also initiated community service projects of various kinds including blood donation camps, charity collection drives and food distribution for the poor. This development, however, is anecdotal, and both the *samayik mandals* and *yuvak mandals* are groups anchored in the religious practices of the *sanghs* but have become sites that reinforce social ties among their members.

The activities at the *derasars* also provide opportunities to *sangh* members to negotiate their social standing within the *sangh.* Being regular in ritual practice through the diligent performance of *samayik* and *pratikraman* is itself seen as a mark of virtue and is perceived as contributing to the social standing of the members. The auctioning of ritual privileges is another site where this is more clearly visible (Kelting 2009). One of the most important events where this comes up for display is during Mahavir Jayanti when the birth of Lord Mahavir is celebrated. It is believed that Trishala Devi, Lord Mahavir's mother, had a number of dreams prior to his birth. In the dream, she saw a lotus pond, the sun, the moon, Goddess Lakshmi and other objects each of which signified a quality of the child to be born. The objects seen in the dream are made of silver, and on the day of Mahavir Jayanti, the *derasars* conduct auctions allowing people the opportunity to temporarily possess and display the objects. Depending on the economic background of the *sangh* members, the bid amounts vastly vary, ranging from a few hundred rupees in smaller *sanghs* to half a million rupees in larger ones. The bidding process inevitably becomes a site to demonstrate individual status and agency.[13] These negotiations extend further in the auctioning of the privilege for sponsoring the *vatsalya* or congregational feasts, which are held at least twice a year on Mahavir Jayanti and the anniversary of the founding of the *derasars.* In large *sanghs* with hundreds of members in the congregation, the expense of the feast is afforded by only some wealthy members of the *sangh*, who then naturally acquire a higher social standing within the community. While the question of status is not central to this chapter, it does reveal that the *sanghs* are not internally homogenous groups but are sites where status is negotiated through the ritual practices in the *derasars* and *upshrays.*

Conclusion: Populating Neighbourhoods and Revitalising *Sanghs*

The shifting relationship between the *derasars* and *upashrays*, the *sanghs* and the neighbourhoods is evident in the trajectory or pattern of urban growth, particularly in the agglomeration of Jain families around the institutions. The medieval walled city of Ahmedabad has more than a hundred *derasars*, making it a site with an extremely high density of Jain religious institutions. The absence of *sanghs*, as

13 Paul Dundas notes that gaining prestige through acts of piety has been found as a historical occurrence among merchants and that this extends to being a matter of credibility in their business transactions as well (1992: 196).

discussed earlier, has led to reduced religious activity and networks around these institutions. Some ascetics and temple trustees have initiated a process of the revival of these institutions. Central to their efforts is the prospect of repopulating the neighbourhoods around the *derasars* in order to create a critical mass of worshippers and, consequently, caretakers for the institutions. The return to neighbourhood formation around the institutions comes in the wake of various other unsuccessful attempts to maintain the institutions. These include remote participation by visiting trustees, appointing caretakers to attend to the basic functioning of the temples and providing outreach services such as awareness programmes. These attempts, however, fail to revitalise the institutions; what it requires instead is multivalent engagements of different members of the *sanghs*, a range of ritual practices as well as the near-constant visits and movements by ascetics. The other component of these revitalisation efforts is the infrastructure of neighbourhood formation around the temples. According to a senior ascetic, many temple trusts maintain housing stock in the vicinity of the temples, which was and continues to be rented out to Jain families at nominal rates.[14] Many such houses now lie vacant with the original inhabitants preferring to move out to the western part of the city. Efforts are being made by local temple trusts and their associate *yuvak mandals* to offer this housing to people such as skilled migrants who seek employment in the city or poor Jain families who come to the city for medical assistance. By providing such people housing and offering them assistance to take care of their basic needs, the institutions hope to regenerate a community around the *derasars*.

Derasars and *upashrays* are central to the collective lives of Jain communities. This has been the case historically as well where the institutions provided a religious anchor to *sanghs*. However, the formation, dissolution and regeneration of *sanghs* across the city

14 Blocks of single-room and tenement-type houses are found adjacent to or in proximity of many *derasars*. In Zaveri Vad, for instance, tenement-type housing is found in Sambhavnath ni Khadki, Chaukumhji ni Pol and Seemandhar Swami ni Khadki, to name just a few.

suggest that neither neighbourhood nor *sangh* are stable formations. Rather, on account of migration, families establish networks similar to their earlier networks while maintaining some continuity with the previous *sanghs* as long as and to the extent the ties remain. What this reveals most importantly is that the religious institutions engender fluid networks that undergird the physical space of the neighbourhood. These form and transform as people move about the city and their lives, transforming the neighbourhood in turn.

References

Cort, John E. 2001. *Jains in the World: Religious Values and Ideology in India*. New York: Oxford University Press.

Desai, Renu. 2011. 'Producing and Contesting the "Communalized City": Hindutva Politics and Urban Space in Ahmedabad'. In *Fundamentalist City? Religiosity and the Remaking of Urban Space,* edited by Nezar AlSayyad and Megjan Massoumi, pp. 99–124. London and New York: Routledge.

Dundas, Paul. 2002 [1991]. *The Jains* (Second Edition). London and New York: Routledge.

Ghassem-Fachandi, Parvis. 2015. 'Urban Thresholds: Crevices, Crossroads, and Magic Remainders'. In *Cities in South Asia,* edited by Crispin Bates, pp. 180–194. London: Routledge.

Kelting, Whitney M. 2009. 'Tournaments of Honour: Jain Auctions, Gender, and Reputation'. *History of Religion*, Vol. 48, No. 4, pp. 284–308.

Mahadevia, Darshini. 2007. 'A City with Many Borders: Beyond Ghettoisation in Ahmedabad'. In *Indian Cities in Transition,* edited by Annapurna Shaw, pp. 315–340. Hyderabad: Orient Longman.

Yagnik, Achyut and Suchitra Sheth. 2011. *Ahmedabad: From Royal City to Megacity*. New Delhi: Penguin Books.

3

In Search of a Neighbourhood among the *Kāshivāsis*: An Ethnographic Account of an *Āshram* in Banaras

Anakshi Pal

The *Kāshivāsis* are *mumukshus*, or seekers of *moksha*, i.e., liberation from the cycle of birth, death and rebirth. They come to the holy city of Banaras to die because of its sacred status and religious significance.[1] The strict guiding philosophy of *Kāshivās*, which governs the social and emotional behaviour and quotidian life of these *mumukshus* who reside at the Kāshi Mumukshu Bhawan in Banaras, lends to its contentious character. This follows from the fact that the central ethos of the life of a *mumukshu* adhering to the main tenet of *Kāshivās* in order to practise the so-called art of dying and, thereby, adopting a specific way of living is based on the idea and practice of detachment. This implies detachment from all forms of material, social and emotional bonds that are regarded as temporal and illusory or as *maya* (Filippi 1947 [1996]; Sharma 2005). These are believed to be entrapments for the soul, making its liberation from the body difficult during the ultimate hour of death. Furthermore, since the prescriptions and proscriptions of *Kāshivās* forbid the formation of all kinds of social bonds, it is also theoretically in the negation of the concept of neighbourhood as an institution, which is primarily *social* in character. Hence, locating a neighbourhood among the *Kāshivāsis* becomes a possibility fraught with contentions and its emergence remains a peculiar development within the social setup of the *āshram* under focus. If conforming to the philosophy of *Kāshivās*—to be able to attain the state of detachment—

1 Of the many significant discussions on this, see Parry 1981; Eck 1983 [2015]; Parry 1994; Justice 1997.

is the primary intention of the *Kāshivāsi* community, then how is the neighbourhood as both a spatial and social formation negotiated?

Taking forward from the editorial introduction in this book, the concept of 'neighbourhood' has generally been understood in sociology as the smallest residential unit defined as 'a limited community with features ... like common territory, members interacting with each other and having a sense of belonging' (Subberwal 2009: N3). The concepts of 'community' and 'neighbourhood' have often been used synonymously in a geographical sense.[2] However, 'community', following from Ferdinand Tönnies (1887), has a more precise meaning; it is a group primarily defined by direct social interactions spanning over several years and diverse spheres of life and exhibiting social intimacy and cohesion (in Bruce and Yearley 2006). The latter could either be (mostly) positive or negative in nature. Yet others have imagined 'neighbourhood' as a sociocultural 'space', extending the notion beyond the idea of a merely geographical 'place' that is not tied to a fixed territory. Such an imagination encourages the conscious creation of an affective social space. In this chapter, I try to locate the neighbourhood as a territorial setup and a social–affective 'space' created and negotiated by the *āshram* inhabitants. The material nature of this space and its affective elements spill-over from one to the other. Kaustubh Mani Sengupta (2017) suggests that the concept is frequently linked with a sense of association and affect. Here, 'affect' does not merely refer to positive emotions such as love, friendship, etc. so that neighbourhoods are imagined only as friendly spaces with affirmative associations. In all of the aforementioned senses of the terms, the Kāshi Mumukshu Bhawan consists of a 'community' because of its shared geographical territory and overlapping spheres of life as well as a 'neighbourhood' that emerges as a negotiated space, which will be discussed in this chapter. The dynamic complexities of everyday interactions that weave such a negotiated space into being will form the main thrust of this chapter.[3]

---

2 This is informed by Subberwal 2009; Allan 2006; Bruce and Yearley 2006.

3 A note of disclaimer: This study acknowledges the fact that the philosophical understanding and views regarding death/dying are restricted to the residents of a particular *āshram* who constitute a segment of the larger Hindu community. The study as such was not particularly sensitive about caste affiliations and none emerged within

The Kāshi Mumukshu Bhawan, popularly known as an '*āshram*', exhibited characteristics of a hospice, a retreat or a hermitage. It had facilities for the care of its residents that could be sought out when required. But unlike a hospital, it did not provide invasive care. Simultaneously, it was a shelter or refuge for people from all over India, and even Bangladesh, who had come to Banaras to live out their final days in the hope of attaining *moksha*. It was a hermitage of sorts since it sheltered renouncers and sages who had completely given up lives of domesticity. The *Kāshivāsis* as a community could be set apart owing to their adherence to the philosophy of *Kāshivās*. The norms and religious principles of the same restricted their social behaviour and defined their quotidian activities and lifestyles. These furthered their practice of the art of dying by foregoing all kinds of material, social, personal and emotional bonds through the attainment of the state of detachment. Those members of the community who deviated from the observance of the basic tenets of *Kāshivās* faced ostracism and collective criticism and were subjected to unspoken judgements by the fellow residents of the *āshram*. Such collective mechanisms, which simultaneously functioned as 'social' push factors, compelled the *non-ideal* 'Kāshivāsis' to put up the 'role' of the ideal *Kāshivāsi*. Here, 'role' refers to the 'complimentary, detailed sets of obligations for interaction' (Parsons and Shils 1951 [2001]: 23 in Appelrouth and Desfor Edles 2011: 26). Therefore, although in essence the philosophy of *Kāshivās*, which governed everyday life at the *āshram*, is mutually exclusive to the idea of the neighbourhood, which is primarily social in character, the latter nevertheless emerges albeit with many peculiarities. This chapter demonstrates how the neighbourhood then significantly influences the social behaviour of the residents to ensure that the philosophy of *Kāshivās* continues to retain its dominance as the driving force behind life at the *āshram*.

---

the scope of the recorded narratives. However, the ideas and views presented within the ambit of this study will differ vastly within different segments of the larger Hindu community with regard to caste identities and other ascribed identities. It might even have similarities with other larger religious communities with heterogeneities within each of them.

The Neighbourhood as a Negotiated Space within an *Āshram* in Banaras

Situated along the main road, close to Assi Ghat in Banaras (Figure 3.1), the Kāshi Mumukshu Bhawan has the appearance of an *āshram*. It was established in 1920 by Pandit Ghanshyam Dutt Ji Chaumal, who was rechristened as Swami Ghanshyamanand Tirth under the tutelage of Swami Ishwaranand Tirth. Initially, Raja Baldev Das Ji Birla provided the land and the financial resources for the construction of the *āshram*.[4] It was meant for providing accommodation to all those elderly people who came to Banaras as their ultimate resting point to spend their final days with the hope of attaining *moksha* (Eck 1983; Justice 1997; Parry 1994; Runthala 2015). At present, it is run by the Kāshi Mumukshu Bhawan Sabha and administered by a manager and the office staff.[5]

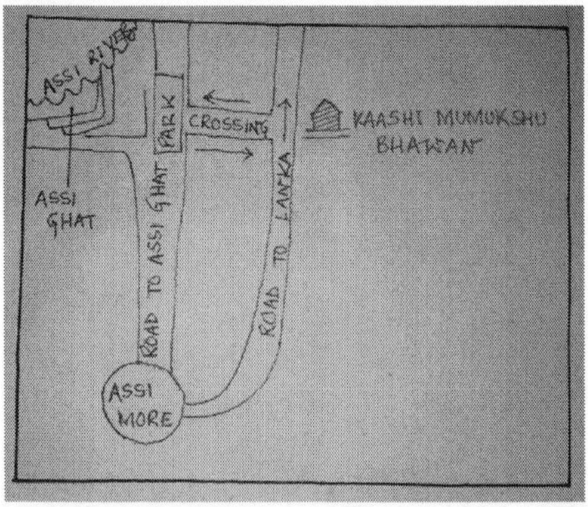

Figure 3.1: A rough illustration of the location of the Kāshi Mumukshu Bhawan near Assi Ghat in Banaras. Image credit: author

The architectural structure of the main gate of the Kāshi Mumukshu Bhawan (henceforth Bhawan) resembles the typical entrance to a Hindu temple (Figure 3.2). It has pale yellow and maroon walls all around.

4 The information has been taken from the pamphlet published by the Kāshi Mumukshu Bhawan Sabha (date unspecified).

5 See *Hinduism Today*, July/August/September 2015. Available at https://www.hinduismtoday.com/modules/smartsection/item.php?itemid=5602 (accessed on 27 April 2018).

Figure 3.2: The main gate of the Kāshi Mumukshu Bhawan near Assi Ghat in Banaras, December 2017. Photo credit: author

Spread over an area of five acres, the *āshram* comprises of the Ishwar Math for Dandi *swamis*,[6] the Ved-Vedang Mahavidyalaya for teaching Sanskrit to students of higher standards and the Prathama Vidyalaya, which provides Sanskrit education to boys of lower standards in a style resembling that of a *gurukulam*, a place of education headed by a *guru*, or teacher-instructor, who imparts knowledge to his students. Residential quarters in the Bhawan are provided at Atithishala, Lohia Chowk, Pakka Chowk, Two Kothis, Paryatak Awas (Tourist Lodge) and Phulwari Chowk; these are gated compounds spread across the Bhawan. This part primarily makes up the geographical structure of the *āshram* neighbourhood. The Bhawan also has a *yagyashala* for *yajnas* (ritual sacrifices made in front of the fire for fulfilling a specific objective) and four temples where ritual offerings and religious festivals are organised and hosted by the residents or the administration. Furthermore, it houses *ayurvedic* and homoeopathic charitable facilities within the campus for the day-to-day medical needs of its (mostly elderly) residents.

6 The Dandi *swamis* are the renouncers or sages who form the ascetic group called 'Dandis'. The Dandis belong to the *Dashnami* (Ten Names) sect, which falls under the Shaiva sect of the sage community. The peculiarity of the Dandis is that this sect only admits men of Brahman birth (see *New World Encyclopedia 2015*. Available at http://www.newworldencyclopedia.org/p/index.php?title=Sadhu_and_Swami&oldid=989769 [accessed on 22 May 2018]).

The first sight of the Bhawan is a feeling of mixed emotions of arrival and departure, as one crosses the road and enters through its main gate where visitors are expected to sign in a register to state the purpose of their visits. Once at the imposing gate, a visitor meets an old Bengali guard named Mishra*ji*.[7] At first, Mishra*ji*'s heavily wrinkled face is indifferent, serious and grumpy. He is accustomed to unforeseen encounters with ignorant strangers who come to enquire about the residents of the Bhawan. On the left, upon entering, the visitor hears lively, chaotic chants in Sanskrit, emanating from the Sanskrit school. The Bhawan comes alive at dawn when the Dandi *swamis* set out for their daily trip to Assi Ghat to take a dip in the Ganges. Clad in saffron with a lot of *rudraksha* bead garlands around their necks, they would walk out of the Bhawan with their bowls for alms and return after their Ganga*snan* (bathing in the Ganges). The elderly residents set about their domestic chores from early morning onwards. Some even perform their daily ritual offerings at the small temple situated at Ganesh Chowk within the Bhawan, in addition to doing the same for their personal deities. For instance, my 'best informant', Itarshi *dadi*, performed religious offerings at the temple almost every day. The *pathshala* opened at around nine in the morning. Mishra*ji* and another old guard usually served in shifts, guarding the entrance alternately during the day. A small tea stall adjacent to the administrative offices, with the usual *chai* (tea) and packaged snacks, was the only place of comfort for the residents in the wintry mornings. The manager usually arrived at 10 am and stayed till 6 pm every day on all seven days of the week. Some of the residents who wanted to maintain a cordial relationship with the manager visited him for a chit-chat before he got too busy. To be in the good books of the manager, I was told, came in handy if, for

---

7 A noticeable Bengali community can be found at a place called Bengali Tola. On asking the locals, many say that the Bengalis, just like other communities, came to and settled in Kāshi to live their lives and die in the sacred city for the promise of *moksha*. This fact is also corroborated by Eck, who writes, 'The part of the city … called Bengali Tola, settled by Bengalis, many of whom have come here for Kāshivasa, living out one's days in Kāshi until death' (1983 [2015]: 226) and again: 'Through the ages, Banaras has been colonized in its various sectors by these Kāshivāsis … the Bengalis [have settled] in Bengali Tola…' (Ibid.: 329).

instance, a resident needed cheap rooms at the Tourist Lodge for fellow villagers or relatives or simply wanted his approval to allow visiting kin to stay for a few days at the resident's quarter.

As I went around the Bhawan one day when I did not find anyone to speak with, I met a few elderly couples who had come from the outskirts of Banaras and other parts of India for treatment or had a scheduled operation in one of the hospitals in Banaras. They put up at the Bhawan for the duration of their medical supervision as it was cheap. Opposite to this was the *yagyashala*; it was cleaned every day by the cleaners and maintained by the gardeners, all of whom were locals speaking animated Bhojpuri. The Tourist Lodge stood across from this, which was the busiest and noisiest part of the Bhawan with innumerable coming-ins and going-outs each day.

Winters are exceptionally quiet times here, as most of the residents from the southern states of India would leave for their homes to return at the end of February. Owing to the intense weather, elderly people would usually come out of their quarters only to enjoy the sun on bright sunny days. Most of them usually set about their daily chores quietly, unless, occasionally, a quarrel broke out with one of their immediate neighbours. Such instances were not uncommon and mostly involved someone more committed in their efforts at being a *Kāshivāsi*, such as Itarshi *dadi,* and one of the local women who had secured membership at the Bhawan primarily because of the many facilities that came with it. Hence, such residents conveniently maintained a 'front', which is defined as 'the expressive equipment of a standard kind intentionally or unwittingly employed by the individual during his performance' by publicly demonstrating their adherence to the proscriptions and prescriptions of *Kāshivās* (Goffman 1956: 13). Here, it is important to specify that the manifestations of the politics behind the identity of a *Kāshivāsi* are dynamic and manifold. To simplify, a clear distinction can be drawn between two kinds of *Kāshivāsis*: (a) those who are primarily committed to the philosophy of *Kāshivās* and, hence, have voluntarily decided to seek shelter at the *āshram* to live their lives as *Kāshivāsis* in the pursuit of *moksha* after having foregone familial ties and (b) those who have sought shelter at the *āshram* involuntarily, being forced to do so because of circumstances which they could not foresee or control—mostly elderly people abandoned by their families—or to escape situations of unemployment and poverty—mostly local women, originally from Banaras—hence, not because of their commitment or wilful decision to live their lives as *Kāshivāsis* (Chopra-Chatterjee and Sengupta 2017; HelpAge India Report 2017).

Meals for residents who were unable to cook and had no domestic or hired help were provided by the Bhawan in tiffin carriers at noon. Before lunch, most of the elderly residents who had been outside in the courtyard vacated the area for the warmth of their quarters. There were a few elderly women who would leave the Bhawan almost daily at about lunchtime, I observed. Some of them said they went to visit their children who lived nearby, while others simply said they had work. However, a few who participated in this study later informed me in confidence that they went out either to beg from foreign tourists at Assi Ghat or in search of odd jobs. Such profitable ventures were looked down upon by committed *mumukshus,* and residents who 'indulged' in such practices were labelled as a bad influence, bringing disrepute to the *Kāshivāsi* community. Evenings were the time for prayers and meditation for serious *mumukshus* who refused to schedule interviews or entertain me during that time. Most of my interviewees also told me that they normally have two meals a day, comprising of light dinner owing to digestive complications, which were seen as an inevitable consequence of old age. Therefore, the only activity within and around the Bhawan, come evening, was of the Dandi *swamis* going for their holy dip in the Ganges.

Nocturnal life in and around the *atithishala* neighbourhood, I was told, was not secure either for the residents or outsiders. On multiple occasions, Itarshi *dadi* expressed her suspicion of the local women (I explore this in detail later). In fact, I gradually understood that the non-local, Hindi-speaking women despised the local women; but they were unable to oust them from the Bhawan because quarters once procured became the residents' properties until death. This further embittered the non-local women, and they vented their disapproval of their local counterparts and distorted their image by making the latter's 'dirty secrets' public. As such, an inkling of the profanity of motives and the heterogeneity in narratives within the *Kāshivāsi* community and neighbourhood began unravelling from within the otherwise 'sacred' and quiet lives of the *Kāshivāsis*.

These complexities and dynamics of everyday life created an intimate and affective space within the *āshram* community. 'Affective space' here implies a space fraught with emotions. This space was mostly ripe with tensions arising out of the social and emotional dynamics shared by various factions within the larger *Kāshivāsi* community. Hence, it can be argued that unavoidable interpersonal interactions of the everyday and conscious or unconscious quotidian activities weave together a neighbourhood. The latter emerge through the everyday politics of interactions and non-interactions, and also through acts of subversion, as will be explored in details in the following section.

The Politics of Space within the *Āshram* Neighbourhood

The Bhawan comprises of a huge area, divided into several compounds, which are separated on the basis of geographical or linguistic communities. For instance, if one goes further away from the administrative offices and turns right (see Figure 3.3), she would arrive at a gated compound where most of the Telugu-speaking residents live. The entire population of the Bhawan could be divided into two linguistic groups: Telugu and Hindi speakers. This was a common trend among other hospices and *āshrams* as well, such as the Kāshi Annapurna Annakshetra Kāsivas Bhawan. A large number of people from Andhra Pradesh and other states of South India donate huge sums of money to these places. Some of the residents were from Bihar and other parts of Central and North India.

Observations from the field revealed sharp differences between the two large linguistic groups spread across and making up the Bhawan neighbourhood. The Telugu-speaking people, mostly from Andhra Pradesh, but a few also from other South Indian states such as Karnataka, hailed from urban areas, while the Hindi-speaking people, mostly from Bihar, came from rural areas. Most of the Telugu-speaking *Kāshivāsis*

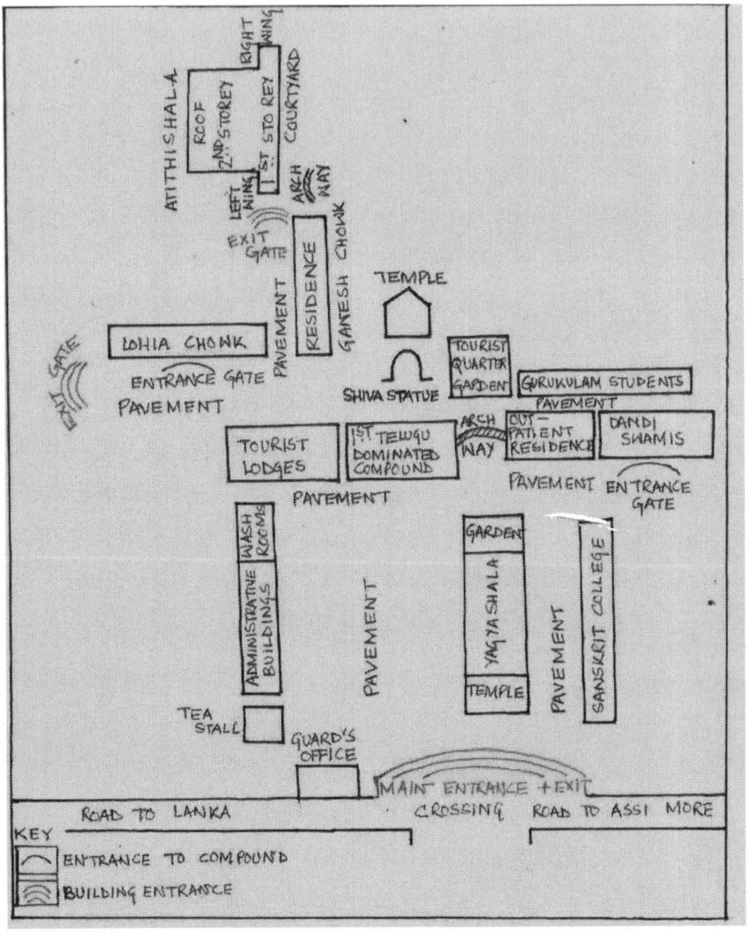

Figure 3.3: An illustration of the route map of the Kāshi Mumukshu Bhawan campus in Banaras. Image credit: author

were moderately or highly educated (Figure 3.4). For example, one of the gentlemen I spoke with—K.A.S.—appeared to be philosophically sound and sophisticated. In fact, he held two MA degrees, a PhD and was a two-time gold medallist. He had also been the head of a language department in a renowned college in his state. It is perhaps not difficult to understand the source of his apparent philosophical sophistication. Two other Telugu-speaking male participants whom I interviewed told me that they had been government officials, one of whom had served as a second-class gazetted officer. In fact, almost all the Telugu-

Figure 3.4: One of the two residential compounds at Lohia Chowk in Kāshi Mumukshu Bhawan, Banaras, where the majority of the residents are Telugu-speaking *Kāshivāsis*, January 2018. Photo credit: author

speaking people, regardless of their genders, demonstrated similar sophistication in their religious beliefs and views about the notions of death and *moksha*. In sharp contrast, the ideas and beliefs about death and *moksha* of the Hindi-speaking residents were strictly learnt from oral traditions and popular beliefs about the sacredness of dying in Kāshi. They also learnt from religious texts such as the Ramayana from a very young age, either by reading them themselves or, as was the case for the majority, imbibing from the teachings of mythologies at religious gatherings in villages.

Regardless of whether they came from resourceful families or not, most of the women were illiterate, although some had been teachers in primary or high schools. Being literate was a matter of great pride for them, such as Saraswati *dadi*, who, after every response, would repeat '*main pari-likhi hu naa*', or 'I am a literate woman after all'.[8] However, most, like Itarshi *dadi*, had taught themselves to read and write by

8 Interview with Saraswati Agarwal on 26 December 2017 at the Kāshi Mumukshu Bhawan premises.

following what their children were taught by their tutors. So, while the Hindi-speaking women residents of the neighbourhood could hardly read and write, their Telugu-speaking counterparts were moderately literate. For instance, it was a common sight to see both men and women, mostly Telugu-speakers, sitting outside in the courtyard of the compound on bright wintry mornings and writing the word 'Ram' a hundred times in Telugu or Hindi in their notebooks. When I asked one of the women why they were doing so, she told me it helped them keep the name of the Lord in their conscious minds and prevent futile thoughts of worldly needs, worries and woes from occupying them. Her handwriting was neat, with a style of its own. Itarshi *dadi*, on the other hand, had been a member of the ruling political party in her village and had occupied an important social role within her community; but she had had no formal education. She had taught herself to read and write, with much difficulty, during her leisure time. But she still sought help from K.A.S. or me when filling out forms for withdrawing money from the bank.

Rooms at the Kāshi Mumukshu Bhawan could be obtained by depositing a fixed sum of money with the authorities. This process could be tweaked, I was informed, by exploiting one's contacts in the administration. Once a room has been obtained by an individual or family, it belonged to them unto death. Rooms were also rented out to couples or groups of threes, like in the case of Itarshi *dadi* who had come thirty years ago with her husband and mother-in-law. It was considered illegal to oust any person who had obtained a room through the aforementioned procedure. Even for couples, their rooms could only be vacated upon the death of both partners. These quarters usually comprised of small rooms with tiny kitchens. Both the residential quarters had mud floors, but the veranda on the first storey of *atithishala* was cemented (Figure 3.5). There were two common bathrooms and two toilets at one end of the building. The Hindi-speaking residents with financial resources could even own luxury commodities like television and fridge and construct attached bathrooms or obtain better quarters; however, it was very rare.

Figure 3.5: The *atithishala* compound in Kāshi Mumukshu Bhawan, December 2017. Photo credit: author

In contrast to the quarters of most of the Hindi-speaking people who occupied single-room tenements on the ground floor of the *atithishala*, the Telugu-speaking people occupied apartment-like spaces on the first floor. The latter were few in number and consisted of more than one room, usually a separate sitting room and a bedroom, with a kitchen and an attached bathroom, all on cemented floors. The Telugu-speaking people often had housemaids too. They were also well-spoken and conversant in English. In addition to the sophisticated and nuanced nature of their ideas of death and *moksha*, their narratives were not too contingent upon mythological stories, unlike the Hindi-speaking group. The latter could only explain these complicated concepts with reference to mythological accounts, unlike their philosophically informed counterparts. This obvious distinction in lifestyle, following Bourdieu (1979 [1984]), can be understood as confirmation through differences in tastes, consumerist choices such as having a dining table or opting for three-room quarters at the Bhawan, and the philosophical outlooks of the latent class hierarchies even within a social group such as the

Kāshivāsis. In essence, the ideology of *Kāshivās* proscribes attachment to material commodities. Hence, opting for luxury commodities, aesthetically appealing products or the exhibition of one's educational credentials as evidence of class status or academic qualifications is against the philosophical and ideological tenets as it demonstrates an individual's attachment to materiality.

Thus, while the philosophical proscriptions potentially impinged upon individual tastes and choices, these were also conveniently ignored to maintain the distinctions of class and status at the risk of contradicting the dominant ideology governing general life at the *āshram*. As the *āshram* community existed in a shared 'place', in terms of their larger territoriality, showcasing such overt distinctions became significant to carve out different 'spaces' within the neighbourhood that set resourceful classes apart from the rest. This also demonstrates the everyday negotiations and subversions, where the neighbourhood and its politics as a social and emotional space subdue the dominant narrative of *Kāshivās* to pave the way for different groups to mark out their geographical and social boundaries within the shared premises. Although these *mumukshus* were seriously committed to the philosophical idea of *Kāshivās* as a way of living and art of dying, they were still entrapped by their attitudes of 'social snobbery' reiterated through their narratives and non-interaction (Ibid.). Owing to these 'distinctions', they enjoyed a lot of power within the neighbourhood and simultaneously a lot of social respect also accrued to them. This followed from a pure admiration for things and qualities that are impossible to be cultivated and are well beyond the means of those residents who did not hail from resourceful families. This reflects the class hierarchy among the residents of *atithishala*. It added to the complexities that contribute towards the formation and sustenance of a neighbourhood that is not merely spatial but also social. This is explored in the section that follows.

Everyday Scenes of Familiarity and Strangeness

One of the few things that significantly emerge upon reflecting on the everyday interpersonal interactions within this neighbourhood is that the Telugu-speaking group opened up several opportunities for local women to be hired as domestic helps. The local women who lived in one of the tenement-like rooms on the ground floor of *atithishala* saw these opportunities as lucrative occupations. However, such menial labour was viewed by the serious, committed *mumukshus* as unbecoming for a *Kāshivāsi*. Working for profit was a proscription one needed to follow in order to be recognised as a 'true' *Kāshivāsi* within the community, as this was a clear indication of an individual's existing attachment to materiality. In fact, I was also informed by several female, non-local Hindi-speaking participants, including Itarshi *dadi*, that some of the female residents even 'invited men to their quarters at night'. The prevalence of similar whispers and gossips reconfirm that majority of the residents of the *atithishala* neighbourhood socially disapproved of the behaviour of the local women. They also re-emphasised their differences with the latter through their narratives and behaviour to show themselves as everything that the locals were not. On the surface, such emotions were couched under strong narratives of religiosity, which claimed that it was only by letting go of material motives, financial scheming and 'indecent behaviour' that one could successfully earn the essential and indispensable 'good karma' for the attainment of *moksha*. On their part, the few local women who spoke with me also presented as sincere a narrative of their daily lives as any other within the Bhawan.

These narratives apparently contradict the seemingly pristine narrative of the 'nonchalant' *Kāshivāsi* community that intends to live a simple 'good life' in Banaras for the promise of a 'good death'.[9] One wonders if the attempts by the *āshram* residents to hide from public view certain details surrounding the everyday life in the neighbourhood were purposive and conscious in nature, as these ensured the preservation of the ideological rubric of the *Kāshivāsi* community in the long run. It is possible, given the general mindset in Banaras where *Kāshivāsis* are socially revered and service to them is considered 'good karma' as they are believed to be living a life of penance and sacrifice. It shall be evident in the following discussion on the peculiarities of the neighbourhood within this particular social setup.

9 For a detailed discussion on the notion of 'good death,' see Justice 1997.

An examination of the figure of a 'neighbour', imbued with both social and emotional qualities, reveals the peculiarities of the Bhawan neighbourhood. Through ethnographic observations and subsequent analyses, I show that the philosophy of *Kāshivās*, which is the dominant guiding narrative for a particular way of living and art of dying among the *Kāshivāsis*, actually negates the very essence of a neighbourhood, if it is imagined as a group that is by nature 'social'.

Observations of the everyday life within the Bhawan and personal interactions with the Telugu-speaking group revealed that despite being better equipped at conversation with refined examples, sophisticated ideas and outlooks, they were also seriously disinterested in discussing their lives as *Kāshivāsis*. The Telugu-speaking group considered this to be a futile exercise as experiences were regarded as strictly personal and individual practices were seen as private efforts at achieving the desired state of detachment. Conversing with fellow residents was something this group strictly avoided. The restricted social behaviour of the Telugu residents and their reticence followed from the belief that conversations led to attachments and is a waste of the little precious time they have to devote towards the thought of God in meditation. K.A.S. said,

> You cannot grow closer to two things at the same time, *amma*[10], you have to understand! It is only by moving away from the world, from my relationships, that I can reach closer to God. Hence, I chose to lead the life of a *Kāshivāsi*....[11]

Similarly, many regarded casual conversations as fallible traps and ready obstacles for the disciplining of minds. The practice of disciplining one's mind and channelising one's thoughts was crucial for the committed *Kāshivāsis*, and such a state of mental discipline could only be attained by strictly checking one's social interactions and bodily behaviour with and around others. Unchecked social behaviour led to the formation of personal and social bonds with residents of the immediate geographical space of the neighbourhood, inviting diversions and bringing ruin to

10 '*Amma*' is used in Telugu as mark of respect and affection for women.

11 Interview with K.A.S. in his quarters at the Kāshi Mumukshu Bhawan in Banaras, December 2017.

their daily efforts at channelising their conscious thoughts towards God. Hence, they consciously rejected the basic means of interaction, which was seen as only natural as they had already overcome the greater pulls of familial bonds and personal relationships upon deciding to take up the life of a *mumukshu* in Banaras.

Consequently, such a conscious avoidance of interpersonal interactions certainly meant that 'neighbourly' relationships were not intended to be cultivated by an ideal *Kāshivāsi*. Therefore, almost every single day, it was a common and typical sight upon arriving at the courtyard of this specific compound to find several men and women scattered across the cemented courtyard, bent over their notebooks and tirelessly writing the word 'Ram' multiple times. No one exchanged a single word with the others or even stared around purposelessly. If there occurred an intrusion in the form of a stranger, such as myself, trying to desperately find someone from this group to talk to, they would simply raise their eyes to look once. In no time, the apathetic gazes went back to doing what they did each morning, filling out pages after pages with the name of Lord 'Ram'. If on a lucky day one of them accepted a request for an interview in the form of a casual conversation, it only meant very brief, shy answers. During such encounters, they acted with childlike restlessness to return to the comfortable monotony of their routine—practising a detached way of living by disciplining their minds to be ready for that long-awaited meeting with *murchu*, or death, by fixating their thoughts on God.

Thus, united by a sense of solidarity, they constituted the larger 'umbrella community' of the *Kāshivāsis*. In this process, what emerged was a neighbourhood defined by the absence of all apparent forms of sociality. I argue that they were united by a sense of solidarity in foregoing all forms of social interaction consciously. But the neighbourhood, which nevertheless emerges, is a peculiar formation in such a case. Although the absence of communication between the residents of the Bhawan neighbourhood was striking, it was through their routinised ritual of writing the name of the Lord 'Ram' multiple times that they actually emerged as a collective, exhibiting a shared behaviour through which they expressed their we-feeling of the neighbourhood. Their conscious silence and self-imposed reticence were symbolic of their intersubjective understanding (Appelrouth and Desfor Edles 2011; Schutz 1932 [1967]) of the world around them being full of illusions, or *maya* (Filippi 1947 [1996]; Sharma 2005) that one can easily sink into by getting entangled in more relationships. In this way, they also created a shared space that was *social* by virtue of its collective language of silence, which became symbolic of this particular community. It demonstrated their conscious efforts at practising the art of detachment as a way of living, as social and personal bonds came to be collectively recognised as a hindrance on the path to a more intimate relationship with the Supreme Being and towards the attainment of the ultimate wisdom that lies in recognising the temporal nature of this illusory world.

Therefore, these shared rituals and symbolism actually converted these isolated individuals into a collective. The exquisite loneliness that might seemingly be pronounced in this typical everyday scenario within this peculiar neighbourhood, where each was on his own pursuit of *moksha*, was in reality misleading. The absence of communication and their silence did not necessarily give rise to loneliness but contributed towards creating a shared form of sociality that went into the involuntary and unconscious making of a neighbourhood, which is seemingly asocial in character and where non-communication defined the collective pursuit of a community for salvation. *Moksha* then became a shared objective that was to be attained in isolation but was not necessarily a lonely venture. Despite this significant peculiarity, the neighbourhood was certainly not a homogenous space in terms of its interpersonal interactions. In fact, social and emotional dynamics varied greatly within and between groups, as will be explored hereafter.

Efforts at interacting with the residents revealed that in sharp contrast to the Telugu-speaking people, the Hindi-speaking people were eager to talk about their lives and ideas unless they felt too defeated by life situations to make any conversation whatsoever. Even so, they were ready to converse with whoever came knocking at their doors, including with one another. However, these people mostly demonstrated a general feeling of hostility and animosity towards one other. Although a typical scene on any cold wintry morning when the sun appeared to be generous enough was to find several old and middle-aged women scattered across the rather large courtyard, conversing with one another, one would soon realise that they were divided into small groups of twos and fours. Interactions with one of these tiny groups could invite hostility towards you when approaching a different group the next day. Itarshi *dadi* mockingly referred to these gatherings, mostly comprising of the local women, as the panchayat (the Hindi word for 'village council') that engages in gossiping about everyone in the Bhawan and spreading rumours all around, thereby inviting criticism from their serious *Kāshivāsi* neighbours.

The local women were despised, even feared, by the non-local Hindi-speaking faction, as previously noted. This followed from the belief in black magic among many female *Kāshivāsis* and their suspicion that the local women performed black magic on their neighbours. For instance, Gayatri Devi Aggarwal told me that she had been plump before she came to the Bhawan but felt sick, she suspected, after some of the women, possibly one of the locals, placed black magic on her food. Itarshi *dadi* also had similar belief but did not express any fear as she believed that those who have faith in 'true' God cannot be defeated by evil magic. In fact, Aggarwal *dadi* and Itarshi *dadi* warned me on several occasions not to accept food offered by anyone, especially the local women of the neighbourhood, as they strongly believed consuming such food would make me fall prey to black magic.

This kind of thinking, I argue, was rooted in the belief that the local women were not committed to the philosophy of *Kāshivās*. Their ways of living and everyday activities clearly fell outside the ambit of religio-philosophical orientation that governed the quotidian reality within the community and the neighbourhood. As such, the local women as a faction within the neighbourhood often came to be marginalised and kept on the periphery because they simply used their *Kāshivāsi* identity as a convenient 'front' (Goffman 1956) owing to the social respect and material benefits that came with it. This naturally portrayed them as dishonest and untrustworthy, especially before their female non-local counterparts. The fear of the local women as practitioners of black magic also arose due to the absence of communication between these two factions of the *atithishala* neighbourhood. One group appeared as the unfamiliar 'other', which in turn fuelled speculations about it being in possession of such supernatural quality. However, Sheila Devi, a local woman, was treated by Itarshi *dadi* in a motherly way despite the fact that she was also keeping up the *Kāshivāsi* identity as a cover. I was told by Itarshi *dadi* that Sheila Devi had been wicked previously and used to roam around with a knife, attacking anyone who approached her. It was she who had taken away her weapon and taught her to behave and live decently. On her part, Sheila Devi also spoke fondly of Itarshi *dadi*, referring to her as *Mai* (Mother). Thus, the 'other' was only dangerous as long as she was unfamiliar.

Furthermore, these beliefs can also be interpreted as conscious attempts to demonise the 'other' to the rest of the world. Such attempts were made even more aggressive by the fact that these local women were known for picking fights easily and using slangs to verbally abuse their neighbours. They were also suspected of spying on their neighbours to report any breach of *āshram* rules to the authorities. One such incident was when Itarshi *dadi*'s family came to see her and stayed back for the night at her insistence. The next morning, the authorities reprimanded her for keeping members of her family inside the Bhawan without paying rent. Needless to say, Itarshi *dadi*'s ego was seriously hurt, and she refused to speak with anyone that entire morning. She later confided in me her suspicion about a local woman who she believed told on her for letting her family members stay the night. She also said that the complainant herself was sheltering her fugitive son for many years and that the son, a lame man, was having an affair with the daughter of another local woman who was also living in her mother's quarters for several months.

Many of the 'true' *Kāshivāsis* committed to the idea of *moksha* and in serious pursuit of it regarded the behaviour of these women as 'distasteful' and 'un-*Kāshivāsi*-like', as previously stated. According to them, this was the hour when they were required to rein in their thoughts and direct them towards God instead of spending time rumour-mongering; any digression was 'bad karma'. The Telugu-speaking people, particularly, avoided mingling with these women and also rarely interacted with other members of the Bhawan neighbourhood who lived on the first storey of the three-sided *atithishala* building. They disapproved of the 'uncouth' language and slangs used by the local women who frequently argued loudly with one another. For instance, one winter morning a fight broke out between Itarshi *dadi* and one of the local women when the former put out her washing on the clothesline in the courtyard, which the latter saw as an attempt to encroach on the space where she sat every day. She started hurling abuses in the air without direct reference to Itarshi *dadi* and threatened to throw the clothes in the gutter. In response to this indirect provocation, Itarshi *dadi* came out and directly dared her to touch her clothes, in which case she said she was still capable of throwing the latter in the gutter instead (Figure 3.6).

Figure 3.6: The ground floor of *atithishala*, mostly occupied by the locals and other Hindi-speaking *Kāshivāsis*, and a few quarters on the second storey, inhabited by Telugu-speaking residents, in Kāshi Mumukshu Bhawan, December 2017. Photo credit: author

The Hindi-speaking people as a group, however, held their Telugu-speaking 'neighbours' in high regard because they demonstrated similar commitment through their daily routines, quotidian activities and beliefs about living their lives as a *Kāshivāsi*. This ensured their assimilation within the neighbourhood and its larger social and religio-philosophical ethos, which transformed the physical space of the neighbourhood into something essentially social in existence. In the process, the neighbourhood as social, in addition to being spatial, exerted an external force so that the norms of the *Kāshivāsi* community are not easily breached but commonly observed, or at least efforts are made to publicly feign adherence to such norms. In case of deviance within the neighbourhood, such factions were met with sanctions in the form of social reprimands and common labelling that denied them the status of 'true' *Kāshivāsi*. Thus, their symbolic silence, coupled with their avoidance of the Hindi-speaking people, made them distinct and bestowed an elevated status upon them. On the contrary, rather than being driven by a certain religio-philosophical commitment, the less advantaged locals, mostly women, sought the *āshram* out as a resourceful space that offered them free food, medical facilities and a market to sell their labour for easy profit. Faced with the problems associated with having an idle or alcoholic husband at home and the danger of abandonment that unemployed women often encounter, living the life of a *Kāshivāsi* could also be interpreted as an escape from the drudgeries and pathos of family life. However, when asked why they were at the Kāshi Mumukshu Bhawan, their narratives, after having suggested as much, still concluded with a reply delivered in an almost rehearsed manner—'I am here for *moksha*.'

Therefore, the primary objective is not necessarily to adopt the way of life of a *mumukshu* but to put on this identity as a convenient, mandatory garb and a performance in an attempt to get assimilated within the larger community and neighbourhood. Their everyday enactment of the role of the *mumukshu* becomes a routinised and rehearsed attempt at 'impression management' (Goffman 1963) or the 'verbal and non-verbal practices [being employed] in an attempt to present an acceptable image of our self to others' (Appelrouth and Desfor Edles 2011: 196). In addition to material security, it brings in social prestige and religious status, which was otherwise absent or denied to them.

Hence, the *Kāshivāsi* identity is best suited as a politics of convenience for the disadvantaged poor and unlucky elderly residents, masking their loss of social status by elevating their individual statuses socially.

In such situations, 'role-playing' becomes a viable option for all those who seek some sort of social acceptance (Parsons and Shils 1951 [2001] in Appelrouth and Desfor Edles 2011). Thus, when the primary roles within the families and communities of these locals failed to yield any personal, social or emotional returns, these roles became secondary in nature and the role of the '*Kāshivāsi*' became central, at least on the surface.

Conclusion: Negotiated Neighbourhood of *Kāshivās*

This chapter traced how, despite being a theoretically contentious possibility within an *āshram* governed by the dominant philosophy of *Kāshivās*, the neighbourhood nevertheless exists, albeit with many peculiarities. The residents of the Bhawan, both the committed *mumukshus* and the rest, negotiate the creation, existence and reproduction of a neighbourhood that cannot be merely categorised as spatial. Not only do their asociality and absence of communication define the shared understanding that reinforces their belief in detachment and their commitment towards a specific way of living and practice of dying, but they too indulge in subversions of the philosophy of *Kāshivās* that guides these beliefs and practices. This is readily done to accommodate social hierarchies, differences and distinctions. Acts of subversions are also often affective in nature and complicated in character because the residents resort to the philosophical prescriptions and proscriptions to justify their expressions of affective behaviour towards one another, when in theory, all kinds of affective bonds are discouraged within *Kāshivās*. Such affective encounters within the neighbourhood is demonstrated either as positive attempts at friendliness to 'correct' the deviant behaviours of others or as quarrels and silent antagonism/hostility. The latter were really expressions of social sanctions that further reiterated the presence of a neighbourhood that is social and contained within the spatial. In this form, the neighbourhood constantly re-emphasises the philosophical ideals and presents novel ways through which the *Kāshivāsis* reinvented their quotidian acts to fit within the larger philosophical worldview of *Kāshivās*.

The *āshram* as an institution, primarily dedicated to *Kāshivās* in its ideal form, comes very close to Michel Foucault's idea of 'heterotopia', which, in contrast to utopia (perfect yet unreal site), he defines as follows:

> [Heterotopias] ... are something like counter-sites, a kind of effectively enacted utopia in which the real sites, all the other real sites that can be found within the culture, are simultaneously represented, contested, and inverted. Places of this kind are outside of all places, even though it may be possible to indicate their location in reality. Because these places are absolutely different from all the sites that they reflect and speak about.... (1967 [1984]: 3–4)

In this sense, the *āshram* is not a space without a place, unlike the example of the ship that Foucault refers to; but instead, it is a space contained within a place, defined by the peripheries of the physical structure of the building. Yet, the world within is an inversion in its ideal form because death seems to be something that is evaded in the outside world and the popular trend is to avoid death, particularly with the invasion of the culture of thanatophobia.[12] In relation to this normalisation of the culture of thanatophobia that has come to define societies and quotidian lives almost everywhere, the *āshram*, comprising of *Kāshivāsis*, is running against the tide. Here, the idea is to embrace death as the completion of a natural cycle beginning at birth (Filippi 1947 [1996]; Saraswati 2005). In this way, it contains the fear of death (Moore and Williamson in Bryant [ed.] 2003) through its espousal of it, as it reiterates those values that do not alienate death but highlight it as a natural progression of cyclical time. However, I think it is only in a distilled state of suspension that the *āshram* can be categorised as a 'heterotopia'; because, as observations in this chapter reveal, it is pervaded by the politics of affect and sociality. The latter, as I have argued within the scope of this chapter, weaves the fabric

12 The *Collins English Dictionary* defines 'thanatophobia' as 'an abnormal fear of death'. Available at https://www.collinsdictionary.com/dictionary/english/thanatophobia (accessed on 30 April 2018).

of such socio-spatial institutions as the neighbourhood despite such a possibility being contentious, theoretically speaking. This fractures the heterotopic potential as the latter could only be realised when the *āshram* as a site represents the condition of *Kāshivās* in its ideal form. But this is hardly the case in practice, as the anxieties and fears related to death and dying are reflected through the everyday performances and activities of the *Kāshivāsis*. Therefore, in conclusion, the neighbourhood emerges as a negotiated space within a potentially heterotopic site. It is fraught with complexities and cannot possibly be read through a singular prism of understanding.

References

101 India. 2016, 'Widows of Varanasi II Death in India II Unique Stories from India', 25 July. Available at https://youtu.be/nJ8KTfEaC7Y (accessed on 27 May 2018).

Allan, Graham. 2006. 'Community'. In *Sociology: The Key Concepts,* edited by John Scott, pp. 35–38. London and New York: Routledge, 2006.

Appelrouth, Scott and Laura Desfor Edles. 2011. *Sociological Theory in the Contemporary Era.* USA: Sage Publications, pp. 20–35, 51–74, 174–260, 261–269, 278–284, 297–311.

Barthes, Roland. 1957 [1972]. *Mythologies.* Translated by Annette Lavers. New York, Farrar, Straus and Giroux: The Noonday Press.

Berger, Peter L. and Thomas Luckmann. 1966. *The Social Construction of Reality* (Excerpts), pp. 285–296. In Scott Appelrouth and Laura Desfor Edles. 2011. *Sociological Theory in the Contemporary Era.* USA: Sage Publications.

Bourdieu, Pierre. 1979 [1984]. *Distinction: A Social Critique of the Judgement of Taste.* Translated by Richard Nice. Cambridge, Massachusetts: Harvard University Press.

Bruce, Steve and Steven Yearley. 2006. 'Community'. *The Sage Dictionary of Sociology.* London, Thousand Oaks, New Delhi: Sage Publications.

Cacioppo, John T. and William Patrick. 2009. *Loneliness: Human Nature and the Need for Social Connection.* New York and London: W.W. Norton and Company.

Chopra-Chatterjee, Suhita and Jaydeep Sengupta. 2017. *Death and Dying in South Asia: Ageing and End-of-Life Care of the Elderly.* London and New York: Routledge.

Cooley, Charles Horton. 1902. *Human Nature and the Social Order*. New York: Scribner.

Das, Veena. 1976. 'The Uses of Liminality: Society and Cosmos in Hinduism'. *Contributions to Indian Sociology*, Vol. 10, No. 2, pp. 245–263.

———. 2012. *Structure and Cognition: Aspects of Hindu Caste and Ritual*. New Delhi: Oxford University Press.

Davies, Douglas J. 2005. *A Brief History of Death*. Madlen, MA: Blackwell Publishing.

Dennis, Norman. 1958. 'The Popularity of the Neighbourhood Community Idea'. *The Sociological Review*, Vol. 6, No. 2, pp. 191–206. Available at https://booksc.xyz/book/18478555/b8f2a0 (accessed on 25 August 2019).

Dumm, Thomas L. 2008. *Loneliness as a Way of Life*. Cambridge, Massachusetts, London, England: Harvard University Press.

Durge, S. 2011. 'Old Age Problem in India'. *The Viewspaper*, 21 February. Available at http://theviewspaper.net/old-age-problem-in-india/ (accessed on 22 May 2018).

Durkheim, Emile. 1897 [1952]. *Suicide: A Study in Sociology*. Translated by John A. Spaulding and George Simpson. London and New York: Routledge.

———. 1912. *The Elementary Forms of Religious Life*. Translated by Karen E. Fields. New York, London, Toronto, Sydney, Tokyo, Singapore: The Free Press.

Eck, Diana L. 2015. *Banaras: City of Light*. India: Penguin Books.

Elias, Norbert. 2001. *The Loneliness of the Dying*. Translated by Edmund Jephcott. New York and London: Continuum.

Exley, Catherine. 2004. 'Review Article: The Sociology of Dying, Death and Bereavement'. *Sociology of Health & Illness*, Vol. 26, No. 1, pp. 110–122.

Filippi, Gian Giuseppe. 2005. *Mrtyu: Concept of Death in Indian Traditions*. Translated by Antonio Rigopoulos. New Delhi: D.K. Printworld (P) Ltd.

Foucault, Michel. 1984. 'Of Other Spaces: Utopias and Heterotopias' (Translated by Jay Miskowiec), *Architecture/Mouvement/Continuité*, pp. 1–9.

Gawande, Atul. 2014. *Being Mortal: Medicine and What Matters in the End*. India: Hamish Hamilton.

Ghosh, Anindita. 2007, 2008. 'A World of Their Very Own: Religion, Pain, and Subversion in Bengali Homes in the Nineteenth Century'. In *Behind the Veil: Resistance, Women and the Everyday in Colonial South Asia*, edited by Anindita Ghosh, pp. 191–221. London and New York: Palgrave Macmillan.

Goffman, Erving. 1956. *The Presentation of Self in Everyday Life*. University of Edinburgh: Social Science Research Centre.

Goffman, Erving. 1963. *Stigma: Notes on the Management of Spoiled Identity.* London: Penguin.

Hawkley, Louise C. and John T. Cacioppo. 2007. 'Aging and Loneliness: Downhill Quickly?' *Current Directions in Psychological Science*, Vol. 16, No.4(August),pp.187–191.Availableathttp://www.jstor.org/stable/20183194 (accessed on 11 September 2013).

HelpAge India. 2017. 'How India Treats Its Elderly: A HelpAge India National Report—2017'. Available at https://www.helpageindia.org/wp-content/uploads/2017/06/Elder-Abuse-How-India-treats-its-Elderly-2017.pdf (accessed on 28 May 2018).

Hinduism Today. 2015. 'To Die in Varanasi: The Hope for Liberation from Rebirth Has Inspired a Retirement Community and a Hospice Industry'. July/August/September. Available at https://www.hinduismtoday.com/modules/smartsection/item.php?itemid=5602 (accessed on 27 April 2018).

Justice, Christopher. 1997. *Dying the Good Death: The Pilgrimage to Die in India's Holy City*. Delhi: Sri Satguru Publications.

Kakar, Sudhir. 2004. *The Inner World: A Psychoanalytic Study of Childhood and Society in India.* Delhi: Oxford University Press.

Karki, Anita. 2009. Loneliness among Elderly Women: A Literature Review. Unpublished Bachelor's Thesis: Degree Programme in Nursing, Laurea University of Applied Sciences, Espoo, Otaneimi.

Kaushik, Meena. 1976. 'The Symbolic Representation of Death'. *Contributions to Indian Sociology*, Vol. 10, No. 2, pp. 265–292.

Kearl, Michael C. 1989. *Endings: A Sociology of Death and Dying.* New York: Oxford University Press.

Kivett, Vira R. 1978, 'Loneliness and the Rural Widow'. *The Family Coordinator*, Vol. 27, No. 4, pp. 389–394. Available at http://www.jstor.org/stable/583442 (accessed on 24 September 2013).

Kubler-Ross, Elizabeth. 1969. *On Death and Dying: What the Dying Have to Teach Doctors, Nurses, Clergy and Their Own Families*. London and New York: Routledge.

Mead, George Herbert. 1934. *Mind, Self and Society: From the Standpoint of a Social Behaviorist*. Chicago and London: The University of Chicago Press.

Moore, Calvin Conzelus and John B. Williamson. 2003. 'The Universal Fear of Death and the Cultural Response'. In *Handbook of Death and Dying: The Presence of Death,* Vol. I, edited by Clifton D. Bryant, pp. 3–13. Thousand Oaks, London, New Delhi: Sage Publications.

Mukti Bhawan (*Hotel Salvation*). 2016. Film directed by Subhashish Bhutiani.

New World Encyclopedia Contributors. 2015. 'Sadhu and Swami'. New World Encyclopedia. Available at http://www.newworldencyclopedia.org/p/index.php?title=Sadhu_and_Swami&oldid=989769 (accessed on 22 May 2018).

Parry, Jonathan P. 1981. 'Death and Cosmogony in Kashi'. *Contributions to Indian Sociology*, Vol. 15, pp. 337–365.

———. 1994. *Death in Banaras*. New York: Cambridge University Press.

Parsons, Talcott C. and Edward A. Shills. 1951 [2001]. 'Categories of the Orientation and Organization of Action', *Toward a General Theory of Action* (Excerpt), pp. 36–50. In Scott Appelrouth and Laura Desfor Edles. 2011. *Sociological Theory in the Contemporary Era*. USA: Sage Publications.

Pathak, Dev Nath. 2018. *Living and Dying: Meanings in Maithili Folklore*. Delhi: Primus Books.

Perlman, Daniel and Letitia Anne Peplau. 1981. 'Toward a Social Psychology of Loneliness'. In *Personal Relationships in Disorder,* edited by Duck and Gilmour, pp. 31–56. London: Academic Press.

Reckon Talk. 2015. 'Moksha Bhavan: The Place Where People Check-In to Die'. 17 November. Available at http://www.reckontalk.com/moksha-bhavan-varanasi-death-indian-holy-city/ (accessed on 22 November 2017).

Rokach, Ami. 2007. 'Coping with Loneliness among the Terminally Ill'. *Social Indicators Research*, Vol. 82, No. 3 (July), pp. 487–503. Available at http://www.jstor.org/stable/20734469 (accessed on 30 June 2017).

Rubenstein, Carin, Phillip Shaver and Letitia Anne Peplau. 1979. 'Loneliness'. *Human Nature* (February), pp. 58–65.

Runthala, Shalu. 2015. 'Mukti Bhawan: Moksha: Banaras'. *The Times of World*, 30 September. Available at https://www.thetimesofworld.com/mukti-bhawan-moksha-banaras/ (accessed on 22 November 2017).

Sahay, K.N. 2005. 'Mystery of Death'. In *Voice of Death,* edited by Baidyanath Saraswati, pp. 37–63. New Delhi: D.K. Printworld (P) Ltd and Varanasi: N.K. Bose Memorial Foundation.

Saraswati, Baidyanath. 2005. 'Introduction'. In *Voice of Death,* edited by Baidyanath Saraswati, pp. 1–13. New Delhi: D.K. Printworld (P) Ltd and Varanasi: N.K. Bose Memorial Foundation.

Schutz, Alfred. 1967. *The Phenomenology of the Social World* (Excerpts), pp. 270–277. In Scott Appelrouth and Laura Desfor Edles. 2011. *Sociological Theory in the Contemporary Era*. USA: Sage Publications.

Segal, Robert A. 2004. *Myth: A Very Short Introduction*. Oxford: Oxford University Press.

Sengupta, Kaustubh Mani. 2017. 'Community and Neighbourhood in a Colonial City: Calcutta's *Para*'. *South Asia Research*, Vol. 38, No. 1, pp. 40–56.

Sharma, R.C. 2005. 'Upanisadic Concept of Death'. In *Voice of Death,* edited by Baidyanath Saraswati, pp. 17–24. New Delhi: D.K. Printworld (P) Ltd. and Varanasi: N.K. Bose Memorial Foundation.

Singh, Ravi Nandan. 2016. 'Many Lives of the Dead in Banaras: Towards an Anthropology of the Indefinite Social'. *Contributions to Indian Sociology,* Vol. 50, No. 1, pp. 27–51.

Subberwal, Ranjana. 2009. *Dictionary of Sociology.* New Delhi: Tata McGraw Hill. pp. N3, P5, R6, R7, S9, S12.

Tagore, Rabindranath. 1931. *The Religion of Man: Being the Hibbert Lectures for 1930.* New York: The Macmillan Company.

Tewari, A. 2009. 'The Old Age Crisis in India'. *Youth Ki Awaaz* (*YKA*), 17 July. Available at https://www.youthkiawaaz.com/2009/07/old-age-problems-india/ (last accessed on 22 May 2018).

'Thanatophobia'. *Collins English Dictionary.* Available at https://www.collinsdictionary.com/dictionary/english/thanatophobia (accessed on 30 April 2018).

Vitebsky, Piers. 2017, 2018. *Living Without the Dead: Loss and Redemption in a Jungle Cosmos.* India: HarperCollins.

Wilson, Liz. 2003. 'Introduction --Passing On: The Social Life of Death in South Asian Religions'. In *The Living and the Dead: Social Dimensions of Death in South Asian Religions* edited by Liz Wilson, pp. 1–12. Albany: State University of New York Press. Available at https://books.google.co.in/books?hl=en&lr=&id=p_nJssfEwDsC&oi=fnd&pg=PR7&dq=liz+wilson+introduction+passing+on&ots=3QD7t3gwlj&sig=-98RFfTIwfZwPV6S5CMZm27AzU4&redir_esc=y#v=onepage&q=liz%20wilson%20introduction%20passing%20on&f=false (accessed on 3 November 2020).

Wirth, Louis. 1938. 'Urbanism as a Way of Life'. *American Journal of Sociology,* Vol. 44 No. 1, pp. 1–24.

Wood, William R. and John B. Williamson. 2003. 'Historical Changes in the Meaning of Death in the Western Tradition'. In *Handbook of Death and Dying: The Presence of Death,* Vol. I, edited by Clifton D. Bryant, pp. 14–23. Thousand Oaks, London and New Delhi: Sage Publications.

4

Gossip and Intra-Denominational Politics in a Christian Neighbourhood in Greater Kolkata: A Sociological Reflection

Abhijit Dasgupta

Focused on a Bengali Christian *pārā* (neighbourhood) under the Kolkata Metropolitan Development Authority (KMDA) in North 24 Parganas district of West Bengal, the chapter looks into the mesh and grid of the neighbourhood and processes through which gossips are circulated. The chapter examines the relationship between gossip and ridicule and their relation to neighbourhood arrangements where human lives reside in close proximities leading to contention over spaces through affiliation of one's faith and belonging. In such a setting, the chapter asks how gossips influence the question of Christian place-making, preaching and the aspiration of the Christian Protestant community.

Anchored through editorial introduction in this book, neighbourhoods emerge as a critical body of inquiry due to their shared landscape and close proximity (Abraham 2010, 2018; De Neve and Donner 2006; Sengupta 2018). A neighbourhood in this context is characterised by the engagement of actors and institutions interpreting and interrogating the same urban space that experiences various forms of easy access to knowledge, information and family secrets creating relationships of both trust and antagonism. Mobilising these insights and perspectives, the chapter attempts to study the way gossip and ridicule as a part of the everyday life of the *pārā* affects the sociopolitical fabric of the Christian *pārā*. The chapter critically reveals the processes through which such gossip affects the Christian socialities that then influence new forms of social relations and power dynamics in the neighbourhood. In what ways do the gossip-induced Christian socialities affect the idea of place, enabling us to understand the linkages between gossip and the creation of new Christian places of worship in the *pārā*? To analyse these questions, the study invests its ears on gossips as an archive of the everyday *pārā* life, allowing the researcher to study gossips as a way to demonstrate the link between socialities and neighbourhood community building. The neighbourhood in these gossips becomes a site of social control, surveillance and contestation at multiple levels. At a broader level, the objective is to understand the relationship between faith and place operating through the grid of the neighbourhood.

The chapter allows us to enter into the overlapping worlds of the *pārā* and the peculiar nature of gossips and ridicule that affects the relation between faith and place. This will be done by analysing a schism[1] in one of the Protestant churches known as the E Protestant church (EPC), Church of North India (CNI). The encounter and engagements in the *pārā* space over the formation of a new church created after a schism in the EPC raises questions about how gossip as everyday practice is closely associated with the question of power, authority and structure of the Christian institutions. In what way is it linked to the position of the priesthood that impacts the neighbourhood's spatial imagination? In such sharing of neighbourhood spaces and in understanding the above questions, the practices of 'gossip' and 'ridicule' are being used by the *pārā* people not just as idle, petty activities, but, as Gluckman (1963) reveals, gossip is seen here rather as a tool in the hands of the people to bring about change in the *pārā*.

Debating Neighbourhood

Taking a leaf from the introductory chapter, we understand that urban neighbourhood is the staple of sociological and anthropological

---

1 I have borrowed the term 'schism' from the scholarship of the anthropology of Christianity, primarily from Courtney Handman's (2014) book *Critical Christianity: Translation and Denominational Conflict in Papua New Guinea*. She discusses the social groups that *Guhu Samane* Christians inhabit and engage, allowing them to produce denominational schism that, according to Protestant Christians, is part of the practice and not a lacuna of any kind credited to the nature of Christianity.

research since the early 20th century when the Chicago school (also known as the ecological school) rose to prominence in urban studies. However, the Chicago school with its 'problem-centred approach' did not pay much attention to the everyday life of the neighbourhood, ignoring many themes of diverse meanings crucial to anthropological meaning-making (Foot 1943; Wirth 1938). In the South Asian context, multiple meanings of the neighbourhood and the way they reveal local politics, power dynamics and aspects of gender negotiation, along with various sensory experiences of 'smell' and 'sound', have only been taken seriously in recent times (Abraham 2010; Gandhi 2016; Ghosh 2015).

Through an ethnography of neighbourhood 'gossip' and 'ridicule' and their effect on space formation and belonging, the study undertaken here deduces its argument from the micro-politics of social relations, power and space.[2] Rajnarayan Chandavarkar (1997) highlights the importance of studying neighbourhood, not only based on old categories that workers brought with them by way of rural ties—for example, caste and kinship—but also the experience of staying in the neighbourhood, which introduced them to new networks of power and domination. Likewise, Abraham (2018) and Sengupta (2018) argue that although there has been a shift from rural to urban—and a tendency to study urban communities in great details—it did not bring about new categories with which to study the urban neighbourhood. Since then scholars have followed the trajectory of Chandavarkar to offer interesting insights on the social dynamics of neighbourhoods.[3]

In the context of West Bengal where my field is located, residential settlements based on caste and ethnicity are well captured in both colonial and recent scholarship. In Bengal, *pārās* derived their names from the physical attributes of the place, for example, *pukur* (pond), *bagan* (garden) or *bazaar* (market). In fact, *pārās* were also named after occupational and caste lines, for example, *Kansaripara, Kumartuli,*

2 One is informed by the writings of Foucault 1975; Srinivas 1952 and De Neve and Donner 2006.

3 Also see Abraham 2010, 2018; Chatterjee 2017; Chopra 2007; De Neve and Donner 2006; Jamil 2017; Khan 2007.

Jeleypara[4] and the erstwhile white and black towns that created two separate sections in the city with contrasting infrastructure (Sengupta 2018; Banerjee 2016). In this discourse, the relation between religiosity and urban spaces is either ignored or reduced to the discourse of communalism and communal events. Hansen (2013) points out that although religion and ethnicity dictate the formation of urban spaces and sociality, their influence on urban scholarship, particularly in terms of urban organisation and structure, has been largely overlooked. The dominance of class, race or caste, in the context of India, overshadows religion, which continues to be 'undefined black box in human geography' (Tse 2014: 201).[5] The lack of scholarship on religion, particularly in the context of neighbourhood, space, place for religious minorities in India like Islam and Christianity, is even more serious as they continue to be seen from the fixed lens of 'fundamentalism' and 'conversion', respectively (Robinson 2012: 17). Contrary to the Christian neighbourhood, the scholarship on Muslim neighbourhoods has in the recent past received some scholarly attention.[6] However, the discourse is tilted towards the narratives of 'ghettoisation' and studying separate enclaves for the Muslim population. While Muslim neighbourhood has been a topic of interest for anthropological scholars in bringing out ways through which specific neighbourhoods are spatially stigmatised and blotched with fear and distress, one asks if the same categories can also be used in understanding neighbourhoods inhabited primarily by Christians.

Krishnapur Christian *Pārā*

The fieldwork for this study has been carried out in a neighbourhood known as Krishnapur Christian *pārā* in North 24 Parganas district, which shares its boundaries with Kolkata. Located under Greater

4 *Kansari* is a Bengali Hindu caste, traditionally brazier and coppersmith by profession. *Kumartuli* is commonly known as potters' quarter. *Jeleypara* denotes neighbourhood of the fishermen community.

5 I am thankful to Kamalika Banerjee, a research scholar at NUS, Singapore, for introducing me to this set of literature.

6 For example, Chatterjee 2017; Jamil 2017.

Kolkata, the Krishnapur Christian *pārā* and its nearby areas comprise three mainstream churches: HFC, under the Roman Catholic Church; EPC, a Protestant church under the Church of North India (CNI) and a Pentecostal church known as AG. It also has two house churches—SDA and CHS—and many informal prayer gatherings that attract both Hindus and Christians. The EPC, which was built in 1829, is the oldest church in the neighbourhood. While It has a strength of 222 families, the HFC has 119 families and AG has 100 members who mostly live in and around Krishnapur. In 2015, the Krishnapur Christian *pārā* was under the jurisdiction of Rajarhat Gopalpur Municipality, but in 2018 it came under Ward Number 26 of Bidhannagar Municipality. During the initial days of my fieldwork, as I attempted to understand the demographic profile of the Krishnapur Christian *pārā*, it was seemingly dominated by Protestants, mostly the Mondals. However, many other non-Mondal families, both Catholics and Protestants, started to move into the *pārā*, particularly after the opening of an iron and aluminium factory in Jessore Road. In fact, it is also believed that the first convert to Protestantism from the region was also a member of the Mondal family, Kalachand Mondal, who is credited to have donated a large amount of land for the construction of the Protestant church (EPC).

The *pārā* under study is dominated by Mondals. The Bengali surname 'Mondal' can be found among Hindus, Muslims and Christians. The term *mandal* means 'chief of the village'; sometimes this designation meant representative of the Zamindar (landlord) who used to distribute land and collect revenues. Some Mondals claim a connection to the *Namasudra* Scheduled-Caste community, but it is wrong to connect all Mondals to the Scheduled-Caste category because some trace their lineage from *Vaishya Kappali*, *Teli* or *Sadgop* caste also. The Christians of the Krishnapur Christian *pārā* identify themselves as Schedule Caste. It can be traced back to the Protestant conversion waves in Bengal. In fact, the use of *Tiyar* caste and the term 'lower caste Hindoos' appear in the London Missionary Society eleventh report and in the writings of O'Malley (2003) that discuss the conversion narratives in the *pārā*.

Sengupta (1971) documents that there was a consensus among historians and missionary writings that much of the first wave of Protestant converts in Bengal did not come from 'respectable' families.

The converts came from low social backgrounds, mostly from *Tili, Jogge, Kaibarta* and others, and they were termed both by Raja Ram Mohan Roy in *The English Works* and Lord Minto in *The Minto Papers* as socially ignorant classes. Aligning to such discussion, voices from the field can also be raised. I met Peter Mondal in a programme conducted by the Youth Association of the EPC. Peter remarked that the *pārā* is called *tapashil pārā* (Scheduled-Caste neighbourhood) as more or less everyone in the *pārā* is a Scheduled Caste. Similarly, Rakesh Mondal, who owns a chicken shop in Mission Bazar, a locality near the Krishnapur Christian *pārā*, points out thus:

> Our ancestors were from the scheduled-caste community. Although we were SCs, we do not *yet* have SC certificate. We are SCs and also Christians. In some churches, demands for OBC [other backward classes] certificates are being raised, but not in our church. My forefathers got converted to Christianity for better standards of living, which included access to education, health and food.

Contrary to western anthropologists working on Christianity, like Robbins (2007: 10), many Christians from the *pārā* do not see their conversion to Christianity as a moment of 'rupture' or complete interruption from the past; rather, they continue to practice many Hindu rituals within the confines of Christian meaning-making mechanism. Protestants, who are the majority in the Christian *pārā*, often refer to themselves as 'Hindu Christians' and show evidence of many popularly believed Hindu rituals and symbols as an important part of their daily lives, for example putting vermillion on the forehead and wearing red-and-white conch bangles etc.

As the spaces in the colonial city of Calcutta were organised on the basis of the communities' direct link to the colonial power, the Christians of Calcutta enjoyed a great deal of patronage from the British government in jobs like custom, police, railways and so on. However, the Christian community cannot be understood as a homogenous category as it included Europeans, Chinese, Armenians, Anglo-Indians and few other Christian communities who lived in various parts of the city. The areas of traditional Christian concentration include Elliot Street, Free School Street, Park Street, Chowringhee, Wellesley Street and so on. However, the study of Christianity in Kolkata has been largely confined to the study of Anglo-Indians and their stories of belonging, identity and migration.[7] Such scholarship has rendered the other Christian population of the city invisible, for example, Bengali Christians who are Christians by faith and speak *Bangla* as their mother tongue. Far removed from any colonial characteristics of Christianity and being relegated to the suburbs of Kolkata, these Bengali Christians are mostly found in some of the areas of DumDum, Thakurpukur, Entally, Sealdah, Krishnapur, Keorapukur and so on. Studying one of such Christian neighbourhoods in the suburbs of Kolkata allows me to refer to Sengupta's (2018) analysis of the archives of Thomas (1997) on the poor in Calcutta. The archive argues that many *pārās* in the city had been dominated by a single family and ethnicity that had control over the land, politics and everyday social life. Much akin to Thomas (1997), the Christian *pārā* is dominated by a single Mondal Protestant family.

The neighbourhood of Krishnapur Christian *pārā* has a strong foothold of Christians who have been living here for generations. The Christian population is primarily Bengali Christians, both Protestants and Catholics. It also comprises many non-Bengali Christians from Odisha, Darjeeling, North East, Chhattisgarh and so on. In fact, the fluid and porous boundaries between Christians and Hindus within and without the *pārās* and the Bengali Christians' peaceful relation with their Hindu counterparts have paved the way for the entry of neoliberal projects such as real estate business and residential projects in the *pārā* and its nearby areas. Such kinds of projects have allowed many Hindu residents to own property and buy lands, resulting in the settlement of many Hindu families in and around the Christian *pārā*. In fact, many Christian families have sold their lands and properties to their Hindu neighbours and moved out of the *pārā*, allowing many Hindus to settle in the *pārā*.

Despite the in-migration of many Hindus, Christian domination is still visible. The domination of three major churches and the vibrant celebration of feasts and festivals set this *pārā* apart. In the evenings, many Catholic and Protestant prayer gatherings become active places

7 See Andrews 2013; Blunt and Bonerjee 2013.

of socialities as they attract both Christian and Hindu residents of the *pārā*. On my many visits to this Christian *pārā*, I often wandered around observing and familiarising myself with the *pārā* space. This space is marked by a host of activities: people going to church in groups on Sunday, sharing about new developments in church, gossiping about neighbours, exchanging sporadic greetings from verandas and courtyards, to mention a few. As one wanders in the street, one also notices quarrels and disputes between construction workers of upcoming high-rise apartments and residents of the neighbourhood due to close proximity of houses and easy effect on the senses. The local *pārā* bodies like clubs are spaces where young men meet, exchange cigarettes and play card games as they bemoan the lack of employment and everyday drudgeries of the *pārā* life. On the other hand, teenage boys are seen loitering around the *pārā* lanes, some on motorbikes and others on cycles, speaking in local *pārā* colloquialism. The sight of women standing near their doorways and exchanging pleasantries while suspiciously examining my presence and labelling me as an 'outsider' was not a new experience for me, as in most cases neighbourhood relations depend on familiarity along kinship lines, face-to-face interactions and physical proximity.

Gossip in the *Pārā*: Smell, Sight and Surveillance

The close proximity of neighbourhood lives, the shared spaces of belonging between members of different families and the constant interplay of sensory experiences constitute a neighbourhood grid. The general nature of gossip about mundane everyday life can be manifested in various conversations and activities. The nature of gossip obtains intensity when people who engage in such practices belong to the same family, or extended family as in this case of the Christian *pārā* where the majority belongs to one family—Mondal. Their background in conversion—it was Kalachand Mondal, their ancestor, who first converted to Christianity, and later on, the entire Mondal family accepted the new faith—has not brought a major break in their relations with the local Hindus. Similar Bengali ethnic, cultural affiliation supported by a communitarian, peaceful relationship with the Hindus of the same and nearby *pārās*, along with porous boundaries within the Christian community itself, contributes to easy communication of knowledge with one another, escalating the practice of gossiping as a part of everyday life.

There is a rich discussion on gossip.[8] Nevertheless, there is hardly any definitional consensus on 'gossip' as a sociological category. For example, while Paine (1967) defines gossip as an act to promote individual interests, others like Ben-Ze'ev (1994) understands the act as a source of fun with the focus more on the process than the outcome. Gossip in the general sense is perceived as a critical talk between two people to evaluate a situation against a third party (Haviland 1977). For Haviland (Ibid.: 28), it includes 'news, report, slander, libel, ridicule, insult, defamation, and malicious and innocent gossip.' Writing from a functionalist perspective, Gluckman (1963) argues that gossip emerges as a means to reinforce group membership and delineate boundaries, which regulates and sanctions the practice of moral policing. Gluckman (Ibid.: 308–309) emphasises that gossip is closely tied to 'the blood and tissue of [that] life'. His understanding of gossip is not a random, arbitrary act; rather, people use gossip as a 'social weapon' to derive change according to their group interests. Though the fieldwork of this study indicates some nature of Gluckman's functionalist framework, one also notices *pārā* gossip to carry a veneer of meanings that is difficult to be spun into one single thread. In the field, as I tried to understand the way gossip as a 'social weapon' was being performed in the close association of the neighbourhood, I realised that the topics included land disputes, surveillance over young college girls, the inefficiency of priests, tittle-tattle over food smell, loud sounds of construction work. Many *pārā* people, often in casual gossip, narrated to me their displeasure and annoyance about everyday *pārā* life and politics, which, however, do not usually lead to hostilities, except recently, when an allegation against an EPC priest led to a schism in the Protestant church, which will be discussed shortly.

In one of my conversations with the *pārā* people, Arun Mondal, a senior resident of the *pārā*, remarked,

---

8 See Bergmann 1987; Dunbar 2004; Eder and Enke 1991; Gluckman 1963; Haviland 1977; Paine 1967; Stewart and Strathern 2004; Vaidyanathan et al. 2016.

> I have four brothers: Asim, Anil, Ashok and Alok. All four are married and live in this *para*. Asim and Ashok have two sons each. Anil has two sons and one daughter, Ashok has one daughter and I have one son. All the sons are married and settled here. Similarly, my cousin brother's sons and daughters are also married. All of them have settled in the Christian *para*. So you can see we have a big family and everyone lives in close distance. We can literally hear, see and smell each other. Last evening, Anil's son John was scolding his teenage son for not going to tuition and his son was crying profusely. We could hear everything. I told my wife, Rita, to close the windows. You know, it's too much of unwanted noise at times. When I was raising my son, I never beat him up. You should raise your children with love, care and other Christian virtues. I felt bad for his son…I thought of going down to speak to Anil, but I did not say anything. After all, it's their personal matter. I am just telling you because you are working on our *para* and this will be useful for your studies.

Quite similar to Arun's story, Antony also recalled that many of the *pārā* residents are his brothers. He complained to me that despite being his brother and going to the same church, his cousin Michael Mondal has been unfair to him over their ancestral land. Antony lamented that when the land was distributed between the brothers, he was cheated and given the tail end of the land where no air or sunlight is available. He told to me in a hushed tone, pointing towards Michael's house, which was partially visible from his bedroom window:

> Look, I know I have been cheated. I have told another brother of mine that Michael has forged the documents. If there is any court case, I will speak against him. I know the local councillor. I will not sign on the land mutation documents. Let him suffer for his deceit.

While coming back from a Sunday church service, Antony pointed me towards a newly built house church and narrated to me the story of a young pastor who fought against a senior *pārā* priest and brought down the image of the *pārā*. He remarked of the new house-church *padri* as 'narrow, improper, and with false representation of Christianity'. He quickly ran to his main entrance and, even, refused to look towards the new house-church building. He called the house church '*bhondo girja*', or fake church, and advised me to never visit such places lest the image of Christianity is tarnished in my mind. He continued,

> Some sections of the *para* people do not read the Bible. They will only hear from random people and buy into their interpretation of it. I do not like people who blindly believe in other people's lectures.... Our ancestors had done so much to get funding from the Diocese to construct the church, but people like these are a nuisance who do not understand the true meaning of Christianity. Do not meet them; they will not be able to say one line from the Bible correctly.

Gossip of several kinds came to my ears during the fieldwork, some also from the Hindus who now live with the Christians as neighbours. Suresh Ghosh, a Hindu who lives in one of the new apartments, said, 'You come here every Sunday, you can only smell pork and beef being cooked. The smell is everywhere, and you cannot even complain.' He pointed out that the benefits of just being Christian have a collateral social cost:

> These Christians are so lucky, they get admission in all leading convent schools. One of the Christian girls in the *para*, Rebecca, got 65 per cent in higher secondary exam, but she got admission in a leading college in Park Street, while my niece who got 80 per cent failed to get admission in a good college. They are reaping the benefits of their forefathers' choice to convert to Christianity. At times I even question their Christianity. They are just like me and you, as in, their weddings and funerals follow a lot of Hindu practices.

Another kind of gossip takes the form of social surveillance. This form of gossip manifests in the enforcement of the invisible *pārā* rules that embody Christian virtues such as grace, benevolence, humility, high moral character, which are almost always meant for young female members of the *pārā*. For example, a young female undergraduate student, whom I shall call Samantha Das, refused to talk to me when I met her briefly after a church programme. She was uncomfortable talking on the neighbourhood road for fear of being talked about and rumoured to be going around with me. She was scared her neighbours might complain to her mother that she was being 'over-friendly' with a stranger. Her close association with me could also affect her image of a 'good Christian girl', and her family might be made answerable to unpleasant questions of her 'liberal behaviour'. She said, 'I can make my mother understand the reason why I walk with you, but the neighbours will develop their own brand of stories and sell them all over the neighbourhood, making sure to label me a loose girl.'

For fear of being ridiculed by her neighbours, Samantha insisted that we take an auto and go to a coffee shop outside the *pārā* and discuss our work. As soon as we departed the *pārā*, her body language changed and we talked freely about many things, including her relations with other churches, disputes in her paternal family and so on.

Rebecca Mondal was another local Protestant girl from the *pārā* that I met. Her parents separated when she was young, after which access to different parts of the *pārā* was curtailed for her by many of her kinship relations. Her father's family lives near the Pentecostal church and, as a result, when the church organises any programme, she hesitates to take part. She said,

> My uncles have never bothered to visit me after my parents separated; they even refused to help me with my college admission. If I go to the Pentecostal church programme, I will feel uncomfortable in their presence, as they will talk about me and my mother behind my back. Although I like the pastor of the church and enjoy his sermons, only because of my uncle's participation I cannot go this time. Living in the same *para* with so many members of the family is difficult.

The aforementioned narratives reveal to us that the neighbourhood space is vexed with a plethora of gossip, which highlights different experiences of staying in it. Arun ridiculed his nephew for poor parenting (the way he treated his son). Antony's anger was against his brothers who 'cheated' him by giving him a poor deal on their ancestral land. Antony's displeasure with false representation of the new church and blaming it for its poor representation of Christianity are few concerns that reached my ears as everyday gossip in the *pārā*. Others include Suresh complaining to me about the smell of pork and beef and the reservation for Christian students in convent schools and colleges, which he thinks is unfair. For Samantha, she had to carry the image of a 'good Christian girl', and any compromise of that image, by walking the streets of the *pārā* with a young stranger would result in embarrassment to her mother and vitiate the general atmosphere of the neighbourhood. Rebecca, on the other hand, is caught in the web of kinship and broken family. Due to the presence of her paternal family in the same neighbourhood, she had to deprive herself of her faith by not participating in the programme held at the Pentecostal church. Such cases of social control and influence, with attempts to define social boundaries, especially for women, have been captured by anthropologists (Abraham 2018, 2010; Abu-Lughod 1986; Khan 2007; Vatuk 1972). The presence of gossip in the aforementioned narratives is perhaps part of everyday life, but most of the time they do not play out openly to affect the *pārā* relationships. People voluntarily comply with many verbal and casual rules of the neighbourhood as they feel it is expected of them to keep themselves in tandem with the goodwill of the neighbourhood. However, during my fieldwork in February 2018, an incident in the *pārā* brought out the close link between neighbourhood gossip (and its intertwined relations)and the functioning of local Christianity involving a church priest and his congregation members.

Gossip and Schism in EPC

As the chapter seeks to measure the pervasiveness of gossip as part of everyday life in the neighbourhood, either in small acts of social control or critical acts of hostilities and disputes, this section highlights one specific gossip that became one of the major topics of tension between the Protestants of the Christian *pārā* and its neighbouring localities. Gluckman's articulation of gossip as 'social weapon' and Haviland's (1977) understanding of gossip as a conversation between two people against a third-party involving news, insult, defamation and so on will help us make sense of this specific case.

During my fieldwork in 2017–2018, the EPC in the Christian *pārā* was being served by a non-Bengali priest (*padri*) from the city of Ranchi, Jharkhand. He was known in the *pārā* for his strictness and was quite inflexible when it came to amending rules to fit the daily expectations of some members. The *padri* was often less approached for family programmes and kept out by members ostensibly for his poor Bengali speaking skills and unfamiliarity with the city.

As a result, the Sunday service of the church usually had low attendees, often mostly women, but at times youths when they are responsible for the sermon. Male attendance at Sunday service was usually low, mostly only seen at specific events.

The *padri* was aware of poor male participation in church service and often demanded, in casual meetings and informal discussions, answers for their absence. This attitude of the *padri* was often not welcomed by the *pārā* people as many of them argued they were busy with their daily routine and preferred to profess their faith and belief in a more personal way rather than attending institutionalised church service. Raj Makhal, a resident of the Christian *pārā*, said,

> Most of us work in shops or run businesses, which usually close late at night. So, Sunday morning is difficult for us to attend church. We can always pray and read the Bible at home when we want. At times, we arrange prayer meetings at home and pray according to our convenience.

Another resident, Emmanuel Mondal, said, 'I avoid going to church on Sunday as I do not want to meet some of my neighbours. Moreover, I do not like members of the organising committee of the church and do not have a good relationship with them.' A couple of days into my fieldwork, conversations with the residents about poor Sunday service attendance indicated a general dislike for the non-Bengali priest. This dislike was not only due to his authoritarian nature and inability to speak in colloquial Bengali like the *pārā* people but also because he was seen as an outsider (he came from the state of Jharkhand). The *padri*'s inability to preach spontaneously and engage in free and casual conversation in Bengali through jokes and humour compelled Ratan Mondal, a forty-five-year-old EPC member, to express his displeasure over the presence of the non-Bengali priest in his church. He said,

> The last [Bengali] *padri* was very close to us. We could go to him and discuss any family stories and experiences. We used to invite him for family prayers and share with him our pain and problems. He used to crack jokes and laugh with us. But this *padri* is very strict and is always serious....He neither understands local political problems nor is he well aware of the local language.

It may be worth pointing out in this context that all other churches in the city under CNI have Bengali priests, which perhaps makes Christian members of the EPC more critical of their *padri*. The lack of Bengali priest motivated few *pārā* residents to make allegations against the *padri*, which often led them to justify their absence from the church. The allegations include the current *padri*' lack of conversational and networking skills and his unfamiliarity with the city and other priests. For example, Rohit Sarkar, a congregation member of the Protestant church who migrated to this *pārā* in the late 1980s, worked (during the course of the study) as a grocery owner in the local market. He complained to me that the '*padri babu* is only good at reading scriptures and verses from the Bible, which he has learnt by heart, but when we call him to house prayers, he is unable to talk to us properly. We miss our old *padri* a lot.'

This kind of displeasure against the *padri* did not seem to radically change the clergy-laity relationship, but at the same time, one cannot pass off the gossips around it as the peripheral commotion of the everyday *pārā* life. The cumulative complaints against and disinterests in the *padri* made him very unpopular particularly among a specific section of the *pārā* population, which eventually led to the rise of an aspiring local Bengali pastor from the Mondal family who tried to flock, like a good shepherd, the congregation members towards a new church that he was establishing around that time. This aspiring pastor Mohan Mondal, who had freshly graduated from a theological college in Siliguri, West Bengal, and was back home to establish a new church, which was called CHS. He used the vitiated atmosphere in the *pārā* to his advantage by demanding the removal of the non-local EPC priest. Mohan's tactic—of winning the hearts and minds of the *pārā* people and uprooting some members of the EPC—was operationalised by taking recourse to gossip. His modus operandi was to selectively interpret the *padri*'s personal information and disseminate them among the *pārā* people through the medium of gossip. Personal information that was the target of ridicule included the *padri*'s English name and surname, which were made fun of by a certain section of the *pārā* people in private conversations that were passed of more acceptably as mere jokes. His English name was variously interpreted to mean *bideshi* (foreigner), *bohiragato* (outsider), *saheber sontan* (white British man's son) and so on. With people in their private domain calling the EPC *padri* with different 'names', demonstrating the origin and source of any gossip become very difficult because of the ambiguous, fluid nature of the gossip medium, which, over time, becomes firmly entrenched in the everyday fluid network of the *pārā* social life.

The linguistic politics and the domination of the Bengali-speaking Christians facilitated Mohan to informally start a prayer meeting every Sunday with loud song and music, which developed curiosity among many *pārā* Christians. In the Bengali-speaking *pārā*, such sociality with a Bengali local pastor from the same Mondal family started to attract a lot of local people. As Mohan's new church started to indulge in song and dance with the accompaniment of loud music, it often caught the attention of many Hindus and Christians in the *pārā* who started visiting him informally every Sunday evening for an hour or so. Such a trend continued for a while until the Christmas of 2017 when one day Mohan formally accused the EPC *padri* in the church general body meeting for renting out the church land for a price without seeking permission from the church organising committee. At the time of the allegation, Mohan was still a member of the EPC. He accused the *padri* and his team of corruption and labelled them 'unfit' to run the church. He said the priest from outside was only interested in making money and would eventually destroy the hundred-year-old church by selling off the lands that their forefathers had donated. Such remarks against a senior *padri* by a local *pārā* person became scandalous, and soon the meeting was dissolved. Tensions broke out in the *pārā* and different kinds of gossips started to circulate among the *pārā* people. Some people believed in the stories circulated by Mohan that the *padri* was unemotional and uncaring towards the church property, an insinuation that he was not a good enough priest to understand the needs and desires of his congregation. Another section, though, decided not to question the authority of the *padri* and was rather fearful of questioning him as he was appointed by the Diocese of Calcutta with necessary rules and regulations.

Before the next meeting was called, the *pārā* people were divided into two groups. Mohan stuck to his narrative that 'a *padri* from outside is selling our church by inviting foreign companies to use our land'. Again, after a few days, another meeting was called in the EPC where voices from both sides of the land dispute were heard. The matter was resolved after an agreement was reached between the two parties that the decision to rent out church land for commercial purposes rests collectively with the organising committee and not unilaterally with the *padri*. Although the matter was resolved behind closed doors, this incident remained major hearsay in the *pārā*. Mohan and his congregation members in the *pārā* and in a common discussion forum continued to propagate the stories of the *padri* selling church land and destroying the peace of the church. The gossips—the *pārā* people discussing the personal life and family of the EPC *padri*, such as questioning his relationship with God, his pastoral training, his family history of conversion, his knowledge about the Bible—did not remain distant from the ears of the *padri*. It is interesting to note that the everyday practice of gossiping was not restricted to the profane and mundane world. In fact, the discussion on gossip became a sermon theme in the church, which itself emerged as a cause for concern for the community.

As gossips entered the more formal setting of the church, I remember that for two consecutive Sunday service sermons, the EPC *padri* condemned the act of gossiping and berated the way his priesthood and family background were being made topics of daily *pārā* discussions. On one such sermon, he termed gossiping as unchristian practice, cited from the Bible—The words of a gossip are like choice morsels; they go down to the innermost parts (Proverb18: 8)—and told the congregation stories about how people who gossip add more sin to their life on earth and hence do not find a place in heaven. In the sermons, he gave the example of Christian virtues of respect for elders, love for neighbours, being charitable and so on. On one occasion, the *padri* gave a sermon with life as an example:

> When a man accepts Jesus Christ in his life, he is often faced with many difficult choices. He at times also has to leave his family to act as per the calling of God. When I was a teenager, I understood the calling of God and left home to serve people who, most of the time, are outside the world of familiarity. So, one must show support and care for such people.

He argued that for devoted Christians, love is not just a feeling or an emotion but an action that they display before people they like, just as the *padri* loved his congregation and, therefore, came from far to serve them. He said he loved his congregation so much that he even made it a point to attend Sunday service every week irrespective of personal or health problems. He gave the example of his bike accident in which he twisted his ankle but did not miss Sunday service as it was the day of the Holy Communion.[9] Similarly, he expected the congregation to show love and affection not just in words but also in action by refraining from gossiping, which, he said, is divisive in nature and can drive a wedge between them. Although the *padri* did his best, in sermons and informal discussions, to critique the practice of gossiping as an act that is against the doctrines of Christianity, nothing seemed to help. Many members of the EPC church understood this period as a crisis in their spiritual journey; and to enrich their spiritual needs, some sought refuge in the new church that Mohan Mondal built. With people migrating to Mohan's new church because of gossip against the EPC *padri* and the latter's sudden departure before his tenure ended, relationships between members of the neighbourhood were visibly strained.

As the EPC *padri* left the church and the *pārā*, Mohan tried to portray an alternative understanding of the church. Speaking in favour of house churches, he criticised the bureaucratic ways in which the EPC conducted itself, which, according to him, was a hindrance to spiritual growth and an obstacle towards improving faith sensibilities. By quoting verses from the Bible—'[A]nd on this rock I will build my church' (Mathew 16: 18) and 'For where two or three gather in my name, there am I with them' (Mathew 18: 20)—he motivated the *pārā* people to join his new church, which he feared, in the initial days, might face

---

9 For Christians who have undergone the ritual of baptism, the Holy Communion is a ritual service of Christian worship at which consecrated bread and wine are shared by congregation members. For Bengali Catholics, the Holy Communion is known as '*Christor prasad*', and for Protestants, it is '*probhur bhoj*'. For the Christians of the Krishnapur Christian *pārā*, people might not attend regular Sunday service but they are usually present on the day of the Holy Communion, which usually takes place once a month during Sunday service.

isolation from the larger Christian community of the *pārā* even as they were moving away from the shadows of CNI. By mobilising through his local Mondal social capital and family connection, he managed to attract a lot of people from the Christian *pārā* and elsewhere and, over time, earned their trust and support.

In a social landscape that is predicated in the presence of a non-Bengali 'outsider' priest in a neighbourhood dominated by Bengali-speaking Christians, along with a strong bulwark of family hegemony, the Mondals seemed like a clear example of how urban space is fiercely produced and reproduced in everyday life along kinship and ethnic boundaries. In this case, gossip is culturally determined, as Mohan was able to understand the local *pārā* dissatisfaction and discontent against the priest and convert gossip into a productive tool to consolidate his position. Although Mohan's new church started functioning on his terrace and attracted enough members every Sunday, a large section of the *pārā* people who were invested in the three mainstream churches refused to see Mohan's house church as a place worth visiting by 'real Christians'. This negative attitude towards Mohan's church was perhaps because it was not registered and did not serve the Holy Communion, which led some Christian residents, like Antony, to label it as '*bhondo girja*' (fake Church). The partaking of *probhur bhoj* is a key criterion for the *pārā* Christians to be counted as Christians because only the ritual 'confirmation' of baptism could make them eligible to partake of it.

One could explain Mohan's engagement with the prevalent gossip as a political act. He channelised this 'political act' through allegations of corruption levelled against the serving priest to exert power and authority to form and organise his own church. Such act not only aggravated the already bitter relations between the EPC *padri* and some section of the *pārā* people, but it also showcased the importance, in the local *pārā* milieu, of achieving the position of priesthood, which is closely tied to one's social and cultural capital in the world of neighbourhood politics where contestations and challenges are spatially controlled. The way the practice of gossiping unfolded in the *pārā* complicated the established ways of seeing them. One needs to see gossip as crucially embedded in the everyday conversations, social relationships, subjective identity formation and, above all, social conditions in which one is located. It is constantly playing out in the local *pārā* at the level of personal aspirations, taking new forms and shapes, often uniting and/or dividing people and affecting relations with faith and place.

Bringing Together Faith and Place

Mohan's CHS, in some sense, was birthed by the schism in the EPC church. The schism allowed CHS to transform itself from an invisible body of religiosity, restricted to a rooftop prayer gathering, to an active church in the *pārā*. The new church participated in various *pārā*-based programmes, which indicates a new Christian place-making approach, highlighting how gossip resembles the religious sentiments of certain sections of the *pārā* Christians. The schism allowed the new church to become prominent in the Christian *pārā* culture, and it soon became a household name in the *pārā*. People in the *pārā* referred to Mohan 'as the man who stood against corruption in the EPC' and often got invited by needy households to pray for and help their members in understanding their spiritual growth and relations with Jesus. As the EPC *padri* left the *pārā* and people started to flock to the CHS church, one woman named Rupa Mondal went around telling everyone, after attending CHS for a week, that her back pain had been miraculously healed. She said,

> Before joining CHS, I had been suffering from acute back pain for months; I could hardly move or do any household chores. I heard that one new church has come up in the *para* and is run by a local person. It is hard to find local people involved in the teaching of Christ. I went there as I knew the family. Mohan prayed for me every time I went there. He told me to read Mathew 4:23–25 and prayed for me for half an hour. I prayed every day and read the verse twice a day, and see today I am all fit. Now I can jump, play and do all kinds of work.

Along a similar line, Aaron Mondal said,

> In CHS, we can pray the way we want to pray; there are no restrictions. We can sing, dance, jump, kneel, cry and feel the spirit of the Holy

> Spirit without any restrictions, while in other churches there are a lot of rules and regulations, which make the connection between individuals and God difficult. When I pray here, I feel I transcend all earthly problems ... I feel light, and at times I feel I do not live in the chaotic *para* anymore.

Liza Pramanick also had a similar story to tell:

> I come here every Sunday from DumDum. I have heard that Mohan has the power to pray effectively, and if I pray with Mohan, my worries and pains will go away. I come here to improve my relationship with God, to feel the Holy Spirit and to understand in what ways I can refrain from committing sin.

Although people come to Mohan from far and wide, he was not so venerated by members of the three mainstream churches of the Krishnapur Christian *pārā* because they perceived the new church with suspicion and often questioned its functioning as Mohan was not an ordained priest.

However, today CHS is a crucial part of *pārā* activities and is invited at all kinds of Christian gatherings. In fact, Christmas and Easter services at CHS attract a lot of Christians and Hindus from within and outside the *pārā*. In addition to that, the church also carries out charitable activities like visiting villages to preach the word of God and donating warm clothes to the poor. Meanwhile, the once-overlooked house church received a fresh coat of paint as members started offering tithes[10] generously. The church stands quite in contrast to other residential buildings in the *pārā*. The entrance reads 'Jesus is my Saviour' and welcomes everyone at its prayer meetings. The CHS church is big on worship, particularly Sunday service where singing and loud music is part for the course. Some other things that make CHS stand out are advertisements across the neighbourhoods, repetitive house prayer meetings, Bible and Sunday classes and prayers of various kinds. Such fervent engagement with prayer indicates that mainly through prayer

10 Tithe denotes one-tenth of annual income that church members give to their churches as a form of offering. It is believed that one-tenth of all income belong to God, therefore, one should give away that fraction every month without fail.

could one develop a lasting relationship with a place of worship amidst different kinds of urban complexities. Due to his familiarity with the local people, Mohan is better able to draw a close connection between local analogies and Bible text, citing examples that have direct bearings on the individual and family crisis of his new congregation members.

Elsewhere, Hovland (2014: 335) argues that place-making in the context of Christianity can be understood based on seven features, which include 'linguistic, material, temporal, personhood, translocal, transcendent, and worldly concerns'. To these markers, I add that the structure of neighbourhood and its endogenous power politics demonstrate gossip to perform the task of urban place-making more visibly in an everyday part of urban life, creating socialities with the new power structure and belonging. By successfully employing the practice of gossiping against the EPC *padri*, Mohan was able to create, for his congregation, one of the key places of worship in the Christian *pārā*. The formation of this new church grew very much out of the endogenous power politics of the *pārā* based on kinship, ethnicity and language. It is based on the fundamental question of who can preach for whom and what difference can preaching by a local pastor from an extended family, caste, kinship have on Christian subjects compared to preaching by an 'outsider' (Kumar 2015).

Conclusion

The place-making process takes a concrete form through an everyday mundane exchange of information and sharing of knowledge, most notably through political contestation of shared proximity affecting the question of representation and preaching among neighbourhood Christians. Christian neighbours, in their acts of living and interrogation within the grid of the neighbourhood, cultivate a sense of place-making that involves a reconfiguration of scarce resources, for example, the position of a priest that commands certain power and authority in the neighbourhood. The position of the priest and its complex relation with the local Christian's understanding of spiritual journey encourages the emergence of new religious buildings and actors, thus enabling Christianity to make a political difference in the neighbourhood. Therefore, in this way people do not merely live in the neighbourhood, but they, through their everyday gossip mechanism, actively transform an invisible house of informal gatherings into one of the new Christian places of worship, allowing neighbourhood gossip and Christian 'schism' to come together to make a meaningful intervention of place-making in a Christian neighbourhood in Kolkata.

References

Abraham, J. 2010. 'Veiling and the Production of Gender and Space in a Town in North India: A Critique of the Public/Private Dichotomy.' *Indian Journal of Gender Studies*, Vol. 17, No. 2, pp. 191–222.

———. 2018. '*The Lives of Other*: The Production and the Influence of Neighbourhood Cultures in Urban India.' In *The Palgrave Handbook of Urban Ethnography,* edited by Italo Pardo and Giuliana B. Prato, pp. 95–112. Switzerland: Palgrave Macmillan.

Abu-Lughod, L. 1986. *Veiled sentiments: Honour and Poetry in a Bedouin Society*. California and London: University of California Press.

Andrews, R. 2013. *Christmas in Calcutta: Anglo-Indian Stories and Essays*. New Delhi: Sage Publications.

Banerjee, S. 2016. *Memoirs of Roads: Calcutta from Colonial Urbanization to Global Modernization*. Delhi: Oxford University Press.

Bergmann, J.R. 1987. *Discreet Indiscretions: The Social organization of Gossip.* New York: Walter de Gruyter.

Ben-Ze'ev, A. 1994. 'The Vindication of Gossip'. In *Good Gossip,* edited by Robert Goodman F. and Aaron Ben-Ze'ev, pp. 11–24. Lawrence: University Press of Kansas.

Board of the Directors to Thirty First General Meeting, 'The Missionary Society usually called the "The London Missionary Society"', 11th report, 34th report, and appendix.

Brandon, V., S. Khalsa and E.E. Howard. 2016. 'Gossip as Social Control: Informal Sanctions on Ethical Violations in Scientific Workplaces'. *Social Problems*, Vol. 63, pp. 554–572.

Blunt, A. and Jayani B. 2013. 'Home, City and Diaspora: Anglo-Indian and Chinese Attachments to Calcutta'. *Global Networks*, Vol. 13, No. 2, pp. 220–240.

Chandavarkar, R. 1997. 'The Making of the Working Class: E.P. Thompson and Indian History'. *History Workshop Journal*, Vol. 43, No. 1, pp. 177–196.

Chatterjee, A. 2017. *Margins of Citizenship: Muslim Experiences in Urban India.* Oxon and New York: Routledge.

Chopra, P. 2007. 'Refiguring the Colonial City: Recovering the Role of Local Inhabitant in the Construction of Colonial Bombay 1854–1918'. *Buildings and Landscapes: Journal of the Vernacular Architecture Forum*, Vol. 14, No. 1, pp. 109–125.

Dunbar, R. 2004. 'Gossip in Evolutionary Perspective'. *Review of General Psychology*, Vol. 8, No. 2, pp. 100–110.

Eder, D. and Janet L. Enke. 1991. 'The Structure of Gossip: Opportunities and Constraints on Collective Expression Among Adolescents'. *American Sociological Review*, Vol. 56, No. 4, pp. 494–508.

Foucault, M. 1975. *Discipline and Punish: The Birth of the Prison*. New York: Vintage.

Gandhi, A. 2016. 'The Language of the Crowd: Public Congregation in Urban India'. *Distinktion: Journal of Social Theory*, Vol. 17, No. 3, pp. 308–315.

Ghosh, A. 2015. 'News, Gossip and Humour: Street Perspectives from Colonial Calcutta'. In *Cities in South Asia,* edited by C. Bates and Minoru Mio, pp. 245–264. Abingdon/New York: Routledge.

Gluckman, M. 1963. 'Papers in Honour of Melville J. Herskovits: Gossip and Scandal'. *Current Anthropology*, Vol. 4, No. 3, pp. 307–316.

Handman, C. 2014. *Critical Christianity: Translation and Denominational Conflict in Papua New Guinea*. California: University of California Press.

Hansen, Thomas B. 2013. 'Strangers, Neighbours and Political Order in the South Asian City'. In *Interrogating India's Modernity: Democracy, Identity and Citizenship. Essays in Honour of Dipankar Gupta,* edited by S. Jodhka, pp. 20–39. Delhi: Oxford University Press.

Haviland, J.B. 1977. *Gossip, Reputation and Knowledge in Zinacantan*. Chicago: University of Chicago Press.

Hovland, I. 2016. 'Christianity, Place/Space, and Anthropology: Thinking Across Recent Research on Evangelical Place-making'. *Religion*, Vol. 46, No. 3, pp. 331–358.

Jamil, G. 2017. *Accumulation by Segregation: Muslim Localities in Delhi*. Delhi: Oxford University Press.

Khan, S. 2007. 'Negotiating the Mohallā: Exclusion, Identity and Muslim Women in Mumbai'. *Economic and Political Weekly*, Vol. 42, No. 17, pp. 1527–1533.

Kumar, Ashok. M. 2015. 'Dalits Preaching to Dalits: Lutherans Mode of Combating Caste Marginality in Andhra, South India'. *Indian Anthropologist*, Vol. 45, No. 1, pp. 61–73.

Neve, D.G. and H. Donner. 2006. *The Meaning of the Local: Politics of Place in Urban India*. Oxon: Routledge.

New International Version. 1967. Available at https://www.biblestudytools.com/niv/ (accessed on 28 December 2019).

O'Malley, L.S.S. 2003 [1914]. *Bengal District Gazetteers: 24 Parganas*. Calcutta: The Bengal Secretariat Book Depot.

Paine, R. 1967. 'What Is Gossip About? An Alternative Hypothesis'. *Man*, Vol. 2, No. 2, pp. 278–285.

Robbins, J. 2007. 'Continuity Thinking and the Problem of Christian Culture: Belief, Time and the Anthropology of Christianity'. *Current Anthropology*, Vol. 48, No. 1, pp. 5–38.

Robinson, R. 2012. 'Introduction'. In *Minority Studies*, edited by R. Robinson, pp. 1–48. Delhi: Oxford University Press.

Sengupta, K.M. 2018. 'Community and Neighbourhood in a Colonial City: Calcutta's *PARA*'. *South Asia Research*, Vol. 38, No. 1, pp. 40–56.

Sengupta, K.P. 1971. *The Christian Missionaries in Bengal 1793–1833*. Calcutta: K.L. Mukhopadhyay.

Stewart Pamela J. and S. Andrew. 2004. *Witchcraft, Sorcery, Rumors, and Gossip*. Cambridge: Cambridge University Press.

Srinivas, M.N. 1952. *Religion and Society Amongst the Coorgs of South India*. Oxford: Clarendon Press.

Tse, J.K.H. 2014. 'Grounded Theologies: "Religion" and the "Secular" in Human Geography'. *Progress in Human Geography*, Vol. 38, No. 2, pp. 201–220.

Vatuk, S. 1972. *Kinship and Urbanization: White Collar Migrants in North India*. Berkley and Los Angeles: University of California Press.

Whyte, W.F. 1955 [1943]. *Street Corner Society: The Social Structure of an Italian Slum*. Chicago: University of Chicago Press.

Wirth, L. 1938. 'Urbanism as a Way of Life.' *American Journal of Sociology*, Vol. 44, No. 1, pp. 1–24.

Part II

Dalit Neighbourhoods: Histories, Subjectivities and Contestation

5

Locating Dalit *Bastis*: The Sites of Everyday Silent Resistance and Works from the Late 19th-Century to the Mid-20th-Century United Provinces

Vijay Kumar*

Khatiks are traditionally considered as butchers. Colonial ethnographers and census commissioners in late 19th and early 20th centuries inform us about various occupational identities of Khatiks in Uttar Pradesh (UP) or the colonial United Provinces: Khara and Kairanga (leather dyers), Chalan Mahraos (tanner and leather workers), Bakar Kasao and Chik (Bakarqassab, Goat sellers and butchers), *mewafarosh* (fruit sellers), *kabariya* (sellers, buyers and store-keepers of rubbish), *ghor charaos* (who take care of and clean horses), Sunkhars (poulters and pig breeders), Chaukidars (watchmen), drum-head makers, Rajmistri or Rajgar (masons), Sombatta (ropemakers) and Bekanwala (pork bacon vendors who were 'in the process of formation'). The last three groups of Khatiks resided in Cawnpore (Crooke 1907: 120; Sherring 1879 [1974]: 352 and 400; Blunt 1912: 351; Blunt 1969: 238; Briggs 1920: 29 and 38; Burn 1902: 232). The *bastis*, or their residential neighbourhoods, were socio-spatially known by their caste names, markers of untouchability and by their traditional occupations. These *bastis* of Khatiks were also settlements of unregistered day labourers and unorganised works. Here, in this chapter, I am going to focus on these Khatik *bastis* in rural (*dehat*) and urban-town (*shahr-kasba*) settings by drawing examples from Kanpur, Lucknow, Banaras, Agra and Ambala (a city in Haryana). By using police and census reports, ethnographic works and

* I dedicate this chapter to Imrati and all *raddiwalis* and *lifafewalis*.

oral account, the chapter discusses the histories of everyday protests and politics around these *bastis*. Also, for ethical-legal reasons, I have used the term Scheduled Caste to avoid derogatory caste names found in the colonial registers and in other primary sources.

Evolution of Khatik *Bastis*: Social Relations and Works

The seasonal migration of day labourers, particularly those who are branded as criminal castes in various parts of UP and British India, was a source of anxiety for both civil society and the colonial State. They were recognised as unwanted guests and undisciplined mass in civil society. In non-native villages, towns and urban centres, they migrated with their stinking untouchable bodies, pigs, animals, stigmatised social status and criminalised past (an official common sense after the implementation of the Criminal Tribe Act, 1871). The caste of Khatiks was one such case. In the early and mid-19th century, such migrations were for the construction of civil and military buildings, forts, canals (like the Ganga canal), roads, government factories and railway stations. By the late 19th and early 20th centuries, the provincial government often allocated lands to these workers known as *raj-mazdoors* (lit. construction labourers). These lands were located in canal-irrigated agriculture zones (for example, Sharda Canal), the vicinities of railway *malgodams* (stores), colonial *karkhanas* (leather tanneries and bristle factories), construction sites, wastelands of railway stations and army cantonments (Kerr 2006: 96; Lucassen 2006: 47–83; *The Pioneer* 13 December 1928). These allotments were usually temporary and were taken back with the termination of the contract, completion of the construction of buildings-bridges or at the will of the State.[1]

However, in practice, the Dalits, who constituted the majority of these day labourers and landless people, continued to stay and live there, giving these *bastis* specific caste nomenclatures such as Khatikpara in

1 File No. 22/44-45, List No. 4, Box No. 44, Agra Commissioner and Collector Records, Agra Regional Archive (hereafter ARA).

the Agra Cantonment, Khatikmandi or Bakaramandi in Meerut (at Lal Kurti, an old name for army cantonment), Khatikans in Kanpur (Cawnpore), Lucknow, Banaras and in various other parts of Eastern UP and across North India. Such Khatik *bastis* also evolved with same names near New Delhi Railway Station and Ambala Cantonment Railway Station (near Grand Trunk Road).

These *bastis* invariably had unplanned layouts and were located at the edges of the cities, revealing the stark spatial contrast between Dalits and urban elites. *Kachche makans* (mud and wooden houses), *sarkari* (government) latrines, and the uncovered *ganda nale* and *naliya* (drainages) were some key fixtures of these *bastis*. The *ganda nala* (dirty drain) quite often functioned as the address, the spatial identity, of houses they live in. For instance, Jamna, a fifty-five-year-old Khatik woman, told me that whenever a *chithi* (letter) or *dak* (postcard) came, the *ganda nala* was the permanent landmark in those letters and postcards. The *nala* had been existing since before her birth, she added. Beyond letters and postcards, the *nala* circulated as a political site too, prominently featuring in electoral promises made by politicians. Remained eternally open, the *nala* has become a part of the social memory of the city, a memory that Khatiks wish to forget.

The question of *nala* or drain leads us to the larger concerns related to cleanliness and public health. In September 1932, Mahatma Gandhi launched the Achhutoddhar (Dalit upliftment) programme in which one of the aims was to clean the Dalit *bastis*. Instructions were passed to caste Hindus to clean the houses of *achhuts* (lit. untouchables or Dalits). Local leaders, caste Hindus and urban elites politicised these calls during Gandhi's fast and during the Cawnpore Municipal Corporation election (September–December 1932). However, soon after the municipal election, *swachchhata* (cleanliness) and *achhutoddhar* were happily forgotten (*Vertman* 24 November1932: 5 and 8 December1932).

In most of North India, a *basti* of one specific Dalit caste is invariably located adjacent to another Dalit *basti/s*. These *bastis* are connected not merely in terms of their shared social hierarchies but also through *galis* (by-lanes), which is another significant feature of these *bastis*, along with the aforementioned open drain. For example, the Colonelganj Khatik *basti* is surrounded by the *bastis* of various other Scheduled Castes, through small *galis*. These *galis* also link Khatik *bastis* to community centres, *dharmshalas*, temples, shops, *akhara*, walls and *sarkari nal* or *barma* (public tap or hand pump). In contrast, the *bastis* of Muslims and caste Hindus are situated at a distance across the road. Despite this physical distance, the local Hindi newspaper and a congress committee report, during the period under study, confirm a good social relation between lower Muslims and Khatiks who used to share the *basti* space and purchase food from each other's shops, although local caste Hindus disliked them. Until 1944, the Khatik *bastis* at Colonelganj and Latouche Road did not have any public water tap.[2]

The segregated space of the *basti* witnessed social distancing being practised not only by conservative sections of higher Hindu castes but also by reformist elements. For example, Karol Bagh (Carol Bagh) of Delhi is an old centre of numerous Scheduled-Caste communities. Since the late colonial time, there were many socioreligious reform agencies (this includes institutions run or funded by church missionaries, Arya Samaj Trust, Hindu Mahasabha and Sanatan Dharma Sabha) active in the fields of social reform, conversion and reconversion in these *bastis* of Karol Bagh. Ironically, none of these institutions existed inside the Dalit *bastis*.

Small shrines of caste specific gurus, gods and goddesses (*kuldevo-devika chabutra*) are another crucial feature of these *bastis*. Two such goddesses are Shitala Devi and Masani Devi. In colonial ethnography, Sheetala/Shitala was known as the goddess of smallpox or deity of the 'Cool One' against smallpox to maintain the body temperature

2 For instance, when Ambedkar arrived at Kanpur for the All India Scheduled Caste Federation Conference on 29 and 30 January 1944, the Khatiks and Muslims of Colonelganj and Latouche Road were obstructed by local Hindus. In November 1943, the license of a Khatik sugar shopkeeper was cancelled by local officers on the ground of discrimination. Similarly, in December 1943, *Vertman* urged the local authority to give sugar and oil licence to Hindu shopkeepers at Anwarganj, Latouche Road and other areas where Hindu shops are less than Muslim shops (*Vertman* 25 November 1943: 2 and 10 December 1943). The Khatik *basti* at Colonelganj had a Muslim house that was protected by Khatiks during the communal riot in 1931. See File No. 3; S. No. 75, List No. 6, Vol. 1, Part 2, 14 April 1931. Subject: Communal Riots at Cawnpore Report of Evidence (Tondon, *Private Papers*. New Delhi: National Archive of India [hereafter NAI]).

(Arnold 1993: 122–123, 274–280 and 291–294; Misra 1969; Nicholas 1981; Wadley 1980). Masani was the goddess of *shamshan ghat*/funeral place and crossroad. During the fieldwork for this research, it was found that many Khatiks celebrate Diwali, Holi and Basora (Sili Sat) festivals with the worship of these two goddesses at the crossroad and without any Brahman priest, by offering pigs, chickens, goats, eggs, rice, wheat, sugar and other food items to these goddesses. Since the colonial time, these offerings were easily available in the Dalit *bastis*. A small mud-brick structure or open shrine of Shitala near a *pipal* tree (sacred tree) is another common feature of the Dalit *bastis*. In addition, crossroads (*chauraha*) around these *bastis* function as the sacred centre of Masani, where common men avoid to walk. These goddesses, their *chauk-chaurahas* and shrines are believed to be the spiritual guardians of not just individuals and families residing in these *bastis* but also of Dalit *bastis* as a whole. Khatiks believe that Chaurahewali Mata Masani controls the enemies who try to infiltrate the precincts of the *bastis* with bad omens, evil spirits and demons.

While in the Brahmanical belief system, these goddesses are the source of pollution, diseases and black magic, in the Dalit belief system, these goddesses are the source of the power of impurity. The presence of Masani, Shitala, Chauraha and pig generates power for Dalits. By using *chauraha* (as a space of worship that is often considered as the place of Masani or evil spirits) and pig (which is considered an impure animal), the Dalit religio-spatial complex represents a counter to Brahmanical religious culture and, therefore, can also be interpreted as a resistance to the hegemonic Brahmanical worldviews.

Unlike officially planned residential colonies with segregated living and commercial areas, these *bastis* have residential spaces interspersed with informal markets like *bakaramandi* (goat and other animal markets), *coolie bazar, labour chauk* and *adda* (field labour markets), *tanga stands* (for local transportation, tours and travels), *sabzimandi* (vegetable and food market) and *kabari bazar* (rubbish market). The *akhara* (local gym and wrestling arena) is a popular centre of communication, friendship, bodybuilding, physical health, public entertainment and *dangals* (wrestling tournaments). One such *Khatik akhara* is located at Colonelganj, Kanpur. Another is at Aminabad,

Lucknow, where three brothers—Ram Prasad, Hiralal and Motilal Sonkar—became popular wrestlers by participating in local *dangals* or wrestling competitions. In the 1920s and 1930s, the Harijan Sevak Sangh and Arya Sabha also came to be associated with some *akharas*, keeping in mind particularly Dalit communities (Gooptu 2001; Kumar 1988 [2017]: 119; Rivariya 2006: 47, 104, 115; for Arya Sabha's gyms, see Turner 1933: 505–508; for Harijan Sevak Sangh's gyms, see Cawnpore Harijan Sevak Sangha 1934: 67–68). These activities allowed the intermingling of the criminalised Khatiks with non-criminalised Dalits in and around these *bastis*.[3] For example, three Khatik sub-castes—Jaisawla, Manikpur and Dalman—and their sub-caste *chaudharis* (headmen) immigrated from Rai Bareilly and Pratabgarh to Lucknow and maintained their social relationship (eating, smoking, intermarrying under the Lucknow panchayat) with Lucknow Khatiks (Blunt 1912: 345–346). Near the Cawnpore railway station, the Khatiks of Latouche Road are day labourers, pig breeders, leather workers and vegetable sellers. Many of them are also known as *Dariyabadi* because they came from Dariyabad (near the Yamuna at Allahabad) to Kanpur. Khatiks working as mason and construction labour at Colonelganj migrated from Kanpur Dehat (rural Kanpur) and Bundelkhand.[4]

In the 1880s Cawnpore, the government established slaughterhouses in Colonelganj for cows and buffaloes and in Fazalganj for pigs, goats and other animals. These slaughterhouses supplied meat, beef and pork to the Civil Lines and army kitchens under the supervision of food inspectors and health officers. Hides and bristle went to the government tanneries for leather, bristle, shoe and brush markets in Europe and to the army. While most Muslims were employed in these slaughterhouses, Dalits worked as leather tanners and dyers (Khara and Kairanga). In addition to these government-established units, self-employed Khatiks and other Scheduled Castes too came up with their unauthorised

3 'At Saharanpur, some fruit-sellers—whose trade, it may be presumed, has been encouraged by the large public garden at the station—have separated themselves from the common herd of Kunjras, or "costermongers," and decorated their small community with the Persian title of Mewafarosh.' The Kunjra/Kanjar were also a criminal caste (Growse 1883: 416).

4 Interview with Sunit Kumar Sonkar on 19 November 2018; Bellwinkel-Schempp 1998.

and uninspected home tanneries and home slaughterhouses in these *bastis*.[5] Along with them, some Scheduled Castes used to sell their pigs and bristles to Khatiks whereas some of these dressed bristle and wool in Khatik home units. In these home tanneries and bristle factories, women members of these Scheduled Castes too worked as part-time semi-skilled dressers, cleaners, washers and tanners.[6] The bristles of black, grey and white colours are used for paint, hair, shoe brushes, respectively; they are obtained from the bodies of pig, sheep and goat, dead or alive. Besides, studies on Dalits and leather-bristle industries during colonial time confirmed an important role played by Khatik leather-bristle collectors and sellers. For instance, Mohinder Singh mentions that Khatiks maintained a local network of leather and bristle collectors from villages (Singh 1947: 92). Bellwinkel-Schempp (1998) notes that there were about five or six Khatiks-owned bristle firms in the late colonial Kanpur, few of them directly connected to European, mainly British traders and dealers. Two old partnership firms were MM Mithu Lal, Roshan Lal, and Mangal Devi, and Messrs Mukundlal and Dorilal. For British and local customers, Mittu Lal was also known as 'King of Bristles' in the 1940s. Khatiks dominated the bristle business in Kanpur (Tripathi and Arora 1957, Vol. 2: 150–153). Many of these factories, firms and shops emerged out of the Kanpur Khatik *bastis* in the process outlined earlier when Khatiks opened unauthorised units informally in the late 19th century.

In terms of their origins, these *bastis* came up when landless Dalits migrated to urban areas from different parts of UP in search of work and livelihood. They squatted on wastelands in towns and cities and converted them into *bastis* and established their home tanneries and industries. Dirty water, waste, flies and smell of hides from these home industries and slaughterhouses soon became unbearable for village-town-urban elites and colonial officers—mostly caste Hindus, dominant Muslims with European officers—who lived in civil lines, railway stations and cantonments.

---

5 See the case of Pyare Lal and Ramprasad Khatik (fruit and meat sellers) who migrated from Faizabad to Meerut in 1901 and later to Delhi in 1932 (Rivariya 2006: 130; Singh 1947: 92; Rawat 2012).

6 Interviews with Khatiks in and from Kanpur, Benares, Allahabad, Agra, Meerut, Aligarh, Ambala and Delhi during my fieldworks.

Colonial and Brahmanical Rules against Dalits: Everyday Politics and Resistance

By the late 19th century, in the dominant perceptions of caste Hindus, colonial health officers, city bosses and village-town-urban elites, these Dalit localities acquired stigmatised labels of *malin bastis* (dirty hamlets), *suarbaade* (pig stables) and as epicentres of diseases, epidemic, pollution, unhygiene, untouchability and rowdies.[7] In 1908, it was reported that 'while sweepers and tanners are often made to live apart from the rest of the village the result is inappreciable so far as sanitation is concerned'.[8] Indeed, the skins of dead animals from home leather tanneries are the main source of foul smell and garbage litters in the streets. Jamna, my respondent, told me that leather production is a long process: tanning, dyeing, drying take about 15–20 days in home leather tanneries. For non-Dalit public, her uncles, who were involved in the leather business, smelt like living rotten dead bodies. And their houses, where they used to keep leather, were like graves or coffins.[9]

In 1917, the Benares Municipal Department regularised the home leather tanneries and factories by enacting rules. These rules were based on issues of public health and certification and eventually led to the closure of these home factories in *bastis*.[10] Moreover, the Epidemic Diseases Act, 1897, and Epidemic Rules, 1929, made village elites and native village officials responsible, in their respective villages, for the prevention of epidemic, ahead of district magistrates, health and sanitation officers. These village elites and officials were given the following rights: to burn infected clothes and other belongings of infected people, to prevent them from sources of water, to disinfect

---

7 *Vertman* 5 December1943; File No. 28/1897, Box No. 401, List No. 44, Commissioner's Office Allahabad (hereafter COA), Allahabad Regional Archive (hereafter RAA).

8 File No. 222/1908, Box No. 91, List no. 1, General Administration Department (hereafter GAD), Uttar Pradesh Archive (hereafter UPSA), Lucknow.

9 Interviews with Jamna, the elder daughter of Imrati, in Delhi, on multiple occasions during my fieldwork. For similar experiences of leather workers belonging to another Scheduled Caste (Kapoor 2016: 240–257).

10 File No. 140, Box No. 83, List No. 1, Department (hereafter Dept.) VIII, Varanasi Regional Archive (hereafter VRA).

private dwellings, to prohibit the burial of corpses in tanks, to prohibit the sale of articles of foods or to seize and destroy such food articles, to prevent infected people and their children from accessing school premises, fairs, places of public entertainment, public assembly, religious and public places. They were also instructed to respect 'the social and religious usages of occupants', which they usually ignored. In this scenario, in the name of prevention, sanitation and public health, both village elites and colonial officers forced poor and landless Dalits to leave or stay out of the borders of villages, towns and cities. Until the 1930s, it was a general belief among village-town-urban elites and upper castes that Dalits spread diseases through black magic and filth. Such a prejudiced stereotype made members of these castes vulnerable to and victims of discrimination (*Harijan Sevak* 6 July 1935; Gandhi 1955: 10; Rawat 2012). In the late 1920s and the 1930s, we also find sanitation awareness campaigns at Scheduled Caste *bastis*, launched by the Harijan movement, Hindu Mahasabha and Arya Samaj, to teach these *basti* dwellers the tenets of '*adrash*' Hindu life (with instructions to use soap and toothbrush and to clean and wash their houses, clothes and bedcovers every day (Gooptu 2001: 182–183).

In colonial North India, particularly UP, the practice of *begari*, a caste-based forced labour, was only done by Dalits. Such a system of exploitation and extortion was sustained and maintained by the colonial government in the name of custom and tradition. It generated a system of free or grossly underpaid labour for the colonial State. It also empowered landlords and village elites by reviving their traditional privileges. But the system deprived Dalits the dignity of labour, labour rights and colonial labour markets. Therefore, the denial of work was the beginning of a silent protest by Dalits. It was an assertion for self-respect and dignity of labour. Due to the increasing demand for illegal *rasad-begar*, Dalit *rasad* suppliers and day labourers (small tenants, beldars, mazdoors, coolies and carters), in the early 1920s, mobilised under the leadership of Dalit organisations like Adi-Hindu Sabha and various other caste *sabhas*, for legal agitation against the *rasad-begar* system (Niaimishrai 2013: 208–217; Pandey 1982: 198–223). However, before this long legal struggle, Dalit day labourers had to take a stand against such issues.

Everyday resistance at Khatik *bastis* in Banaras and Kanpur were some of the good examples of Dalit protests. For instance, whenever the civil, railway, police and cantonment officers removed the *thelas* (carts/pushcarts) of Khatik *sabzfarosh* (green stuff vendors and hawkers), *mewafarosh* (fruit vendors), *thelewalas* (cart pullers) and *tangawalas/ekkawalas/ghor charaos* (carriage men) from stations or beat the Khatik *kabaris/kabariyas* (peddlers and collectors of rubbish) who roamed near stations and civil lines, their field labourer cousins from their caste, families and *basti* would collectively deny loading and unloading orders from lorries and *mall garis* (carts and stock carts) for civil, railway, cantonment and police stations.[11] At times, fruit vendors collectively protested against the demand for *rasad* and exploitation by big traders and local police. For example, in Banaras, there were many Khatik *bastis*. Among them, the Khatik *basti* at Mandivadih was a *basti* of various types of labourers and workers. The Khatik fruit-vegetable vendors numerically dominated this *basti*. This *basti*, near Mandivadih Railway Station and Allahabad–Banaras highway (at Grand Trunk Road), often acted as the site of protest against injustice. Here, Shivamangal Ram Vaidh and Shivalal, local Congressmen and followers of Gandhi, were two important leaders of Khatiks who had organised many such small strikes and silent protests. These caste members were connected to the Banaras Khatik Sabha and had staged a protest at Vishweshwar Ganj in 1936. This particular protest was triggered by the discriminatory behaviour of an upper-caste Hindu police officer and the exploitation of small vendors by a Muslim fruit trader who was also notorious for habitually harassing and exploiting women. There are many such instances when Dalit *bastis* became the site of protests.[12] Many of these protests and resistance were quite subtle and less demonstrative in nature. For example, the *beiman* (corrupt) civil contractors, *chaprasis*, storekeepers and banias in the railway *malgodams* and *anazmandi* (grain markets) used to cheat labourers

11 At Benares, on 'Sep 3, a strike took place among ekka, tonga and motor drivers. It lasted only twelve hours' (Government of UP. *United Provinces Police Abstract of Intelligence* [hereafter PAI], Allahabad: The Government Press, 17 September 1927).

12 Vaidh 1978 [2005]; Interview with Sunit Kumar Sonkar, Kanpur, on 19 November 2018.

of their daily wage. As a protest against this malpractice, Khatik day labourers, *thelewalas* and *redewalas* (carters) would sometimes intentionally make holes in the grain *boras* (bags) so that they could, later on, gather the strewn grains for free.[13] Sometimes they would leave the grain *boras* and other goods on wet floors or exposed them in the rain. My respondent, Jamna, said her father, Toti Ram, and his fellow *thelawalas* and *redewalas* often did such things.

In the early 1950s, when the Khatiks were excluded from the UP Scheduled-Caste list, they started a mass movement against the UP government. This coincided with the visits of the newly constituted Backward Classes Commission (Kalelkar Commission) members to collect on-ground information on the conditions of Dalits. When members of commission reached Kanpur, Allahabad, and other parts of UP, the Khatiks uncovered dead bodies of animals, burnt *katrans* (waste leather shreds) and opened the gates of their home tanneries, leather factories and slaughterhouses, exposing the visiting Central team to the smell of leather, pork, pig and stinking untouchable bodies.[14] By doing this, Khatiks capitalised upon the sensorial qualities of their *bastis* and turned these location-specific qualities into weapons of mass protest. Over time, the history of the *basti* has built layers of such unique forms of protests. Indeed, few such layers have gone into shaping the built environment of these *bastis* too. For example, normally Khatiks (those working as sub-contractors) had a good relationship with Britishers who helped them in the development of everyday life and Dalit *bastis*. Sometimes Khatik masons and day labourers would pilfer construction materials from sites to teach their corrupt and cunning masters a lesson or two. Some of these Khatiks built Dalit shrines, temples, *akharas*, schools, ponds, water tanks, restrooms (*dharmshala* and *sarais*), cemeteries (*kabristan* for Muslims) and funeral grounds (*shamshan ghat* for low castes and Dalits) in and near their *bastis*.[15] These represent

13 There used to be a Khatik sub-caste called Kaseruwale during the post-colonial period. 'Kaseruwale, who keep a donkey for transportation' (Singh 1998: 1715).

14 Interview with Rajnath Sonkar Shastri on 6–7 May, Kanhaiya Lal Sonkar on 28 May, Ram Das Sonkar on 30 May and 17 June, Ashok Nirwan on 22 September, 2–4 February 2012.

15 In the context of Karori Mal and his grandfather Bihari Mal Mistri, Yatinder Sonkar mentions these buildings. Interview with Yatinder Sonkar on 14 October 2016, 28–29 January 2017.

the living symbols of Dalit power and silent protest. They soon acquired the status of new community spaces within the *bastis*.

The *bastis* also functioned as an immediate environment for the blossoming of new forms of solidarities among migrants in an urban landscape and also doubled as the springboard of Dalit aspirations. In this aspirational zone, the sub-contractor (*thekedars*) was a new identity of semi-educated Khatik leaders who were working as middlemen in the Khatik *bastis*. Recalling from memories, Chhidan, a ninety-year-old Khatik woman, narrated the story of her grandfather, Roopan, a part-time peasant who also worked as a mason at Metha village in rural Kanpur. Due to his caste, he faced social discrimination in his village. In order to get away, he would seasonally migrate, along with his three sons, Darbari, Tulsi and Gulzari, to the city to work as a mason and labourer. Later on, after he became a *thekedar* (sub-contractor), he permanently settled in Kanpur city with his family. His sons, who worked alongside him as day labourers, later got promoted to masons. One of them, Gulzari, a primary school-educated boy, helped maintained his father's accounts (*likha-padi*) and credit-wage distribution (*chittah*) of the labours. Chhidan was born in Kanpur city in the 1930s. At a young age, she was married off to a big *thekedar*'s son at Colonelganj, leaving behind a story of upward social mobility and prosperity all made possible by the networks of kinship, work and other social ties that this Khatik *basti* of Colonelganj offered her and her migrant father.[16]

In the late 19th and the early 20th centuries, these sub-contractors emerged as popular Dalit leaders, as benevolent figures supporting poor Khatik labourers, workers, members of their caste and *bastis*.[17] The sub-contractors broke the old Khatik panchayat system and took over the dominance of Chaudhuris in Kanpur, Lucknow, Benares, Calcutta and other places. For instance, at Kanpur, Bihari Lal Mistri (1820–1905), his son, Dulichand Sonkar, and grandson, Karori Mal (February 1893–September1937), were one such family of sub-contractors who earned money, respect and trust of their Muslim, Khatik and other Scheduled Caste labourers and neighbours. Members of his family were patrons

16 Interview with Chhidan in Kanpur on 19 November2018.

17 For contractors, construction workers and labourers (Kerr 2006: 85–86).

and followers of Swami Siva Narayan Math and a gurudwara. At the Colonelganj Khatik *basti*, Bihari Lal built a gurudwara in April 1870 where he inserted a 'silver coin' (Bellwinkel-Schempp 2006: 15–32; Sonkar [nd]; Sonkar *Private Papers*). This gurudwara and the act of inserting a silver coin became a visual expression of Dalit power and the centre of Dalit sociopolitical activism in Kanpur. A number of Adi-Hindu and Khatik Caste meetings were held in this gurudwara in the 20th century. He donated some of his properties to the Swami Siva Narayan sect, which was a popular religious order among Dalits in colonial UP. In addition to this gurudwara, a strong gurudwara in the *basti* represents an assertion of power among Khatiks, which came with the spread of Sant Siva Narayan Sampradaya among Dalits in Kanpur. While financial power came with the construction of European mills and buildings in Kanpur by Khatik masons, the Khatik gurudwara represents the ideologies of the medieval Dalit bhakti saints and colonial Adi-Hindu movement, which spread among the Khatiks in the second quarter of the 20th century. With the assimilation of Bhakti cult into the Adi-Hindu ideologies, the Khatik gurudwara became a part of Dalit resistance to Brahmanical religion (Bellwinkel-Schempp 2006; Tartakov 2012: 1–12).

In short, Khatiks used the everyday forms of silent protests to counter colonial rules and elite politics. Denial of works, building architecture, *chauraha* worship as the living symbol of protest, small strikes under the leadership of sub-contractors, sometimes even without leadership—all these became the expression of Dalit power in Dalit *bastis*. In this struggle, the *basti* provided an alternative to the colonial and Brahmanical establishments. For instance, in an attempt to define the Dalit *basti*, Jamna said,

> Our [Dalit] *basti* is our *mata* [mother], which gives space not only to Khatiks but also non-Khatiks. It is a space of love, equality, brotherhood, unity, justice and blessing of ancestors, gurus, and *kuldevies* and *kuldevs*. When you live within the *basti*, you have all these things. But when you leave the *basti* and go to a non-Dalit space, you will face discrimination, injustice, depression, separation, loneliness, etc. Therefore, for Khatiks, the *basti* is a world within a world. It acts as a site where they treasure their past and their memories.

Suarbaades (Dalit *Bastis*) in Kanpur

The pig is an essential component of the Dalit *bastis*; it is an integral part of Dalit rituals (*bali*) and an important source of food and income. Most Dalit castes in Kanpur (the centre of the leather-bristle business) and other parts of UP raised pigs. At Latouche Road, near the Kanpur railway station, there was a Khatik *basti*, as noted earlier, where many Khatiks had established themselves in the leather-bristle and pork business. Their pigs scavenged for food and littered public places. They roamed fearlessly in open drains and garbage heaps of the *basti*, city, railway station and military cantonment.[18]

This was also the time when the urban elites, caste Hindus and the Hindi-Hindu agencies were targeting the untouchable *bastis* in the name of morality, public health, city aesthetic and urban poor. For instance, on 5 December 1943, *Vertman*, a Hindi newspaper from Kanpur, published an article on the living conditions of Cawnpore's citizen. On the one hand, the article talked about rich urban elites, industries and big houses, on the other hand, it portrayed the city's poor public health conditions, poor aesthetics and disorder. For the newspaper, such a condition was due to migrant labourers, scavenging pigs, and reeking and overcrowded *bastis*. *Vertman* labelled these *bastis* as *suarbaade* (pig pen), suggesting that they created negative impressions and bad memories in the minds of tourists and travellers visiting the city. The newspaper further criticised Kanpur municipal board, its politics and its chairman for their failure to prevent the *suarbaade* from changing. Subsequently, the chairman of the board, Rameshwar Prasad Baghal, resigned in January 1944.

At Latouche Road, there was a big open space that Khatik pig breeders and bristle traders used to hoard their goods (pigs, pork, bacon, bristles, etc.). At the same place, during the second conference of the All India Scheduled Caste Federation in January 1944, Chairman

---

18 File No. 99, April 1856, Military Dept, NAI; File No. 8, Box No. 31 List No. 6. Post-Mutiny Records of Commissioners' Offices of Meerut Divisions, RAA.; For Khatiks, see File No. Progs. Nos. 934, 1900–1922, Public Records, NAI; Bellwinkel-Schempp 2005: 201–226.

Ramlal Sonkar invited Ambedkar and organised a big public feast in the Khatik *basti*. This was to honour Ambedkar, and every Dalit was invited.[19] By adopting Ambedkarism and participating in Dalit activism, Dalits were challenging Hindu society, caste system and *mai-baaps* of the city. The public feast symbolised a protest against the narrow representation of Dalit *basti* in the Hindi-Hindu newspaper.

It should be noted that such politics of space and neighbourhood were very common and connected to mainstream politics. In the late 19th and early 20th centuries, the Hindi-Hindu writing was a big agency of mushrooming caste-communal consciousness against Dalits, their lifestyle and *bastis*. In the minds of Sanatanists and orthodox Hindus, the body of a Dalit was a body of demon spirits, impurity and diseases. Unclean occupations (pig breeding, pig skinning, leather tanning, bristle making) and unclean food habits (drinking wine and eating pork, beef and meat) were the causes of degradation of Dalits in the Hindu society and Hindu food culture. In this schema, a Dalit *basti* was the centre of all these anti-Hindu *dharma* activities. Thus, according to the Hindi-Hindu writings, Dalits used to face in their everyday life 'exclusion from temples', refusal of Brahmans 'to perform religious ceremonies' and 'exclusion from village wells' (Ambedkar 2016: 184–207; Chaturvedi 1933: 1, 9–10, 25–26, 32; Turner 1933: 627–628). Therefore, in the name of social reform, some Hindi-Hindu agencies used to organise meetings in Dalit *bastis* and forced Dalits to abandon the practice of pig-related activities. One such meeting with a Dalit caste was held in Jaunpur. The Arya Samajists of Jaunpur, who belonged to the Thakur social identity, wanted to mobilise Dalits under their umbrella. These Arya Samajists organised a meeting with members of a Dalit caste and told them 'not to keep pigs or commit thefts' (*PAI*, 22 May 1926).

The Khatik *bastis* were stigmatised as *suarbaade*, incriminating them for their associations with the pig, leather tanning, food habits, and overpopulation. While the pig was a source of impurity for upper castes, it was an important economic resource for Khatiks and their

19 Interview with Ramlal's family at Latouche Road in Kanpur on 28 January 2017; Interview with Yatendar Sonkar at Kanpur on 26–28 January 2017; *Jai Bhim Jai Samaj* (a Hindi weekly newspaper from Kanpur), 15 February 2015.

newly acquired financial power to support their sociopolitical activism in Dalit *bastis*. Also, the visit of Ambedkar in the Khatik *basti* at Latouche Road represented a new sociopolitical consciousness among Khatiks. For urban elites and caste Hindus, the presence of Dalits, pigs and Dalit *bastis* were the metaphors of sociopolitical and moral disorder in their neighbourhoods.

The *Lifafewalis* and Dalit Women

With the growing market and the politics of the late 19th and early 20th centuries, the domain of the print expanded exponentially in the forms of newspapers, periodicals and magazines in colonial UP. Once read, these printed pages eventually found their ways to the Khatik *kabaris* (waste pickers) as well as other Dalit *kabaris* living in and working from Dalit *bastis*, only to re-enter the recycle chain. *Lifafa* (paper bag) making was an important element in that chain.[20] The *lifafa*, made of waste newspapers and pages of used books, emerged as a business opportunity for many Dalits and *banias*. Thus, apart from working in home tanneries, leather-bristle units and fruit-vegetable markets, many Khatik women were involved in *lifafa* making. In Western UP (Agra, Aligarh, Meerut etc.), it was a small-scale cottage industry in Dalit *basti*s. One small room was good enough to store waste newspapers and make *lifafas*. One business unit generally had ten to eighty women who would carry waste newspapers every day from the store. After completing household chores, women generally made *lifafas* at home while men sold fruits and vegetables. Although *bania* and Dalit men in the *bastis* were the nodes of this business, in reality, illiterate Dalit women ran the entire production cycle of *lifafas*. Like Khatik man hawkers, many Khatik woman hawkers would sell these *lifafas* in markets near the *bastis*, town, cantonment, railway station and highway. Whenever *banias*, *bakeriwala* (bakers), *halwai* (sweetmeat makers), shopkeepers and vendors tried to cheat them by paying less than the market rate, these women silently countered by reducing the

20 Before *lifafa*, traditionally *patta* (leaf), leather, cloth and jute bags were used as scrolls to carry things (Baillie 1894: 70; Burn: 277; *Vertman* 25 November 1932).

number of *lifafas* in the bundles. Sometimes under the leadership of woman peddlers, these woman *lifafa* makers also organised strikes against *bania* and Dalit male heads of the *lifafa* business for fair wages. These protests were in the form of hoarding *raddis* (waste paper) and burning them in front of male business heads. These strikes helped the Khatik woman hawkers to replace their male heads and become self-dependent and self-employed businesswomen. The *raddiwali* and *lifafewali* were the new labour identities for such women in Dalit *bastis* and markets in their neighbourhood.[21]

Talking about women in the business, Jamna narrated the story of her mother, Imrati, a Khatik *lifafewali*. Imrati was born in a Khatik fruit-seller family in Khatikpara, Agra. She was the third girl child of her parents, Lala Ram Asiwal (father) and Saroopi (mother). Her father and three brothers used to sell fruits at the *sabzi mandi*, Raghunath Talkies and Raja Mandi Railway Station near Khatikpara. Both her sisters, Kesar and Imrati, learnt *lifafa* making and *lifafa* business in their *basti*. They used to make *lifafes* for their father, brothers and the head of the *lifafa* business in the neighbourhood. As *lifafa* makers, they participated in some of these strikes by *lifafewalis* at Khatikpara, Agra. After marriage, they migrated to Khatikmandi, a Khatik *basti* inside the Ambala cantonment where they resumed *lifafa* making. After India's Independence, Imrati transformed herself from a *lifafa* maker to a businesswoman and head of the business. Her six daughters and other Khatik women worked under her headship.[22]

In the context of working Dalit women controlled by Dalit men and panchayats, Charu Gupta (2015: 107) writes, 'The Khatiks of Lucknow resolved not to allow their women to peddle fruits on the street, instead [of] making them sell only in shops.' However, she

21 Interview with many Khatik women who, after marriage, migrated from Agra, Aligarh, Meerut, Ambala etc to. Delhi. Also, in Delhi, Gangaram Nirvan (1929–2009) led many *lifafawalis* women strikes for fair wages between the 1960s and 1990s. He was an Ambedkarite and also one of the activist members of the Bahujan Samaj Party during its foundation at Karol Bagh. But many times, Khatik women protested alone (Rivariya: 49–50; Interview with Ashok Nirvan, son of Gangaram Nirvan, on 4 January 2012).

22 Interviews with Jamna, the elder daughter of Imrati, in Delhi on multiple occasions during my fieldwork.

does not mention that in the same panchayat, the Khatik woman and her husband, against whom this resolution was passed, wanted to 'shoebeat these men' (complainants and panchs). Similarly, in everyday life and business, women *lifafa* hawkers of the Khatik caste broke the codes of veil, patriarchy and panchayat in Dalit society and male domination in the labour market and home workshops. Indeed, the decline in the influence of both the panchayat and the *chaudharis* reduced their control over the everyday life and businesses of poor Dalits. But everyday needs and markets in towns and cities controlled the Dalits. As Blunt notes, there were a 'series of quarrels' and contested voices in the Khatik panchayat on the issue of professional matters and women dignity.[23] This struggle against Dalit patriarchal domination was made possible by the shared informality of the Khatik *bastis*.

Conclusion

In the 19th and early 20th centuries, Dalit *bastis* emerged as centres of day labours and works. In the beginning, these *bastis* acted as temporary colonies, supplying labour to nearby construction sites. These unplanned *bastis* at the edges of towns, cities, cantonments, railway stations, highways and village boundaries gradually came to be transformed as sites of everyday forms of resistance to Brahmanical and colonial powers, innovatively mobilising their resources and lived sensorial experiences against hegemonic regimes of morality, discipline, domination, the scented white body, purity and hygiene.

In a milieu when the 'white towns' of the Europeans were the spatial metaphor and the landscape of aspiration for the upper-caste and middle-class urban civil society, these *bastis* represent a history of counter sites of such moral-spatial urban orders.

These *bastis* of Dalit labourers were unplanned and unauthorised, inhabited by so-called bad characters and uncivilised poor and thus

23 Blunt mentions one such panchayat conflict: 'a certain woman peddled fruit with her basket on her head—an act considered derogatory to the caste's dignity—women should only sell at shops' (Blunt 1912: 345–346; Blunt 1969: 241).

labelled as *malin bastis* or *suarbaade*. These were the opposite of the colonial aesthetic sense, town planning and beauty of white and semi-white colonies—a space of everyday headache and disorder—and lacking discipline for colonial civil governance, architects and town planners. Consequently, with pseudo sympathy and the idea of '*not near us, not here*', the colonial municipality, railway and cantonment officials and village-town-urban elites intentionally forced Dalits to settle outside the boundaries of civil society (for impurity and power, see Bellwinkel-Schempp 1998 and 2005; Douglas 1966 [1984]: 95–115; Gordon 1985: 139; Kapoor 2016: 240–257; Radhakrishna 2000: 2554).

Indeed, the colonial government worked to fit these indisciplined, uncivilised Dalit day labourers and bad characters in the agricultural and industrial settings, but not in the modern residential spaces of civil society. The colonial government, railway, police and army officers, civil contractors, European and native city bosses, elites, industrialists wanted day labourers, coolies, begar, pork, meat, leather and bristle as commodities and services on cheap rates or free of cost. But they were intolerant to smell, flies, waste and garbage of the Dalit *bastis*.

In this context, I would like to argue, like Scott, Douglas and Bellwinkel-Schempp, that the fear of impurity, squatting, poaching and disorder in civil society generated power, self-respect and dignity of Dalits in the late 19th and 20th centuries. This power was not only in the hands of village-town-urban elites, caste Hindus and colonial State, but limited power was indirectly also in the hands of Dalits (Bellwinkel-Schempp 2005 and 1998; Scott 2013: 64–73). The Dalit *bastis* were the sites of negotiation and empowerment. At these sites, the powers of the dominant and subordinate meet, contest and negotiate with each other.

The Dalit *basti* (localities or slums) was a site of everyday resistance for property rights, unorganised workplaces and invisibility. It was a site of the formation of a homogenous community, economy, market, everyday politics, work, labour relation and labour process. At these *bastis*, pigs, pork, bristle, leather, waste (garbage), dirty water, the smell of hide, stinking untouchable bodies, buildings, Dalit collective solidarity and the rise of sub-contractors were the symbols of Dalit power and the power of impurity. The ignored, unplanned and unauthorised survived, and segregated Dalit *bastis* were living symbols of protest against the idea of purity, caste, race, class, disciplined society, domination, high culture and aesthetic, and white town.[24] Also, the Dalit *basti* provided an opened 'space of solidarity and sociality', where the meanings of masculinity and gender were reworked, reproduced and redefined by invisible Dalit men and women. It also provided a sense of domestic and outside spaces in the caste notion. For Khatik men and women, although Khatik localities were domestic workspaces, the *bastis* of other Scheduled Castes or Banias (a Vashya caste) and local markets at and near the civil centres (like railway stations and cantonments) were the 'outside' workspaces where the Khatiks tried to find the respect and dignity of labour through negotiation, contestation and everyday silent protests in 'informal and invisible ways'.

The alternative workforce (*lifafa* makers and cart pullers) in these *bastis* called on the excluded, veiled and abandoned Dalit women, men and children, including unsettled, criminalised Khatiks to pull out of 'seclusion' and invisibility. In the private regulations of Dalit *bastis*, the unsettled criminalised Khatiks and Dalits were not only connected to their caste panchayats and sabhas but also connected to families, local brotherhood, cousinhood and neighbourhood. Here they maintained their social and market relations with non-criminalised and free Khatiks and other Dalits. Therefore, the Dalit *basti* was one of the sites of contest, negotiation, resistance, empowerment, subordination, liberation and the formation of new occupational identities for most Dalit castes.

The Dalit *basti* was segregated from the rest of the city because of its leather-bristle industry, opened drainage (*gaanda naala*), garbage heap,

---

24 In the late 19th and the early 20th centuries, the colonial racial theory was often used to characterise living conditions and housing styles. According to that, the European settlements, known as White Towns, were centres of westernisation, modernity, order, defense, sanitation and beautification. On the other hand, Indian settlements (*bastis*), known as Black Towns, were centres of dense population, violence, beggars, rowdies, narrow streets, broken huts, dilapidation, unhealthy and polluted environment (Khilnani 1997: 115; Metcalf 1989).

lack of sanitation, health issue, *suarbaade* (Dalit labour *bastis*) and caste politics. Despite all the odds, this chapter attempts to show the strategies and practices in and through which these Dalit *bastis* transformed social lives of their residents as well as the built spaces of these *bastis*. In this process, we see the turning around of established social and spatial codes and value system in the spheres of religion (through the worship of the non-Brahamanic goddess, that too outside the traditional setting of home or temple, at crossroads, and having temples rooted in bhakti lineage), economy (by setting up informal networks of home tanneries, bristle industries and *lifafa* making), politics (making counter claims over bodies and work and through everyday forms of resistance) and aesthetics (mobilising upon the smell of leather to display their anger against visiting colonial representatives). These examples are narrated in this chapter by bringing together evidence from the colonial archive and responses gathered from the field. These responses from the field emphatically suggest that the memory of this resistance and this transformation of a spatial unit called Khatik *basti* is still alive and continues to provide new meanings to our understanding of the neighbourhood.

References

Ambedkar, B.R. 2016. 'Untouchability, the Dead Cow and the Brahmin'. In *The Myth of the Holy Cow,* edited by D.N. Jha, pp. 184–207. New Delhi: Navayang.

Arnold, David. 1993. *Colonizing the Body: State Medicine and Epidemic Disease in Nineteenth-century India.* Berkeley and Los Angeles: University of California Press.

Baillie, D.C. 1894. *Census of India, 1891: The North Western Provinces and Oudh.* Vol. 16, No. 1, Report and Provincial Tables. Allahabad: The Government Press.

Bellwinkel-Schempp, Maren. 1998. 'The Khatiks of Kanpur and the Bristle Trade: Towards an Anthropology of Man and Beast'. *Sociological Bulletin,* Vol. 47, No. 2, pp. 185–206.

———. 2005. 'Pigs and Power: Urban Space and Urban Decay'. In *Urbanization and Governance in India,* edited by Evelin Hust and Michael Mann, pp. 201–226. Delhi: Manohar.

Bellwinkel-Schempp, Maren. 2006. 'Social Practice of Bhakti in Siv Narayan Sampradaya'. In *Bhakti in Current Research, 2001–2003,* edited by Monika Horstmann, pp. 15–32. Delhi: Manohar.

Blunt, E.A.H. 1912. *Census of India 1911: United Provinces of Agra and Oudh.* Vol. XV, Part 1–2, Report and Imperial Tables. Allahabad: The Government Press.

———. 1969. *The Caste System of Northern India.* Delhi: S. Chand and Co.

Briggs, G.W. 1920. *The Chamars.* Calcutta: Association Press.

Burn, R. 1902. *Census of India, 1901: United Provinces of Agra and Oudh,* Vol. 16, No. 1. Report. Allahabad: The Government Press.

Cawnpore Harijan Sevak Sangha. May 1934. *Report of the Harijan Survey Committee, 1933–34.* Cawnpore.

Chaturvedi, Giridhar Sharma. 1933. *Kya Asprashyata Kalpit Hai.* Etawah: Brahma Press.

Crooke, William. 1896. *The Popular Religion and Folk-lore of Northern India,* Vol. 1. Westminster: Archibald Constable and Co.

———. 1907. *Natives of Northern India. The Native Races of the British Empire.* London: Archibald Constable and Co.

Douglas, Mary. 1966 [1984]. *Purity and Danger: An Analysis of the Concepts of Pollution and Taboo.* New York: Routledge.

Dumont, Louis. 1988. *Homo Hierarchicus: The Caste System and Its Implications.* Delhi: Oxford University Press.

Evenson, Norma. 1989. *The Indian Metropolis: A View Toward the West.* New Delhi: Oxford University Press.

Gandhi, Mahatma. 1955. *Harijan Sevako Ke Liye,* edited by Bharatan Kumarppa. Ahamdabad: Navjivan Prakashan Mandir.

General Administration Department, Lucknow, Uttar Pradesh State Archive.

Gooptu, Nandini. 2001. *The Politics of the Urban Poor in Early Twentieth-century India.* Cambridge: Cambridge University Press.

Gordon, Stewart N. 1985. 'Bhils and the Idea of a Criminal Tribe in Nineteenth-century India'. In *Crime and Criminality in British India,* edited by Anand A. Yang, pp. 128–139. Arizona: University of Arizona Press.

Government of UP. *United Provinces Police Abstract of Intelligence.* Allahabad: The Government Press.

Growse, F.S. 1883. *Mathura District Memoir.* Allahabad: The Government Press.

Gupta, Charu. 2015. 'Embodying Resistance Representing Dalits in Colonial India'. *South Asia: Journal of South Asian Studies,* Vol. 38, No. 1, pp. 100–118.

Harijan Sevak (Hindi newspaper from Delhi).

Ibbetson, Denzil. 1916 [1981]. *Punjab Castes: Races, Castes and Tribes of the Punjab.* New Delhi: Cosmo Publications.

Interviews with Khatiks in and from Kanpur, Benares, Allahabad, Agra, Meerut, Aligarh, Ambala and Delhi across several days during my fieldwork.

Jai Bhim Jai Samaj (Hindi weekly newspaper from Kanpur).

Joshi, Chitra. 2008. 'Histories of Indian Labour: Predicaments and Possibilities.' *History Compass*, Vol. 6, No. 2, pp. 439–454.

Kapoor, Shivani. 2016. 'Ira Banam Chamda: Uttar Pradesh Mein Jati aur Gandh ki Rajniti'. *Pratiman*, Vol. 4, No. 7, pp. 240–257.

Kerr, Ian J. 2006. 'On the Move: Circulating Labor in Pre-Colonial, Colonial, and Post-Colonial India'. In *Coolies, Capital, and Colonialism: Studies in Indian Labour History*, edited by Rana P. Behal and Marcel van der Linden, pp. 85–109. Cambridge and New Delhi: Cambrige Univeristy Press and International Review of Social History Supplements.

Khilnani, Sunil. 1997. *The Idea of India*. London: Hamish Hamilton.

Kumar, Nita. 1988 [2017]. *The Artisans of Banaras: Popular Culture and Identity, 1880–1986*. New Jersey: Princeton University Press.

Kumar, Vijay. 2013. The Ideological Transformation of Khatik in Uttar Pradesh, 1920–1960. Unpublished MPhil Dissertation: History and Culture Department, Jamia Millia Islamia, New Delhi.

———. 2016. 'Myth and Reality of Dalit Religiosity: A Case of the Chauraha Worship in North India'. Paper presented at Research Scholars' Workshop, University of Delhi, New Delhi, 3 March.

———. Ongoing Research. An Untouchable Caste: Social and Political Histories of Khatiks in Uttar Pradesh, 1881–1956. Unpublished PhD Thesis: Department of History, University of Delhi, Delhi.

Leader (English newspaper from Lucknow).

Lucassen, Jan. 2006. '"The Brickmakers" Strikes on the Ganges Canal in 1848–1849'. In *Coolies, Capital, and Colonialism: Studies in Indian Labour History*, edited by Rana P. Behal and Marcel van der Linden, pp. 47–83. Cambridge and New Delhi: Cambridge University Press and International Review of Social History.

Mann, Michael. 2007. 'Delhi's Belly: On the Management of Water, Sewage and Excreta in a Changing Urban Environment during the Nineteenth Century'. *Studies in History*, Vol. 23, No. 1, pp. 1–30.

Metcalf, Thomas. 1989. *Imperial Vision: Indian Architecture and British Raj*. Delhi: Oxford University Press.

Misra, Babagrahi. 1969. 'Sitala: The Small-Pox Goddess of India'. *Asian Folklore Studies*, Vol. 28, No. 2, pp. 133–142.

Niaimishrai, Mohandas. 2013. *Bhartiya Dalit Aandolan ka Itihas*, Vol. 2. New Delhi: Radhakrishna Prakashan.

Nicholas, Ralph W. 1981. 'The Goddess Sitala and Epidemic Smallpox in Bengal'. *The Journal of Asian Studies*, Vol. 41, No. 1, pp. 21–44.

Pandey, Gyanendra. 1982. 'Peasant Revolt and Indian Nationalism: The Peasant Movement in Awadh, 1919–1922'. In *Subaltern Studies I,* edited by R. Guha, pp. 198–223. Delhi: Oxford University Press.

Radhakrishna, Meena. 2000. 'Colonial Construction of a "Criminal" Tribe: Yerukules of Madras Presidency'. *Economic and Political Weekly*, Vol. 35, No. 28–29, pp. 2553–2563.

Rawat, Ramnarayan S. 2012. *Reconsidering Untouchability: Chamars and Dalit History in North India.* New Delhi: Permanent Black.

Records of Commissioner's and Collectorate's Offices of the Banaras Division. Varanasi: Varanasi Regional Archive.

Records of Commissioner's and Collectorate's Offices of the Agra Division. Agra: Agra Regional Archive.

Rivariya, Mamchand. 2006. *Khatik Samaj Ke Ratn.* New Delhi: Rivariya Sahitya Prakashan.

Ruth, S. Freed and Stanley A. Freed. 1962. 'Two Mother Goddess Ceremonies of Delhi State in the Great and Little Traditions'. *South Western Journal of Anthropology*, Vol. 18, No. 3, pp. 246–277.

Scott, James C. 1990. *Weapons of the Weak: Everyday Forms of Peasant Resistance.* Delhi: Oxford University Press.

———. 2013. *Decoding Subaltern Politics: Ideology, Disguise, and Resistance in Agrarian Politics.* London and New York: Routledge.

Shastri, Rajnath Sonkar. 2005. *Khatik Jaati ki Utpatti aur Vikas.* Varanasi: Kushal Publication.

Sherring, M.A. 1974. *Hindu Tribes and Castes: Benares*, Vol. I. Delhi: Cosmo Publications.

Singh, K.S. 1998. *India's Communities: People of India.* Anthropological Survey of India, Vol. 5. Oxford: Oxford University Press

Singh, Mohinder. 1947. *The Depressed Classes: Their Economic and Social Condition.* Bombay: Hind Kitab Ltd.

Sonkar, Yatinder. (no date). *The Short Life Story (Hagiography) of Sant Bhai Karori Mal.* Unpublished Manuscript. Kanpur: Sant Bhai Karori Mal Janamutsav Smiti and Khatik Samaj Vikas Samiti.

Sonkar, Yatinder. *Private Papers.* Kanpur.

Tartakov, Gary Michael. 2012. 'Introduction: Invisibles?' In *Dalit Art and Visual Imagery,* edited by Gary Michael Tartakov, pp.1–12. New Delhi: Oxford University Press.

The Pioneer (English newspaper from Lucknow).

Tondon, Purushottam Das. *Private Papers.* New Delhi: National Archive of India.

Tripathi, Laxmikant and Narayan Prasad Arora. 1957. *Kanpur Ka Itihas*, Vol. 2. Kanpur: Kanpur-Itihas Smiti and Gyan Mandir Press.

Turner, A.C. 1933. *Census of India, 1931: United Provinces of Agra and Oudh*. Vol. XVIII, Part 1, Report. Allahabad: The Government Press.

Vaidh, Sivamangal Ram. *Private Papers*. Banaras.

Vertman (Hindi newspaper from Kanpur).

Wadley, Susan S. 1980. 'Sitala: The Cool One'. *Asian Folklore Studies*, Vol. 39, No. 1, pp. 33–62.

6

Making of the 'New City': The Overlapping Structures of Caste and Class in Post-Partition Delhi

Akanksha Kumar

The partition of the Indian subcontinent into nation states in the late 1940s had a catastrophic influence on different dimensions of life. While the traumatic event and its continued ramifications at political, social and psychological levels have been studied from various perspectives, scholars have often ignored the spatial translation of such a colossal phenomenon. Pitching at this blind spot, this chapter aims to understand how this partition, in terms of the large influx of refugees to Indian cities and towns, shaped the urban landscape in Independent India. For this purpose, this chapter focuses on the neighbourhoods of Delhi. The discussion in this chapter further narrows down its ambit by analysing these neighbourhood formations through the dynamics of caste, another less explored theme in the scholarship on Delhi. The chapter claims that caste was a crucial coordinate in the emergence and making of neighbourhoods in Delhi, without which the urban landscape of post-partition Delhi cannot be understood adequately. With this objective, the chapter highlights aspects related to Dalit refugees in the social history of these post-partition neighbourhoods of Delhi.

The discussion in this chapter attempts to trace the history of Dalit refugees and their resettlement in post-partition Delhi. For this purpose, the story of a Dalit refugee colony of East Delhi, namely Jhilmil Colony in Shahdara established in 1950, is the mainstay of this chapter. This story of the partition refugees relates to the establishment of various Dalit refugee colonies. The question of Dalits during the partition and its implications in terms of neighbourhood formation aim to advance the scholarship by addressing spatial complexities and fresh additions to the historiography on the partition as well as on neighbourhoods.

Premised upon the detailed introduction, in this discussion, a neighbourhood is understood as a form of social interaction, in particular, interconnections between neighbours and kinship ties. This aids in studying the creation of urban spaces that witnessed a massive influx of partition migrants from rural and urban areas from across the border. Involuntary or forced migrations are only one aspect of the much larger cultural process and sociopolitical practices. The role of refugees, therefore, should not be limited to recipients of relief and rehabilitation measures alone, but also take into consideration their role as historical actors. Elsewhere, Ravinder Kaur (2007: 1–5) discusses the refugees, their everyday lives, forced migration and renewed embodiment of the migrant's personal and social bearing in post-partition Delhi. The whole journey of the refugees culminated in Delhi with multiple levels of caste, class and gender experiences, and the present circumstances reshape the remembrance of the past. This chapter elaborates on the invocation of the past in the everyday lives of the Punjabi refugees in Delhi. The partition of Punjab and forced migration of more than five million Hindus and Sikhs into India opened an unexplored area within modern Indian history. Kaur looks into the forms of post-partition experiences of Punjabi Hindu refugees to evolve coping strategies when forced to leave their homes in 1947 and the identification process of the refugees that they have developed with their former homelands as well as the Indian State. This chapter, in this light, uses personal and governmental narratives to show that the population movement, which was multilayered with caste and class, was far more complex than it has been imagined.

Moreover, Kaur deals with the untouchable migrants of partition and the conscious absence of the untouchable refugee narratives (marginalised narratives) within modern Indian history. The history of partition refugees has been largely limited to the upper-caste Hindus and Sikhs who were forced to move. 'The emergent quintessential refugee in fictional, autobiographical and official accounts somehow restricts the investigative field of resettlement to the middle-class areas of Delhi where the upper caste refugees were settled by the government' (Kaur 2007: 158). The untouchable refugees and their history during the partition could have two possibilities: one, that the untouchable castes in west Punjab did not migrate in large numbers and two, that they did not settle in the middle- or lower-middle-class areas of Delhi. There are references to migration of untouchables in various accounts, therefore, the second option seems more viable according to the author. However, Kaur brings about certain interesting facts about the experiences of the 'untouchable refugees'; when they arrived in Delhi, they were certainly divided on caste basis and their colonies were also different from the upper-caste Hindu refugees. The credit for the economic and social success that these refugees gained was given to the government; the refugees stated that they would have never been so successful had they been back home in Pakistan. Kaur, however, feels that the Indian State was planning at different levels for refugees where the level of support was determined by their class and caste, for example, the Scheduled Caste refugees were provided mud huts in an area already occupied by untouchable groups in Delhi. This segregation along caste lines, initiated by upper castes, also led to the coming together of untouchable migrants and the existing 'untouchable' groups in Delhi, leading to some kind of integrated community of untouchables.

In terms of the aftermath of the partition and its influence on cities such as Delhi, it ought to be noted that in the beginning the residents were sympathetic to the refugees, but when the refugees became rival in business, the attitude changed (Datta 1986: 278). The Punjabi refugees led the way towards rapid commercial and industrial expansion. Moving further from V.N. Datta's upper-caste/middle-class Punjabi refugee success story in Delhi, Kaur points out that there could be two possibilities as to why the story of Dalit resettlements has not been included in partition writings: one, that they did not migrate in large numbers and the other, that they did not settle in the lower- or middle-class areas with the upper-caste refugees. If they did not settle in the popular refugee colonies, then where did they actually manage to adjust and how did the state-sponsored relief and rehabilitation measures assist them? Also, when they migrated to Delhi, were they included in the Hindu fold and how were their primary identities affected? Within the historiography of post-partition experiences of refugees, it is reflected that Dalit experience has not been explored to a large extend. Dalit refugees from Pakistan have been mentioned in the archival records as 'Displaced Harijans'. Kaur found records of Dalit settlements in the Karol Bagh area of Delhi where these refugees were allotted huts, as well as an area called Raghpur, which was largely a Schedule Caste locality.[1] She mentions that the government helped these Dalits in many ways and so the Dalits gave the government credit for their social and economic success, unlike the upper-caste refugees. This rupture (partition) proved to be a positive turning point in the lives of these refugees. Evidently, the refugees experienced partition differently as well as resettled in separate colonies; the relief given to them was different from the upper-caste migrants. The Ministry of Relief and Rehabilitation had made attempts in this direction. The focus of this study would be to make additions to this and further explore the role of Ministry of Relief and Rehabilitation in rehabilitating Dalits in post-partition 'Harijan Refugee' colonies of Delhi, one of which was Jhilmil Colony. The present study finds that the work of rehabilitating Dalit refugees was handed over to Harijan Sewak Sangh by the Ministry of Relief and Rehabilitation in 1949; the chapter explores their roles as well as focuses on personal stories of Dalit refugees and their journey, through oral history and interviews of the surviving Dalit migrants of the partition.

The archival records refer to Dalit refugees as 'Displaced Harijans'. In a meeting held on 4 March 1949, the Relief and Rehabilitation Department allotted the duty of resettling 'Displaced Harijans' to Harijan Sewak Sangh.[2]

The Harijan Sewak Sangh approved this in its monthly letter of April 1949 where they mentioned that it had become an agency of the Central

---

1 For ethical-legal reasons, all derogatory caste names that fall under the category of Scheduled Castes are replaced as Scheduled Castes or Dalits.

2 Delhi State Archives, File No. 82/49-C.

government for the rehabilitation of the displaced Harijans[3] Harijan Sewak Sangh organised itself to manage the affairs of the 'Displaced Harijans' all over the country. A Displaced Harijans Rehabilitation Board was established with Rameshwari Nehru as its president. The annual report for the year 1951–1952 of the Harijan Sewak Sangh states that the sangh took over the work of the Harijan section of the Union rehabilitation ministry in 1949. It further states, 'It was felt that since most of the displaced Harijans were poor and illiterate, the work of their rehabilitation could best be carried out by non-official agencies working in a missionary spirit.'[4] The Ministry of Relief and Rehabilitation did not directly carry out the rehabilitation work of Dalits but appointed Harijan Sewak Sangh as a central government agency for the task.

It becomes essential to perhaps have a glance at the role and evolution of Harijan Sewak Sangh in Delhi. Linking this history of the Dalit community in Delhi and the Harijan Sewak Sangh, the experiences of partition refugees belonging to the 'lower' strata of society need to be largely included in the existing writings on partition refugees. The attempt made in the present study is to draw a picture of how the State resettled the Dalit refugees in the changed urban landscape of post-partition Delhi whereby special plans were drawn out for resettling Dalits at Jhilmil Colony. The records of Harijan Sewak Sangh reveal that they had encountered a lot of problems in providing houses to the Dalits from West Pakistan. The houses were allotted on a system of Hire and Purchase in which a monthly instalment had to be paid. This was unaffordable for the Dalit refugees, therefore, only mud huts were given for free. The Harijan Sewak Sangh's report mentions that the following colonies were built in Delhi for the resettlement of Dalit refugees (Table 6.1).[5]

3 *Rameshwari Nehru Papers*, Nehru Memorial Museum and Library, File No. 1.

4 *Rameshwari Nehru Papers*, Nehru Memorial Museum and Library, *Reports on Harijan Work Done by Smt. Rameshwari Nehru*.

5 *Rameshwari Nehru Papers*, Nehru Memorial Museum and Library, *Reports on Harijan Work Done by Smt. Rameshwari Nehru*, p. 1.

Name of Colony	Whether Built by Board or Government	No. of Families Accommodated
Rameshwari Nagar	Board	430
Kasturba Nagar (Delhi Shahdara)	Board	74
Lajpat Nagar	Government	14
Kilkori (Vinobha Puri)	Board	189
Kalkaji	Board	50
West Patel Nagar	Government	72
Moti Nagar	-do-	160
Ramesh Nagar	-do-	12
Tihar	-do-	201
Malka Ganj	-do-	22
Miscellaneous (Built in 1954–1956)	-do-	140
Total		1,364

Table 6.1: A list of Dalit refugee colonies in Delhi. Table credit: author

Field visits to a couple of these colonies like Shahdara and Lajpat Nagar also revealed that almost all the Dalit families originally rehabilitated in these places had left after selling their houses to upper-caste refugees for a meagre amount. No wonder majority of these colonies form a relatively affluent and upmarket urban landscape of Delhi today. Very few Dalit families who have been successfully able to preserve their houses till today have done so with great hardships.

There were many reasons why the Dalit refugees were not able to live in these colonies that were originally allotted to them. First, it was difficult for them to pay instalments in the Hire and Purchase Scheme. Second, these houses were allotted on the outskirts of the city where water, electricity and sanitation were a huge problem and long-distance travel for work and labour opportunities were a constant challenge. Thus, a large number of Dalits sold off their houses for gaining some instant profit. As I spoke to a few people left behind in these colonies, it was revealed that these refugees left the places because they were addicted to alcohol and needed money. The socioeconomic conditions of all these Dalit families, therefore, became a reason why they could not preserve the houses allotted to them.

Jhilmil Colony—Shahdara

East Delhi was one of the special landscapes where a number of refugee colonies were built by the Displaced Harijans Rehabilitation Board. This section focuses upon a 'Harijan' refugee colony built in Shahdra, where the Bhaat caste from Sikh community lives today. They got these quarters allotted to them after their stay in the Jamuna Bazaar Slum area of East Delhi. In this slum, a number of Dalit refugees stayed immediately after being displaced from West Pakistan.

Land for building this colony was allotted to All India Harijan Sewak Sangh for the construction of houses for the Dalit refugees. All India Harijan Sewak Sangh had requested for allotment of a plot of land near Shahdara comprising of Khasra No. 315/54 measuring three acres. Harijan Sewak Sangh had asked for twelve acres of land since they thought all of this would be required to construct houses for the displaced 'Harijans' from Pakistan. However, only six acres got approved for the construction of this colony.[6]

In my visits to Jhilmil Colony and in my meetings with Dalits who migrated from West Punjab, initially, I was told that none of those who were originally allotted these quarters lives there any longer. They had sold their houses and left the place, similar to the stories of other colonies. I was told that the place was vacated by them as the living cost was too high to afford by the original allottees, a point that has been discussed earlier in the chapter. The archival records show that the original plan was to construct 500 quarters, but all of them could not be built since the Harijan Sewak Sangh could only get six acres of land to construct these quarters for the 'Displaced Harijans'. I was,

6 Delhi State Archives, File No. 1(34)/49/LSG/DIT CC.

however, fortunate to meet a few families who were originally allotted these houses in the early 1950s.

From these families, I found out that they were refugees living in the Jamuna Bazaar slum before moving into these quarters allotted to them in around 1950. These current occupants narrated that Pandit Nehru had personally come to the colony for the allotment of these quarters. Through interaction with people of the colony, it was revealed that people in this camp also got houses allotted in many different parts of Delhi such as Malviya Nagar, Trilokpuri and Mayapuri. My first interview was with a man from Lahore named Chaman Singh, age seventy-eight. Chaman Singh said he got the quarter allotted as a measure of relief from the government. He said basic amenities like ration, *atta*, *ghee*, *daal* were provided to them at their temporary settlements of Jamuna Bazaar slum area. Only after moving into the quarter did the free rations stop. He said they were five brothers who came from Lahore, but only two quarters were allotted to the whole family. The rest of the family had migrated to Canada; only Chaman Singh lived in the quarter allotted. When asked about his education, he said he is illiterate but can speak Punjabi, Hindi and English!

Chaman Singh shared that all the people from his caste (Bhaat) were allotted these houses; however, almost all of them sold off their quarters and left the colony. He also revealed that the quarters were sold off by them for ten, twenty or even forty thousand rupees. Chaman Singh told me that only theirs and the quarter at the end of the street were the ones belonging to the Bhaat community, rest had left the colony and settled in other places such as Seemapuri, Trilokpuri etc., and some went to Malaviya Nagar. He said that a few of his caste people lived in Kalyanpuri as well.

Chaman Singh had owned a shop; he said he used to sell *churies* (bangles). In his words, 'bangles worth rupees 2000 are lying with me even today'. Chaman Singh used to travel till Gaziabad and surrounding villages to sell bangles. He said he is unable to continue this profession as it's physically demanding, which his old age and poor eyesight no longer permit. He pointed out that almost all the people who had been originally allotted quarters under the government's resettlement efforts have long left the colony. Many shifted to Trilokpuri, the reasons for which, he said, were unknown. When asked why all the people have left this colony, Chaman Singh simply replied, 'How do I know?'

Chaman Singh belonged to the Bhaat community or the Ramgarhia Sikhs, which had mostly migrated to Britain and Canada in the 1950s. The major professions of this caste were carpenter, stonemason and blacksmith. The interviews in the present chapter reveal similar, undefined and vagrant nature of this caste; the community being studied in this section, therefore, reveals an overlapping structure of both caste and class.

Chaman Singh's family received sufficient aid and help from the government for which he expressed his gratefulness towards Nehru: he said, 'We got these houses from him for free.' According to him, getting a quarter from the government after being displaced was a big relief; however, since everyone from his family had left the colony and moved to Canada, he appeared a little discontent with his life, living in the same quarter allotted to him in the 1950s.

In the same row where Chaman Singh lived, I found another quarter that was in the same condition as originally allotted in the 1950s. A big joint family was living there, with the patriarch, the great grandfather of the younger members of the family, still alive. Kharak Singh, popularly known as Mastana, came from Lahore; he was ninety-five years old when I met him. He was also from the Bhaat caste. Since he was much older than other refugees, he had a treasure trove of memory to share with me about his life, his community and the experience of Partition as a refugee. Before moving into the colony, he also stayed at the Jamuna Bazaar slum, Gandhi Nagar and Kashmiri Gate camps. He came to Delhi in 1947 but the quarter was allotted to him in 1950.

Kharak Singh was illiterate, so he survived, he said, by working as a labourer and doing other menial jobs. Although he was not educated, he gave his children formal education. He said he used to give massages to people who had body pain and ankle sprains. His whole family did this job when they were in Pakistan, which he continued here as well. He migrated from Lahore, which is a big city like Delhi, therefore, professionally he adapted quite well here in Delhi. He came to Delhi with his parents and one brother. In contrast to Chaman Singh, Kharak Singh said, 'We only got one quarter from the government in terms of relief; we got nothing else from the government—no rations or anything.'

When asked why he was unhappy with the government when others in the colony were grateful of Pandit Nehru and the government, Kharak Singh replied that he has a 'gift of humanity, because everything he used to do was done with a lot of hard work.... In this world, we cannot ask for anything; everything is a result of hard work. I was a labourer—a hard-working labourer.'

Kharak Singh did not seem to have solidarity or association with people of his caste. He said many from his community came from Gujranwala, Sialkot and Lahore, but he hah had no connection with any of them. In terms of Hindu–Muslim conflict, Kharak Singh shared many interesting views and instances. He said he had had no conflict with the Muslims (unlike the majority upper-caste/middle-class Punjabi migrant community of Delhi). On being probed further, he said his livelihood as a labourer did not allow him to think on communal lines: 'We were hard-working labourers. We used to work for 2.50 or 3 rupees per day. I had three sons who also worked as labourers along with me, and women don't work in our *biradari*.' He said he was not scared during the partition riots as the Muslims were afraid of his Sikh identity.

If not communal riots, then what made Kharak Singh leave Pakistan, I asked him, to which he replied, people from his community had already made up their minds that they would go to Hindustan. Overwhelmed by memories, he 'recited' a partition-era slogan: *Zindabad Jayenge Hindustan, Zindabad Jayenge Hindustan*! (Long live Hindustan! We shall go to Hindustan!)

Later in the course of the conversation with him, Kharak Singh narrated his journey from Pakistan. He said, 'If you want to listen to the whole journey from my mouth, [the following are the stations we passed] ... the first station from Lahore is Mughalpura, [after which are] Harbanspura, Jalo, Wagha, Tari, Khasa, Chiyata and then Amritsar, and from here Beas to Kartarpur.' He remembered all the stations by heart from Rawalpindi to Delhi. Kharak Singh had a vagrant profession, and so even before the partition, he used to travel to Hindustan for work. He said, 'We left our houses just like that; we did not feel the need to sell the houses to the Muslims because it would give them a chance to say '*ke bhai, hindu log apni izzat bhi bech gaye hain*' (Hindus sold their honour as well). Kharak Singh said he did not have any conflict with the Muslims and there was no hatred in his heart for them: *Musalman log apne Imaan par khade hokar kehte the yeh hamaare bhai hain, yeh hamaare chacha hain* (Swearing on their belief, the Muslims used to say these are our brothers, those are our uncles). He said, 'Muslims used to call us chacha (uncle), can you believe it?'

With tears in his eyes, Kharak Singh said he has no hatred or complaint against Muslim friends, and that he still travels to Pakistan and meets them like brothers. It was only the Pathans, according to him, who were problematic. Kharak Singh said the Sikhs and the Pathans were not on friendly terms because the Pathans do not have a good character as compared to the Muslims.

Most Bhaats are now in Britain. he said, and his brothers have also moved there. Like Chaman Singh, he also said that the Bhaats in the colony used to sell *churies* (bangles) or do different things for a living. 'If we don't get work, we also beg!' Kharak Singh told me. It is evident from the conditions of the Bhatt community that they are socially placed very low in the caste hierarchy.

'I don't regret anything,' Kharak Singh said, strongly highlighting his hard-working labourer identity, and added, '*Main mazdoor hoon mehnat karne wala mazdoor, mazdoor ko chahiye mazdoori karni aur dene wala khuda hai*' (I am a labourer who works hard. A labourer needs labour, rest depends on god). These were the last words of Kharak Singh (Mastana). Even though he did not have much in life, he said he does not regret anything because he is a hard-working labourer.

These two interviews show the Bhaats are a vagrant community, one that did not really have any fixed profession. Kharak Singh Mastana's interview revealed that they moved around frequently for work. The Bhaats did different things for a living, including reading palm (palmistry, a lot like a fortune teller), giving massages, making bangles or even begging, if required. Even though this caste is placed very low in the social and/or economic order, it is amazing how they have been successfully improved their lot and recreated themselves by migrating to Britain in large numbers.

In the same locality, I met a few more families from the Sikh community. One such name is Bahadur Singh, who came from Pakistan in 1947. He travelled from his hometown in Multan to Amritsar in a train during the partition riots. He could not speak much, when I met him, because of age-induced poor health; he was 80 years old. He also belongs to the Bhaat caste, but his family lived in a slum nearby. He did not get a quarter because he kept moving for work. He was among the many refugees that lived in Jamuna Bazaar. After Jamuna Bazaar camps, he moved to East Punjab and, finally, came back to Delhi in 1971. Bahadur Singh, like others in the locality, also sold bangles for a living. Like Kharak Singh, he too was unhappy with the aid given by the government.

As most of the refugees I met in this colony belong to the Sikh community, it's important to review the caste structure within Sikhism. Sikhism has a distinct tradition in North India, originating from the Sant Sects of medieval Hinduism. The Sikhs have had a colourful and militant past and hold a prominent place in India's present (Juergensmeyer and Barrier 1979: 1). Hew McLeod (1997) puts forward the question, do Sikhs recognise caste? This is a question that has been dealt with by some scholars, and perhaps a vigilant look at this question would answer some of the questions that the present research is dealing with—Sikhs and their identity.

Ronki Ram argues that caste discrimination in the Sikh community is different from the Brahmanical order because relations are not framed from a purity–pollution dichotomy. Rather, power in Punjab is based on land ownership. Most of the land in Punjab is owned by Jats. Although Dalits constitute 28 per cent of the population, their share in land ownership is almost negligible. Since most of them were agricultural workers, it was difficult to follow untouchability there, but they remained subordinate to Jat Sikhs. This subordination has, therefore, 'made the Dalit population more vulnerable in comparison to other parts of India, these Jat Sikhs are therefore the dominant group in Punjab rather than the Brahmins' (Ronki 2004: 895–912).

The Khatris constitute about three per cent of the Panth, and a large majority of them are Hindus. The bulk of the Sikh community comprises of Jats. The caste that is second in number is the Ramgarhia caste, predominantly formed by Tarkhan (village carpenter), Nai (barber), Lohar (blacksmith) and Raj (mason). In the village, they are the clients of Jats and are considered lower in status (McLeod 1997: 232).

There are two outcastes in the Sikh community: Jats, perhaps the untouchable community within Sikhism, are referred to as Mazhabis, corresponding to sweeper caste, and Ramdasia or Ravi Dasi, which is the another caste known for their the leather work (Ibid.: 233). The structure of caste discrimination in the Sikh community was considerably liberated from the purity–pollution frame of relations, as against the Hindu community's in which that consideration is relatively more prominent (Puri 2003: 2693–2701).

McLeod refers to the Bhaat caste as a tiny caste in Punjab whose members have migrated to Britain in large numbers. This fact has been verified by Chaman Singh and Kharak Singh in the interviews earlier. Although this caste has historically not been in a good social or economic position, they have achieved some upward mobility by migrating to Britain. Both Chaman Singh's and Kharak Singh's brothers have moved to Britain and attained considerable successes, but the condition of those who stayed behind, like Chaman's and Kharak's, remained the same as was in 1950.

Therefore, it could be surmised from the interviews that caste discrimination in Sikh society is indeed a strong enough reality. Sikhism did not lead to the end of the caste system or the creation of an egalitarian community (Puri 2003). Very little is being written about this tiny caste called Bhaat. It is not clear if this caste was included in the Scheduled-Caste category in the post-partition era. Interactions with the family members of Chaman Singh and Kharak Singh reflected that the Sikhs living in the colony were included in the categories of Scheduled Caste (SC) and Other Backward Classes (OBC). The socioeconomic status of the 'Bhaats' reflects that they are below the land-owning Jats or Khatris, who are the dominant castes among the Sikhs.

However, as pointed out by Harish K. Puri (2003), a lot of priests, *ragis* or *sewadars* came from the lower castes, including the Scheduled Caste, but a few surprisingly also came from the Jat caste. In Jhilmil Colony, one of the people I interviewed was the wife of a priest who identified themselves as OBCs. Therefore, the present study demonstrates that the Sikh refugees of Jhilmil Colony are from the lower castes or OBC. This fact also tallies with the archival records and the history of the establishment of this post-partition Dalit neighbourhood.

Conclusion

The Dalit refugees of partition were rehabilitated by Harijan Sewak Sangh under the aegis of the Central government at different colonies across Delhi. The government had claimed to have rehabilitated Dalit refugees in what is today considered popular refugee colonies in Delhi. However, the majority of the original allottees have long sold off their quarters and left the colonies as they could not afford the expenses of living in them. This chapter has highlighted one of many such cases: the results of the work done towards resettling Dalit refugees in a colony in East Delhi.

However, one can raise a few hypothetical questions here. First, would the urban landscape of Delhi be any different today if 500 quarters were built on twelve acres of land in Shahdara, as was originally planned? Second, would the Dalits be living in larger numbers in today's popular refugee colonies of the city if greater efforts had been made in their resettlement? The caste barriers of these refugees denote that their status has remained the same since post-partition, especially when compared to the successes of upper-caste Punjabi refugees who became the beneficiaries of the rapid commercial expansion of Delhi.

Through this study of a Dalit refugee caste in Jhilmil Colony, an attempt has been made to establish the differences in their attitudes, lives and socioeconomic conditions vis-à-vis the upper- and middle-class Punjabi refugees. The present condition of these Dalit refugees has deep social roots ingrained in caste-based structural inequalities. The difference is also noticeable in the manner in which the resettlement was carried out unfairly wherein the refugees of Jhilmil Colony were made to stay at the Jamuna Bazaar *basti* (slum) before being allotted quarters while other refugees were accommodated at temples and *Gurudwaras* (Datta 1986). This highlights the overlapping structures of caste and class in a new and changed post-partition Delhi. This study brings to light the caste and class dimensions of the ever-changing urban space that historically went through innumerable ruptures, resulting in what constitutes and makes the city of Delhi what it is today.

References

Datta, V.N. 1986. 'Punjabi Refugees and the Urban Development of Greater Delhi'. In *Delhi Through the Ages in Urban History: Society and Culture,* edited by R.E. Frykenberg. Delhi: Oxford University Press, pp. 442–460.

Garrioch, D. and M. Peel. 2006. 'Introduction: The Social History of Urban Neighbourhoods'. *Journal of Urban Studies*, Vol. 32, No. 5, pp. 663–676.

Juergensmeyer, M. and N.G. Barrier. 1979. 'Sikh Studies: Comparative Perspective on a Changing Tradition'. A Working Paper From the Berkeley Conference on Sikh Studies, Graduate Theological Union, Berkeley, California.

Kaur, Ravinder. 2007. *Since 1947*. Delhi: Oxford University Press.

Malkki. Liisa H. 1995. 'Refugees and Exile: From "Refugee Studies" to the National Order of Things'. *Annual Review of Anthropology*, Vol. 24, pp. 495–523.

McLeod, H. 1997. *Sikhism*. London: Penguin Books.

Puri, H.K. 2003. 'Scheduled Caste in Sikh Community: A Historical Perspective'. *Economic and Political Weekly*, Vol. 38, No. 26 (June–July), pp. 2693–2701.

Rameshwari Nehru Papers. Nehru Memorial Museum and Library, Delhi.

'Reports on Harijan Work Done by Smt. Rameshwari Nehru', *Rameshwari Nehru Papers*. Nehru Memorial Museum and Library, Delhi.

Ronki, R. 2004. 'Untouchability in India with a Difference: Ad Dharma, Dalit Assertion, and Caste Conflicts in Punjab'. *Asian Survey*, Vol. 44, No. 6 (November–December), pp. 895–912.

Scheduled Caste Survey of Delhi 1961. Government of India. Delhi: Central Secretariat Library.

Part III

Engendering Neighbourhood: Female Neighbours and Contested Subjectivities

7

Living Like Friends and Neighbours: Everyday Narratives of the Neighbourhood

Joyashree Sarma

The Indo-Bangladesh borderlands in Assam are often represented in the larger political and media discourses as places crawling with 'infiltrators', 'illegal immigrants', cow smugglers, militants and terrorists. The Indo-Bangladesh borders in Assam are heavily guarded by security personnel and barricaded with barbed wire fences to securitise the nation against illegal movement and flow of humans, animals and goods along with illicit substances and terrorists. The debate on 'illegal immigrant' 'infiltration' is reflected in the political situation in Assam through the exercise of the citizen enumerating process of National Register of Citizens (NRC), which sought documents from the residents of Assam to prove their citizenship. As the process questioned all residents to prove their 'legal' associations with the nation and the state of Assam, through their ancestry dating back before 24 March 1971, the implications were immediately felt in each and every household as members raced to submit legacy documents, forms, photographs etc. Thus, the Indo-Bangladesh borderlands in Assam are situated within the debates on the securitisation of nation state, identity politics of citizen and 'illegal immigrant'. Another dimension to this debate comes from the understanding that the local, the indigenous and the 'son-of-the-soil' within the state are major driving forces behind the implementation of NRC in Assam to fulfil the demand of the Assamese-speaking population to identify 'illegal immigrants' vis-à-vis the indigenous. The NRC, although mandated by the Supreme Court of India, had a local appeal, imagination and support in the context of Assam. In this study, I seek to understand what meanings do issues of identity translate into the everyday life of the inhabitants of these borderland towns when the enumeration and documentation project of NRC was underway.

Identity in borderlands is often articulated through contestations, fluidity and hybridity due to movement of people and cultures, and even due to shift and change in the borders of a nation state. In the aftermath of the partition of the subcontinent, the Bengal borderland, as Van Schendel (2005: 332) points out, 'became an important battlefield of identities, a place where worldview met and where new forms of self-identification were shaped'. This appears true also of the borderlands of Assam with Bangladesh where questions around the identity of the borderland inhabitants are often shrouded in the movement and migration of people across borders, which were mostly unfenced and unguarded until the 1980s. The borderlands of Assam reflect a homogeneous nature in terms of religion, language and communities, and hence questions of identity and belonging were raked up by the NRC. The social relations in Assam have often been overshadowed by what is considered a conflict between indigenous and immigrants, resulting in clashes and riots between Assamese and Bengali-speaking population, between Bodos and Bengali-speaking population and between tribal and non-tribal groups.

Hence, to understand the translation of the macro politics of identity among the borderland inhabitants, this chapter looks at the everyday interactions by considering the neighbourhood as a site of placemaking, social relations and dynamics between the inhabitants. In doing so, I followed an ethnographic approach to conduct an in-depth study in the neighbourhood of Dakhin Tokererchara in Golakganj, a border town in the district of Dhubri, Assam.

Taking a cue from the introductory chapter, the neighbourhood is 'a space in-between par excellence, a locality that connects the direct experiences of households and families with their participation in wider networks of city, nation and the world' (De Neve and Donner 2006: 10). Hence, the neighbourhood is a pertinent place to investigate the link between public and private spheres. As a place situated in the periphery of the nation state, along a militarised border, it becomes pertinent to understand the localised lifeworld by considering the neighbourhood within a borderland. The neighbourhood as a place of social interaction also opens up the possibility of understanding the relationships and interactions between the local and the global (Appadurai 1996). Sociologically speaking, the understanding of the social structure and social order is derived from the 'lifeworld' and the social interactions between actors in their natural context. Thus, this chapter attempts to explore networks of friends and neighbours in order to understand as to how the politics of identity operates within them. Drawing from ethnographic fieldwork conducted in Golakganj, this study examines the political situation impinging on the neighbourhood and its people. The ethnographic descriptions in this chapter unravel the neighbourhood of Dakhin Tokererchara Pt. III through the fieldwork, which was conducted in late 2017 and early 2018.

The Everyday in the Neighbourhood

The border town of Golakganj is marked by the presence of security personnel deployed by the Central government and local police in the public areas. Located on one end of the main road that leads to the town from National Highway 17, the Sahastra Seema Bal (SSB) has a checkpoint close to the railway station, market, police station, and the local auto and bus stand. From near the busy main road, the SSB watches over the villagers who cross the river and go to the market, haggling between the buyers and sellers in the market and auto-rickshaw drivers shouting and calling passengers. The electricity pillars and town walls display political slogans and party symbols. The names of student unions, such as All Assam Muslim Students Union (AAMSU) and All Assam Koch Rajbonshi Students Union (AKRSU), or invitations like 'Join Bajrang Dal' are written on them (Figure 7.1). As a town situated around five kilometres inside the international border with Bangladesh, the politics of religion and community is hard to miss across the public space (Figures 7.2 and 7.3).

Figure 7.1: 'Bajrang Dal' written on an electricity pole in red on white background (in original). Photo credit: author

Figure 7.2: 'AAMSU' (All Assam Muslim Students Union) written on a tea-shop next to a mosque in Golakganj. 'Golakganj Bazar Jama Masjid' is written in Assamese. Photo credit: author

Figure 7.3: 'Join Deshi Yuba Parishad Assam' (DYPA) written on a pillar and 'DYPA Zindabad' written in Assamese. Photo credit: author

According to Census 2011, the total size of Golakganj is 132.31 sq. km. and the population of Golakganj is 1,10,582, out of which 8,244 fall under the category of urban and 108,332 under rural.[1]

Although the district of Dhubri, under which Golokganj falls, has recorded 79.67 per cent of its population as Muslim, the town of Golakganj has recorded 82.81 per cent of its population as Hindus and 16.29 per cent as Muslims.[2] People in Golakganj mostly speak *Deshi*[3], which is a pidgin of Bengali and Assamese.

The Koch Rajbonghsi community associate themselves with this language, and it is widely spoken in the areas of the erstwhile Goalpara region. The Koch Rajbongshi community traces its origin to the 12th-century Koch dynasty and claims indigeneity to this area and beyond,

1 Census data available at http://censusindia.gov.in/2011census/dchb/1802_PART_B_DCHB_DHUBRI.pdf (accessed on 23 March 2020).

2 Census data available at https://www.census2011.co.in/data/religion/district/148-dhubri.html (accessed on 23 March 2020).

3 I use *Deshi* as it is how the inhabitants themselves refer the dialect as, although some may contest it as Rajbonsghi.

spreading across the contiguous parts of Assam, Meghalaya, West Bengal, Bangladesh and Nepal.[4] There are a substantial number of people from the Rajbongshi community in Golakganj, apart from members of the Bengali-speaking community. The term *Deshi* not only refers to the dialect but is also used to identify a group of Muslims as 'Deshi Muslims'. The Deshi Muslims have been recognised as indigenous Muslims by the Assam government. In the recent times, the Koch Rajbongshis have also been demanding the status of Scheduled Tribe.[5] While Deshi Muslims have been successfully granted the status of an indigenous Muslims by the Assam government.[6] These social dynamics get reflected on the walls and pillars of Golakganj, as political bodies representing both sides of the ethnic and religious divide politicised the public space.

Turning to the specific site of ethnographic unravelling, the area under Dakhin Tokererchara is considered to be a gram panchayat (village council). It covers 145. 27 hectares of land and has 725 households as per the District Census Report of 2011. It is predominantly a Hindu neighbourhood with speakers of both Bengali and *Deshi* languages. While the houses are located closer to the main road are relatively *pucca* Assam-type house, inside the lanes and closer to the river, the houses are *kutchha* or semi-*pucca.* All the houses here have either boundary made of tin or thickly woven tall bamboo fences. Two households that I know, including my host's, consider Assamese as their mother tongue. Generally speaking, women who speak Bengali, *Deshi* and Assamese often converse in *Deshi* among themselves. At the extreme end of the neighbourhood and close to a stream that empties into the Gangadhar river are few Muslim households. I observed that my respondents did not interact with them on a daily basis, but when they do, it was a relation of buyers and seller of labour. I look at the neighbourhood,

4 From the website of Centre for the Koch-Rajbangshi Studies and Development. For further information, see https://kochrajbanshicentre.org/2013/09/16/koch-and-rajbongshi-confusion-or-fusion/ (accessed on 23 March 2020).

5 For details see https://www.sentinelassam.com/guwahati-city/want-st-status-first-all-koch-rajbongshi-students-union/ (accessed on 23 March 2020).

6 For details see https://economictimes.indiatimes.com/news/politics-and-nation/assam-govt-plans-survey-to-identify-indigenous-muslims/articleshow/74091811.cms?from=mdr (accessed on 23 March 2020).

vis-à-vis social relations and interactions, through observation and, at times, participation in the everyday life. It is through my host, Bina, that I could access the neighbourhood and their friendship network. This particular neighbourhood mostly has families who run petty shops, like tailoring and grocery, in the market, a few lower rank state government employees who have retired and daily labourers who live a hand-to-mouth existence.

Bina is in her mid-fifties and runs her household. At noon, her house would often have women visitors who would come to exchange news, ask for cow dung or bring a handful of seasonal local fruits or flowers for *puja*. This was usually the time when her son, Gopal, would have gone out to meet with friends or for work. The visitors would directly go to her backyard through the side entrance where the kitchen and the tube well are located and Bina would be working. Tea would be served depending on the keenness of the guest and the availability of the gas stove. If there was no urgency to cook, a teapot would replace the pots and woks. Bina was born and raised in this house in Dakhin Tokererchara in Golakganj. She inherited this house from her mother who came here from the erstwhile Kamrup district of Assam after her marriage. She knows all the women of this neighbourhood who came after marriage. This fact was revealed during a discussion on marriage and how easy the lives of present-day daughters-in-law are compared to theirs. Her neighbours Runu *mami*[7] and Kanair *bou* (wife of Kanai) reminisce about doing household chores like plastering house with mud and cow dung, threshing and separating rice from sheaves and, in those instances, making Bina a witness to their own lives as newlywed daughters-in-law.

Bina remembers the 1971 liberation war of Bangladesh as a schoolgirl—a time when everyone had conjunctivitis or '*Joy Bangla*',[8] the earth shook violently from bomb shelling, people came in groups with '*toplas*', *khichuri* was cooked for public distribution and she got a frock from 'Indira Gandhi' as aid poured in for the refugees who came from East Bengal. She

7 *Mami* is a form of address for mother's brother's wife—an aunt. Here in this context, it has been used to address a neighbour, not related by blood but by marriage (she married a person considered a brother by Bina, hence his wife is addressed as *mami* by Bina's son, Gopal.

8 *Joy Bangla* was a war cry during the Bangladesh Liberation War.

believes that there was, in the air, a certain kind of smoke that caused the *'Joy Bangla'*, just as she believed when people around told her that Indira Gandhi, the prime minister of India, had sent clothes and food for people who were fleeing the war in East Pakistan (now Bangladesh).

The neighbourhood lanes were the meeting points for women when they take evening strolls after coming back from work, such as cooking at a function, or after getting their cows from the grazing field. The womenfolk share the burden of raising children; they help one another in matters such as tuitions, alcoholic sons, 'uncooperative' daughters-in-law, upcoming religious ceremonies and rituals, concerns related to married daughters etc. They visit one another in the evening, or late afternoon in winter when the sun sets faster. For these group of resourceful women, their world seems to revolve around everyday routine, where each day meant maintaining and protecting the daily rhythm of their households. I would accompany Bina on these visits—to have *prasad* from *kirtans* and *pujas* or to partake in some mundane activities like plucking one another's white hairs and braiding in the sun. It is not uncommon to see them help one another in cooking, especially when there are extra guests in the house or when visited by sickness.

Another dimension of the neighbourhood is the use of gossip as a medium to express veiled attacks on daughters-in-law's characters or someone's ethnicity. One evening, on a visit to a neighbour called Runu *mami*, another woman, Moni *bouma*,[9] also dropped by while on her routine evening stroll. While my host and Runu *mami* are in their fifties, Moni *bouma* is in her late thirties. The conversation between them revolved around general health ailments like pain and cold, food, children and schooling, and attending the *shaad* ceremony of a pregnant neighbour, Sarala *didi*. They all have been invited to bless the woman in the eight-month of her pregnancy. The conversation then turned to discussing the would-be mother, and how good, or bad, she is as a daughter-in-law. When Bina said Sarala's mother-in-law washes her clothes, Runu *mama* added sarcastically that the mother-in-law does it because her daughter-in-law has a government job and contributes to the upkeep of the household. The older women discussed

9 Daughter-in-law (as was addressed by all in the neighbourhood).

the younger daughters-in-law of the neighbourhood, criticising them of not doing any hard work or not taking care of their mothers-in-law. Moni *bouma* disagreed; she said her neighbour's daughter-in-law is genteel and sensitive: '*Ki bhalo bouta, sarakhon ma-baba eita khao, eita nao kore. Nepali mey biya korshe kintu eito bhalo kotha, bebohar*' (What a well behaved and good daughter-in-law she is, fending and feeding her mother-in-law, even though she is a Nepali girl).

To this Runu *mami* added, '*Anu'r* [another neighbour] *chele o Rajbonghsi mey biye korse kintu amader moto e toh khawa-dawa*' (Anu's son also married a Rajbongshi girl, but there is no difference in the style of cooking). She then asked Bina if she has found a match for her son. Bina said she wanted to find her son a bride from her mother's place and nowhere else. Bina wanted for her son an Assamese bride from her mother's place, although her husband was from Golakganj. She sent word to her relatives to find a bride for her son. Bina was very firm that she did not want any Rajbongshi or Bengali bride for her younger son. Her elder son had married a Rajbongshi girl against her will, because of which their relationship had been severed. However, it is interesting to note that Bina and her family communicate in *Deshi*, which is primarily spoken by the Koch Rajbongshi community.

Conversations around marriage have been frequent among womenfolk; however, I am only highlighting instances when ethnic identities were invoked with reference to it. The choice of a partner, as reflected in the discussion by Bina, Runu *mami*, Moni *bouma* and Kanair *bou*, illustrates the importance given to language and ethnicity when a marital alliance is forged. Such instances of boundary making in everyday interactions helps understand the overt references to identifying self and others. The references to ethnicity when discussing marital alliances were the pauses that brought forth the consciousness of difference in their similar routined lives centred around domestic chores. It is through such instances that the awareness of the self and other is expressed and distinguished, and the seemingly coherent everyday of women devoid of politics is raptured. However, it is also in instances like this that the neighbourhood comes across as a place where people, irrespective of their differences, inhabit it, bounded by the everydayness of their lives and transgress the boundaries of community and language.

Neighbourliness as a concept is often considered in terms of its latent and manifest functions based on the overtness and covertness of the acts involved (Mann 1954; Snedden 1926). The overt manifest functions, including social visits and routine assistance, have been categorised as an instrumental exchange by Ring (2006), whereas the latent functions have been linked to more positive actions and attitudes of help. It is the private nature of expressive intersection within which attitudes like intimacy and trust is developed. As per such categorisation of neighbourliness, this neighbourhood exhibited bonhomie, warmth, affection and intimacy as women sought the support of one another, exchanged marital problems, health issues to seek '*moner shanti*' (peace of mind) as Runu *mami* puts it. For the women, the everyday space of neighbourhood lanes and courtyards are places where exchanging news of neighbours' domestic troubles are narrated. These women did not make direct reference to subjects of politics in their day-to-day conversations. Hence, observing the presence of conversations around expressions of ethnicity and consciousness about it was revealed in terms of the larger politics of identity, which they don't seem to bother about but, at the same time, would be implicated in it through casual conversations. Marriage was one of the major topics of discussion that gave out clear indications about ethnicity and boundary-making as instances of gossips lead to covert references about it.[10]

However, it is also imperative to mention that while these women avoided discussing politics in the neighbourhood, the men routed the discussion around politics among friends and neighbours to the market place. The local market place and grocery shops turn out to be an extended neighbourhood where male members from particular neighbourhood share stories and exchange information.

Men and Neighbourly Interactions

Within Gopal's network of friends who were aware of one another's family legacies, certain discussions around politics would appear at

10 For more on ethnic difference and neighbourhood relations, see Bopegamage 1957; Zang 2003.

times, which may not be descriptive but brief in the form of seeking information. This was visible predominantly among men when information and talks around politics take place. I could access the friends circle of Gopal who owned shops in the main market of Golakganj. While two of his friends were Bengali-speaking Hindus, one was a Hindi-speaking man whose family roots are in the state of Bihar.

Monohar *dada*, who runs a jewellery shop in Golakganj market, was happy that his village was put under a newly formed gram panchayat in 2018. He informed the same to Gopal as we entered his jewellery shop in Golakganj market. He lived in a village close to the barbed wired fence along the guarded border. The reason for his happiness was that post the reorganisation of the gram panchayat villages, his village became a Hindu-majority village, and he was thinking of a suitable candidate who can contest with the other candidates. Manohar *dada*'s mother's natal family is in Bangladesh, and *Didima*, his mother, was in tears when she talked about how difficult it has become, after the fences came up, to meeting relatives who live across the border. She recounted that when her husband died a few years ago, her brothers could come only after months as it took time for them to get passports and visas. Manohar *dada*, in a conversation with *Didima* in their house, was quick to add one of his adventurous trip of evading border security and crossing an unfenced stream near the border to reach his uncle in the neighbouring country. It was Bina who led me to their place and introduced me to their family but without giving finer details of legal and bureaucratic entanglements.

Akhil Das, a man in his fifties, ran a grocery shop in Golakganj, sitting amid heaps of rice, pulses and spices. He was hopeful that the citizenship law will help Bengali Hindus in ending their '*risker jibon*' in Bangladesh. In October 2018, when the Citizenship Amendment Bill (CAB), 2016,[11] was facing a lot of protests in Assam, he thought it was a good idea because Hindus in Bangladesh are not safe as they

11 The bill was introduced as CAB, 2019 after the formation of the government by the NDA led allies in the 17th Lok Sabha. After the bill was passed in both the Lok Sabha and Rajya Sabha, the CAB, 2019 became the Citizenship Amendment Act (CAA) on 12 December 2019.

suffer religious persecution. I asked him how he knew about the persecution and he said he had been told about it by his relatives who live in Bangladesh, some of whom had visited him a few years ago.

The stories of Monahar *dada*, Gopal and Akhil Das are common instances of how borderland inhabitants form a circle of friends centred around religion. This holds the trust and mutual respect for one another's political secrets. It is within the same public space of Golakganj that they have their shops and carry out their businesses, which reflect the absence of political talks. The interpersonal relations between people of different religions, languages and ethnicities have been marked by pure civic behaviour of tolerance in the public space. This pure civic behaviour is characterised by avoiding conflict in public, restraining an individual's political opinions and expressing differences aloud. This was not the case in terms of governing the rules of forging friendship and trust between people who inhabit the same public space. Duchesne and Haegel (2007) reveal that the dynamics of public discussions depend on the way participants assume the risk of engaging in conflict with persons who are more or less strangers. Political discussions have the potential to reach both consensus and 'durable conflict'; they have the risk of revealing which group one belongs to, and hence for individuals, the politicisation process is a demanding one. The loudness implies a sense of boldness in homogenous spaces of inhabitance, whereas in public spaces, people from different religious and ethnic backgrounds enter in to exchange while restraining against speaking out personal opinions and political views to avoid conflict.

In contrast to the silence around the political process that public sites like markets, auto-stands and streets in Golakganj exhibit, the loudness of strong political opinions and talks feature in the personal relationships of the people in Dakhin Tokererchara. This is also exemplified in the way neighbourhoods in the border areas are segregated in terms of religion, or in the way market area itself has been demarcated into segments owned by Hindu and Muslim shopkeepers after communal clashes in the early 1990s. In 1992, after the demolition of Babri Masjid in Ayodhya, the communal riots spread to different parts of the country, including the border district of Dhubri.[12] Following it there has been communal tensions resulting in various localised reactions. In Golakganj, the Muslim households moved to one side of the railway track, which in present-day is identified as a Muslim locality, as claimed by a Muslim informant. One of my respondents in my early fieldwork days pointed out to the other side as the neighbourhood of '*Dariyas*' (long-bearded Muslim men). These opinions frequently featured in the Hindu-dominated parts of Dakhin Tokrarcherer where Muslim inhabitants are considered as the 'other' who cannot be trusted. The Muslims are often the topics of everyday conversations in which they are stereotyped as 'kidnappers' of Hindu women.

There were no veiled opinions; no subtle silences but clear indications of affiliations, beliefs and political positions when the private sphere of individual households and lives are explored. The walls in Golakganj, in which open references are made to the undercurrents of politics, resonated the strong and polemical words of the inhabitants. For the men, the market and their networks of friends become their source of informal information and suggestions to fulfil the criteria of the documentation process. It is through these informal networks that the people get to learn which government forms and what procedures are required. Although the NRC offices in the town are the official source of information, the networks and circles become informal sources of information. The extension of the neighbourhood to spaces beyond common lanes, backyards of houses, grocery shops and the market place allow the men to form their own circle of trust. This bonding among people from similar religious and linguistic backgrounds further them to consolidate their viewpoints and political opinions, which are reflected in the homogenous character of their neighbourhoods.

The Politics of Avoidance

In 2015, the enumeration process of the NRC began in Assam with an aim of identifying 'illegal' citizens residing in Assam. The issue

12 See https://www.sciencespo.fr/mass-violence-war-massacre-resistance/en/document/hindu-muslim-communal-riots-india-ii-1986-2011.html (accessed on 10 March 2020).

of 'illegal immigrants' has been at the centre of Assam's politics for long, and this process sought documents to prove one's existence and citizenship based on the cut-off date of 24 March 1971. The first draft of the NRC list was published on 31 December 2017. Following it, a few women in the neighbourhood, including Runu *mami* and Bina, did not find their names in it. Rupali, whose son had an alcohol problem and husband worked as a construction labourer, confided in me that she needed to go to court-*kachari* to get documents as her name was not in the list.

There was a tension in Bina's family as my host did not find her name in the list, although her son's and husband's names were in the first draft. Bina claimed that her father had never voted as he was a priest and would often travel, even as far as present-day Bangladesh, to perform rituals for people who sought his service. Those days, she recalled, there was no 'fencing' and required days of travel by foot, bullock carts, bicycle etc. The anxiety in Bina's household became more evident when her son began negotiating the bureaucratic maze at the local NRC and panchayat offices to check records and acquire papers during the first round of verification process that was carried out in the early months of 2018. Bina was evidently disturbed and compared the NRC process with matriculation exam, passing of which was important as otherwise she would be branded a 'Bangladeshi'. The term 'Bangladeshi' is used in Assam with resentment and hatred, as a way of abuse against people who are thought to be inferior, non-native, not belonging, and as someone who is 'illegal'. It is through the differences of language, religion and ethnicity that the dominant linguistic and tribal groups use it, and the term owes its construction in the anti-foreigner movement of 1979–1985 in Assam. The term might provoke suspicion against people and induce a deep sense of fear and anxiety of being shamed if labelled so.

However, Bina's son was able to track down Bina's mother's voting records from the district electoral office in Dhubri after two days of laborious search. Her son Gopal was advised by the people in the local NRC office in Golakganj to try and see if any documents could be obtained from the district headquarters of the election office. The electoral rolls in which Bina's mother's name was found was dated 1967, and these were obtained after submitting application forms in the election office in Dhubri. The electoral rolls up to midnight of 24 March 1971 could also be used as documents to prove ancestry.[13]

Although Bina was anxious about proving her citizenship, her precariousness and anxieties never found a mention in the conversations with her neighbours (it was strictly confined within the house). In everyday conversations among the womenfolk, the politics surrounding NRC was hardly discussed. They seemed barely concerned, as their discussions immediately after the publication of the first draft of the NRC on 31 December 2017 were about mundane affairs like income generation, health, finding brides for their sons or gossiping about newly married daughters-in-law. In one particular instance, Moni'r *ma*,[14] a woman in her early thirties with four kids and a husband struggling to find regular jobs, exclaimed in a lamenting tone, '*Ki je kortase, sorkar*' (I wonder, what is the government up to?), as she counted the amount required to travel to her village to get her school certificate. But she was snubbed by Runu *mami* to stop 'lecturing' on politics and help with the household work. Moni'r *ma* was replying to my question on whether she had found her name in the list. The document was meant for submission to the NRC office.

The space of the neighbourhood where the women would discuss their worries about their husbands, children and grandchildren to find '*moner shanti*' was mostly devoid of political content that they themselves were implicated in. It appeared that political discussions were not part of their intimate personal spaces, which were confined to domestic issues of health and hearth. Explaining why politics was not discussed in intimate spaces, Rudd (2000: 116) observes that politics was often referred to her during her fieldwork as 'dirty' (*nungra*), meaning unprincipled, as something unsavoury that morally upright people would not touch, a sullied game of bargaining and dishonesty. It was represented as something that could cause disharmony, unnecessary

13 As cited in the official website http://www.nrcassam.nic.in/admin-documents.html (accessed on 23 March 2020).

14 Moni's mother. It is a standard practice in Indian society for neighbours to address one another by their eldest son's or daughter's name.

disturbances and undignified quarrels among people in the family, caste, neighbourhood or village, who ideally should be friends and treat one another with respect (Rudd 2000: 119).

While the nation state proactively sought personal histories of belonging and proof of legality of existence as citizens, the women, despite being aware of one another's personal histories, avoided speaking about it in their everyday interactions. Although stories of migration from across the borders are known to members of the neighbourhood, the bonds of neighbourliness demanded trust, so as not to break the intimacy in their everyday ordinary lives. These are everyday efforts at peacekeeping to avoid any sort of sourness, bitterness and conflict in the everyday affairs of their lives, as, after all, one is bound to live in the same neighbourhood.

Bina was teased by her grandson as 'Bangladeshi', which irked her and compounded her fear of getting deported to Bangladesh. This was the common understanding and fear of the people even as the NRC process was going on. Media reports highlighted the number of people committing suicide was in the rise across the state during the NRC process, suggesting the deaths were due to non-inclusion in the NRC drafts, fear of detention camps and expulsion to Bangladesh.[15]

Although Bina was affected by politics, her suffering was not made visible in public but limited within the household. The women were directly affected by the NRC documentation process when they were summoned for verifications. All of them knew who in the neighbourhood received the notice, but none prioritised and discussed this in their everyday friendship circles. The fear of politics as something that can cause disharmony and rupture in the neighbourhood was real for these women, and hence it was relegated to the more intimate space of the household where fears, anger and frustration of the political situation were discussed by family members and possible solutions explored by way of finding an adviser or locating relevant documents.

---

15 Some of the news that appeared in popular newspapers can be accessed at https://www.hindustantimes.com/india-news/man-commits-suicide-after-exclusion-from-assam-s-nrc-draft-says-family/story-Bz826rGmrdqmsjZCMz4CtI.html; https://www.thehindu.com/news/national/kin-left-out-of-nrc-assam-man-commits-suicide/article24627220.ece (accessed on 23 March 2020).

Thus, the politics of the nation state was negotiated by these women in the local spaces of the neighbourhood by making it invisible in the realm of friendships and neighbourhood politics. It was not that it did not exist but was avoided deliberately. The neighbourhood thus comes across as a place where rules of avoidance are followed to maintain reciprocity of warmth and to withheld secrets to avoid conflict with neighbours. Rossier (2007), while discussing the concept of an open secret in the context of abortions in Burkina Faso, explains that a 'secret' is understood either as the product of conflicts of interest between individual, groups and values or it can be used as a device to hide, conceal from forbidden acts, legal violations and corruption. But the key to sharing a secret, as he argues, lies with whom it is shared, as good confidants are those who are either bound with secrecy through bonds of intimacy or shared transgression. The point that Rossier tries to make is that you either need to have committed a transgression together, and hence hold each other's secret, or one must be in confrontation, holding opposing views, and hence required to hide it from others. Therefore, what is shared or not shared is based on similarity and difference in the situation and views of the people. Hence conflict avoidance, mistrust, intimacy and trust are the factors that shape interactions in a neighbourhood with regard to expressing political views.

The people in this neighbourhood of this particular border town are well aware of one another's personal family histories of movement across the border, which was once fluid (before it was fenced), unguarded and unregulated in terms of movement between the two nations, particularly after the Assam Movement (1979–1985). As Bina said, 'Many of us have been visited by the police with 'notice' but what is the point in discussing all that?' By notice she meant the police asking the residents to enquire about doubtful voters (D voters), which sometimes require them to appear for case hearings in the Foreigners Tribunals court.[16] The women in this neighbourhood have witnessed

16 The border police wing of Assam police is also entrusted with carrying out such tasks, For details see https://police.assam.gov.in/portlet-sub-innerpage/functions (accessed on 23 March 2020).

one another's lives and personal troubles of husbands abandoning, alcoholic sons and sick husbands, and it is the everyday exchange of neighbourliness that prevents them from deliberating the politics of 'legality/illegality' of citizens. The bonds of intimacy and trust with neighbours allow for transgression in the boundary-making practices as the borderland residents in this particular neighbourhood are bound by memories and experiences of a fluid, unguarded and unfenced border. The boundary making is maintained through ethnic references of marriage alliances and ways of cooking and eating in the everyday setting. However, the aspects of mutual trust, intimacy and secret-keeping hold up the inhabitants of the neighbourhood.

The inhabitants of Dakhin Tokererchara are well aware of one another's cross-border movements at various times. They are also aware of some of the existing ties that their neighbours have with people across the border in present-day Bangladesh. Possessing the information of one another's histories and genealogies of settling and resettling have developed an unsaid collective understanding among them. Neither do they talk about it explicitly among themselves nor do they discuss the issues around the NRC documentation process. Thus, the avoidance of speaking about and around politics is maintained in the borderland neighbourhood.

Conclusion

By observing the everyday life of the people of this border town, this chapter attempts to demonstrate the neighbourhood as space where the politics of the nation is mediated and articulated through everyday discussions, memories and personal histories. The neighbourhood has an ambivalent quality of being public and private, as the space beyond the doors of the household becomes public but the household located within it is private and intimate. This is exemplified in the way the anxieties around the listing of names in the NRC was avoided by the women as a topic of public discussion but was discussed with family members in the household. The neighbourhood as a site of placemaking is embedded in the multilayered distinctions of overt and the covert politics, as was observed in the gossips about marriage alliances. The macro politics of identity in Assam, which they deliberately refrained to comment on, is overtly exposed in the subtle references to ethnicity.

While the political situation in the Indo-Bangladesh borderland in Assam impinged the discourse on 'legality/illegality', the residents of the borderland neighbourhoods transgressed the politics of ethnicity and language to sustain neighbourly relations. The search for '*moner shanti*' (peace of mind) in the routine and mundane neighbourly interactions between the women discreetly affirmed the process of seeking understanding and peace among themselves, while avoiding discussion about politics and keeping away elements that might disrupt friendly relations between them. In a heterogeneous neighbourhood, what can be spoken, avoided and expressed involve conscious and deliberate decision-making by neighbours to create intimate spaces of trust and warmth. Although avoidance and silence, in terms of discretion about discussing the political situation, might also appear to be a case of mistrust and fear of neighbours, it was revealed through sustained ethnographic fieldwork that avoidance and secret-keeping were beneath neighbourliness in the borderland neighbourhoods where questions of identity remain critical.

References

Appadurai, A. 1996. *Modernity at Large: Cultural Dimensions of Globalization.* London: University of Minnesota Press.

Bopegamage, A. 1957. 'Neighbourhood Relations in Indian Cities: Delhi'. *Sociological Bulletin*, Vol. 6, No. 1, pp. 34–42.

De Neve, G. and H. Donner. 2006. 'Space, Place and Globalization: Revisiting the Urban Neighbourhood in India'. In *The Meaning of the Local: Politics of Place in Urban India,* edited by G. De Neve and H. Donner, pp. 1–20. New York: UCL Press.

Duchesne, S. and F. Haegel. 2007. 'Avoiding or Accepting Conflict in Public Talk'. *British Journal of Political Science,* Vol. 37, No. 1, pp. 1–22.

Mann, H.P. 1954. 'The Concept of Neighborliness'. *American Journal of Sociology*, Vol. 60, No. 2, pp. 163–168.

Ring, L.A. 2006. *Zenana: Everyday Peace in Karachi Apartment Building.* Bloomington: Indiana University Press.

Rossier, C. 2007. 'Abortion: An Open Secret? Abortion and Social Network Involvement in Burkina Faso'. *Reproductive Health Matters*, Vol. 15, No. 30, pp. 230–238.

Rudd, E.A. 2000. 'Talking Dirty About Politics: A View From a Bengali Village'. In *The Everyday State and Society in Modern India,* edited by C.J. Fuller and B. Veronique, pp. 115–135. New Delhi: Social Science Press.

Snedden, D. 1926. 'Neighbors and Neighborliness'. *Social Forces*, Vol. 5, No. 2, pp. 231–236.

Van Schendel, W. 2004. *The Bengal Borderland.* London: Anthem Press.

Zang, X. 2003. 'Ethnic Differences in Neighboring Behaviour in Urban China'. *Sociological Focus*, Vol. 36, No. 3, pp. 197–218.

8

Home-ing the World and World-ing the Home: An Understanding of Singlehood, Rental Housing and Neighbourliness

Rashi Bhargava and Richa Chilana

Rental housing offers us an opportunity to unravel various ways in which people negotiate spatial and social dynamics in a neighbourhood. While scholars have looked at various discriminatory aspects in relation to identity and rental housing,[1] lived experiences of middle-class single migrant men and women have largely been ignored. Through a focus on the embodied experiences of single men and women (referred to as 'singles' hereafter) in terms of their access to rental housing and interaction or lack thereof with their neighbourhoods, this chapter seeks to explore lived experiences, sociocultural attitudes and perceptions in relation to tenants–neighbours.

As the chapter intends to focus on practices and everydayness of this social reality, it borrows insights from De Certeau's 'ways of operating' (1988) to understand the relationship between singlehood, rental housing and neighbourhood. De Certeau has argued that people (or the 'user'—a term used by De Certeau) actively behave, act and in turn resist the impositions and/or effects of wider forces within the sphere

1 For studies linking residential patterns and class, see Castells (1977), Kurtulus (2007), Sandhu (2003), Soni (2000) and Thrift and Amin (1987). For studies on segregation based on race and ethnicity, see Nick Drydakis (2011), Jackson and Smith (1981) and Peach, Robinson and Smith (1981). For a more recent account connecting religion and urban segregation, see Jamil (2017). For studies on migration, neighbourhood, kinship and residential patterns, see M.S.A. Rao (1991). The list here is by no means exhaustive but only an indication of some of the many issues that were addressed within urban studies.

of politics, culture and commerce. Mobilising De Certeau is pertinent for this study as approaches to the neighbourhood that are informed by Henri Lefebvre's (1991) *Production of Space* do not acknowledge how neighbourliness might get constructed beyond one's immediate physical space.

In recent decades, scholarship in urban studies has looked at neighbourhoods as constantly being made, unmade and conceptualised as spaces where hegemonic discourses, dominant practices and power struggles unfold on a day-to-day basis (De Neve and Donner 2006). Earlier, the shift towards placing emphasis on human agency and autonomy, as against structures and their ability to structure and stabilise what was once deemed necessary, was questioned by geographers like Massey (1994), Duncan (1994) and Duncan and Duncan (2004). Their works allow us to look at the spatial and its potential to transform the social through a space–time framework imbued with power relations. In the Indian context too, scholars have engaged with interlinkages between space and gender, feminism and geography and delineated a feminist framework for understanding urban spaces and processes, arguing that city spaces are gendered scapes and need to be explored accordingly (Chanda 2017; Phadke 2007; Raju and Lahiri-Dutt 2011; Ranade 2007).

Informed by this scholarship, we explore the possibility of engendering neighbourhood and neighbourliness through practices and experiences related to rented accommodations accessed and inhabited by singles. The research looks at the narratives of singlehood and their experiences of accessing rented accommodation and establishing neighbourliness. Coming from diverse professional backgrounds such as academia, publishing industry, social sector, media, film/entertainment/fashion industry, information technology, law and the corporate sector, the respondents for this study are between the age-group of twenty-five to forty years and have migrated to the National Capital Region (Delhi-NCR). Along with the responses gathered from the field, we also drew upon what Okely (1996) calls 'retrospective fieldwork' by recollecting our own experiences as single women and the conversations we have had with other single men and women over the years.

Most of the respondents in this study are/were residing in two urban villages[2] in Delhi: Kishangarh and Munirka. Kishangarh is located between Mehrauli and Vasant Kunj while Munirka Village is located close to Jawaharlal Nehru University (JNU) and the Indian Institute of Technology (IIT), Delhi. Both these villages, often referred to as *Lal Dora*,[3] are located in South West Delhi and are predominantly inhabited by Jats, the primary landholding community in the area. With a boom in the real estate market in the 1990s, one can locate a transition of these villages from rural to semi-urban and the community from an agrarian-pastoral to entrepreneurial (Pati 2017). In these two neighbourhoods, renting out emerged as a profitable venture leading to the mushrooming of one-room sets, now easily accessible to young professionals who have migrated to Delhi.

The *mohallā*, the space of this study, is not just a spatial unit; it comprises familial and sociocultural attachments between its residents. As a *mohallā*, 'it is an evolved reality that resembles the *jati* or endogamous caste enclaves of rural communities, and, like those enclaves, relates to the occupational, religious or geographical origin of the *mohallā* dwellers' (Raju 1980: 287). Despite urbanisation and education, religion, caste and kinship have not lost their hold on the society, which is undergoing a process of 'retribalisation' (Sopher 1964).[4] Most of the houses in the *mohallā* in Munirka and Kishangarh are owned by members of a particular community. In addition to these

---

2 A term used by Herbert Gans (1964), who defined it as a site where 'people are closely related, interact on a regular basis and share similar socio-economic circumstances'. Cited in De Neve and Donner (2006: 8).

3 As cited in Sushmita Pati (2017: 94):

> The land earmarked for village *abadi* and the agricultural land of the village were duly demarcated in the land settlement of 1908–1909 and the *abadi* site was circumscribed in the village map in red ink; therefore, the name *lal dora* [literally, red ink]. It is still in use with *lal dora* as the village residential land and the extended *lal dora* land which was left outside the village as vacant land, but has now seen massive mushrooming of buildings. The borders between *lal dora* and extended *lal dora* are extremely amorphous and, therefore, a source of confusion, and it is this confusion which makes a property legal or illegal.

4 As cited in Raju (1980).

two areas, some of our respondents also reside in Kamla Nagar, Vijay Nagar, South Extension, Anand Niketan and Noida.

These urban areas thrive on rent economy as mentioned above. They do not deny access to singles but might impose their ideas of 'decent' behaviour and social order. The contrary pulls of globalisation and re-territorialisation have led to a desperate urge to revive institutions of family and community for a more secure mooring in a rapidly changing world (Duncan and Duncan 2004; Harvey 1989; Massey 1994). The lived experiences of those at the margins of a normative/familial set-up provide a vantage point to look at how dominant norms and perceptions are embodied and challenged by those who do not conform.

Narratives of Singlehood

The understanding of singlehood has varied across time and space. It is seen as a socially devalued identity (Simon 1987), the absence of a marital bond and motherhood, a socially and sexually deviant state (Gordon 1994), associated with either a lack/void (Bell and Yans 2007), a waiting phase, an intermediary stage (Lahad 2012) and, hence, a pitiable state.

Our respondents confirm similar condescending perceptions of how others look at their single status as a transitory phase, a 'chronic disease', a 'heinous crime' or a 'dangerous situation that needs immediate attention'. Aditya,[5] a thirty-seven-year-old male informant who migrated from Kanpur, has lived in Delhi for almost nine years and is currently working in the corporate sector, pointed out that different generations respond to singlehood differently. For older people, it is like 'getting off the Titanic before it sinks,' but those who are young consider single people as part of their gang or relatable. Sushant, a thirty-year-old male informant from Jaipur who works as an assistant professor in University of Delhi, stated that singlehood is acceptable when one is a student, but when one starts working, she/he is expected to have a family. Anupam, a thirty-seven-year-old male assistant professor

5 All names in the chapter have been changed to protect the identities of the respondents.

from Kolkata, pointed out that a single person is the centre of all social conversations. He said if a person has been single for long, it is assumed that she/he would be incapable of making serious decisions.

The refusal to see single men as complete and mature adults is a recurrent theme in their narratives. We find similar narratives in the responses of single women. Many respondents shared that they often feel they are eyed with suspicion, are negatively labelled and their characters, as well as social, economic, mental and physical well-being, questioned. Some of these labels include reckless, eccentric, indulgent, untrustworthy, vagabond and so on. Although this applies to both women and men, it is accentuated in the case of women who may find themselves in adverse situations and subjected to harsh opinions, questions and criticisms. Abhilasha, a thirty-one-year-old female respondent who has migrated from Dibrugarh, Assam, and is currently employed in the corporate sector, said that single women over thirty years are often presumed to be desperate and miserable: 'Men often consider them to be an easy catch while women look at them either with caution or with pity'. Most of these responses to singlehood by others stem from an inability to understand the motivation behind staying single, which could be a voluntary state of being, as put forth succinctly by Swastika, a thirty-one-year-old migrant lawyer from Moradabad, Uttar Pradesh. She said, 'I think, for society singlehood is a threat.' Single women are considered more threatening than single men to the social order, as is illustrated by the responses. Uncontrolled/undomesticated female sexuality is seen as a threat in a society that priorities the social bonds of marriage and family over individual choice.

Contesting these dominant perceptions of being, our research brought forth a counter-narrative, enabling an insight into the everyday negotiations that have strong spatial connotations to singlehood. Singlehood comes across, in this study, as founded on elements of choice, freedom and control over oneself and one's surroundings. Thus, typical responses that we received from male respondents were about a bigger pool of choice, not being tied up in a relationship/commitment or possibilities of fleeting relationships. For instance, Satyajit, a thirty-seven-year-old academician, said, 'being single offers you the choice to reach out to others with greater flexibility and a bigger basket to choose from as far as instant or temporal companionship is concerned.' Karan, a thirty-year-old respondent who used to stay in Delhi before he got a job in a small town in Haryana, stated, 'being single for me is the possibility to flirt with many people without having to think much about it.' Men were more open to desiring and articulating their desires as compared to female respondents. It was interesting that only two of our female respondents were vocal about their sexuality in terms of admitting that they felt lonely on the days they were horny or masturbated to pleasure themselves.

In terms of desires and aspirations, single women were found to be more vocal about their time, leisure—often unavailable to women in a familial set-up—and self-sufficiency in finding their 'self' and their own happiness. Female respondents emphasised the liberating nature of their status, the possibility of being in control of their lives, being responsible for every decision, be it mundane or extraordinary, and the ample opportunities that are available to them that are often unavailable to married women. Twenty-seven-year-old Prerna from Lucknow, who works in a publishing house in Delhi pointed out that being single means having a lot of 'me time'. For another, being single was to have an identity of one's own. This set of responses gets complicated when Rupali, a thirty-seven-year-old female doctoral candidate, pointed out that being single means taking care of one's physical, emotional and mental health and being solely responsible for one's 'everyday social reproduction', which can be an 'emotionally consuming experience'. Contrary to stereotypical perceptions, in these responses, singlehood comes across as taking charge of one's life and happiness, which could be physically and emotionally draining but also a rich learning experience.

Sometimes in situations such as illness or despair, their very space and sole control over their lives may become difficult to negotiate, and they may find themselves in a vulnerable state. Maitreyee, a twenty-seven-year-old assistant editor from Kolkata who resides in South Delhi, said, 'When I have bad days at work or something happens that really irritates me, I don't project that anger and hurt on another person because it is a terrible thing to do.' She also said that she felt bad about her single status when she felt lonely in a big city. However, such a feeling is temporary as indicated in the response by Rupali, who suggested that being single is not about being on an island with no social relations or support system. She highlighted the significance of her large group of friends in dealing with adverse situations.

Besides the opportunities offered by city spaces, the luxury and liberty of being on one's own term without being burdened by intrusive questions possibly lured some of our respondents out of their parental homes and into the homes they tried to create for themselves. Arpita, a thirty-four-year-old entertainment industry consultant from Ahmedabad, talked about the difference between her place and her parents' dwelling. She craved for the independent house she had, where there were 'no questions, no answers'. Arianla, a thirty-seven-year-old academician who has migrated from Dimapur, associated her parents' house with the carefree days of childhood. The imagination of what a home encapsulates is still predicated on the parental dwelling and there are attempts to recreate the same ambience and aesthetics in their own homes, especially during festivals and special occasions, as was shared by Rhia, a thirty-seven-year-old female assistant professor from Lucknow who hosted her friends on numerous occasions. Thus, the establishment of a home and the process of homemaking were seen as essential to becoming an adult and intimately associated with forging a coherent and well-integrated self. However, in their attempts to create a space for themselves, they faced various challenges that emerged from the conventional association of home with family and familial relationships, which, in the case of our respondents, were missing.

Home and Homemaking

The idea of home, for the respondents in our study, was realised through their arduous journeys of accessing rented accommodation after they migrated to Delhi. The considerations in realising this idea were reflected in the preoccupation with the locality, neighbourhood, security, parks, proximity to the workplace, essential services in the vicinity and so on. Female respondents shared their concerns about staying in a gated community, but both male and female respondents concurred about their preference for a clean, spacious, affordable home that is close to their workplaces and a locality that houses other single men and women. This urge to stay surrounded by other singles could be to save themselves from unsolicited attention and bias, but it could also be another version of creating a neighbourhood of similar and like-minded people. From the responses, it can be said that belonging is often restricted to their homes and not so much to the neighbourhoods because of the all-pervasive panoptic gaze. Rhia, who is staying in Kishangarh for the past five years, said that she shifted to her current rented accommodation mainly because she already knew a number of single people from JNU who were staying in the same locality. She also shared that after staying in the same area for so many years, the entire neighbourhood knew about her and her single status, but very few (overtly) commented on it (although she has noticed a change in the way her neighbour—a family of four—interacts with her). In the initial years of her stay, there used to be an exchange of pleasantries on an everyday basis and sweets/food on festivals, but this does not happen anymore. Interestingly, there is no change in the way the same family behaves with her single male neighbour.

Neighbourhoods are 'space-based communities' where living at close quarters with another may or may not create a sense of community; it is rather a 'form of communing' (Betancur and Smith 2016). One of the reasons why people with similar conditions or economic status are part of the same neighbourhood is because people consciously seek those like them to live around and try collectively to maintain the status quo of that space. Kavya, a twenty-five-year-old female respondent from Mohali who is currently pursuing a research degree alongside her job as a lecturer, pointed out,

> I don't usually worry about who lives next to me, but I prefer renting a room in localities which also accommodate a number of students and single working professionals. It gives me some assurance about the mobility that I will be allowed to have. If my parents are participating in the decision, they usually make sure that there are not many 'boys' [read: single men] as my neighbours, or living in the same building, for that matter. Although, it's not been my priority to worry about it. Lately, they don't ask much.

She also pointed out how other single tenants seldom ask questions but married neighbours are curious about her career, choices, routine, lifestyle and so on. Those with teenage kids do not interact at all, considering singles a bad influence. With regard to the parental dwelling, one might be engaged in some sort of 'communing' or interaction with the neighbourhood as one is a part of a normative familial set-up, whereas in the case of single tenants, attempts are made to ward off unsolicited attention, which might take the form of curiosity, interference and criticism. Rhia shared,

> When I go back home for vacations, nobody will force me to interact with my neighbours but there is an understanding that I will meet my parents' friends and generally talk to them about what is happening in my life. But when I am in Delhi, I generally avoid conversations with my neighbours unless it's absolutely necessary which seldom happens.

Most singles in our study admitted that they do not interact with their neighbours because of the tremendous curiosity these people have about their lives. Sometimes, it may lead to an aversion to interacting with families as pointed out by Satyajit, thus guarding their private space even more closely.

The freedom to dress and undress and being alone in their private space was one of the most liberating experiences of staying alone, according to most of our respondents. Anupam pointed out that being single and having a house of one's own meant 'solitude, being able to move around my house with or without clothes, listening and playing music 24×7'. Another thirty-nine-year-old male respondent, Kaito who is working in the private sector and originally from Kohima, said, 'Delhi is too hot. The less you wear the better. So home is also about the freedom to dress and undress.' While our male respondents indicated comfort with their naked bodies by pointing out how they used to roam around naked in the house, female respondents spoke of being braless as liberating.

The ways of inhabiting these spaces also challenge the conventional division of space into public/private. Our respondents made certain parts of their home exclusive/personal/intimate by limiting socialising to the living room. Sonakshi, a twenty-five-year-old from Bareilly who works as a consultant in Delhi, pointed out that the only reason she bought furniture was to limit access to her bedroom, thus indicating how within the private space of her home there were some sections such as the living room that she saw as 'public'. We often think of space in terms of boundaries and boundedness (Massey 1994), and in the case of our respondents, the need to create an exclusive space indicates that others, and possibly they themselves, do not see their homes as completely private. A number of respondents shared how people saw their homes as a readily available space unlike those of married people. For instance, Niharika, a twenty-five-year-old who works in the entertainment industry, shared that one of her friends had remarked 'it [Niharika's house] feels like home but can also double up as a club'. In a similar tone, Anupam shared, 'My male friends, single or married, would request me to give them the keys of my room if they had to meet someone special whom they could not meet in other places. My room keys would become more precious than me.' He added that such liberty may never be taken with a married person's house. This indicates how a home harbouring a normative heterosexual couple assumes a certain sanctity as against that of a single person. Thus, it was indicated how single and married people's homes were seen as belonging to two opposite ends of the spectrum of signification.

A non-geographical/non-spatial understanding of home was shared by our respondents who suggested that home could be their entire paraphernalia, a bundle of possessions, an SUV with a guitar and a tennis racket or just a person you want to share a significant portion of your day with. Home could also be one's own self. For example, Maitreyee said, 'Home can be a person you come back to after a crazy day just to find your peace.' When asked if societal perceptions would change when they own a house, most of them replied that their singlehood would still be stigmatised.

The various dimensions of home that were reflected in the responses of single men and women challenged the conventional understanding of the home, which is seen as rooted, fixed and stable and a place that signifies a sense of belonging. It is an assertion of the desire for autonomy and the need to be away from surveillance and control. It is a process, a result of your physical and emotional labour, a 'temporary safe harbour', but also a painful process as indicated in the following section because of societal perceptions about singlehood.

Biases and Un-belonging

The narratives shared by our respondents unveiled the singlism[6] they faced in their attempts to establish a home in rented accommodation. Singlism created hurdles in their desire to access rental housing, and even when they attained access, the panoptic gaze of the landlords and neighbours made them uncomfortable or forced them to toe the line. Pointing to one such process, some of our respondents shared how 'gossip' and 'gossip-mongering' can and sometimes emerged as a constraining factor while undertaking many of their activities. Rupali, who had temporarily shifted with a male friend, was told by her domestic help that many in the locality thought she and her friend were married to each other and hence residing together. Gossip, thus, can be seen as an indicator of societal perceptions and norms and might act as an instrument of surveillance and control especially in places that house closed communities. Many a time, there are other people such as landlords, Resident Welfare Associations (RWAs) and neighbours who would devise mechanisms to control those who seem to have crossed the boundaries set for them.

However, both single men and women are subjected to different forms of surveillance in their rented accommodations. For example, Rohan, a twenty-six-year-old assistant professor who shifted to Delhi from Champaran, Bihar, shared how, when he shifted to his present rented accommodation, there was also a compulsion to hire the help who used to work in the landlord's house, and if that wasn't done the help hired by the tenant was forced to leave. This can be seen as an attempt on the part of the landlord to keep an eye on single tenants; this surveillance is perceived to increase further when women are on their own with no family (read male) members to oversee them, as in the case of migrant working women. Hence, women who migrate to metropolitan cities might find it difficult to carve a space for themselves, especially within an already established space like a neighbourhood,

6 Singlism is a term coined by Bella DePaulo and Wendy Morris (2005) to talk of the stereotyping, bias/discrimination against single people. It happens because of the unquestioned faith and belief in the family system and values.

and often when they do, they are subjected to surveillance either by landlords or neighbours. Swastika pointed out that since she is the only single woman in her locality, all her neighbours keep an eye on her movements. A neighbour used to knock on her door in the middle of the night to tell her that her talking on the phone and walking in her flat was audible and disturbed those around. She said, 'I had a neighbour tell me that everyone knows what type of things go on at my place and that there are boys coming in at ungodly hours, and also this is a respectable neighbourhood where such kind of activities won't be tolerated.' Niharika also shared something similar about her guests being questioned every time they come visiting her.

> Of late, the guards in our colony have started questioning our male friends as to where they're headed, to meet whom, what the purpose of their visit is, etc. It is annoying and embarrassing for guests to be questioned in such a manner and I believe this happens only because we're *bachelors* living on our own. I have never seen guests of *family* households being questioned in a similar fashion.

These responses lead to a scenario in which the behaviour of single tenants is judged against the quotidian ideas of decency, which was more severe in the case of single women tenants. Their attempts to create a space of their own was determined by the wider structural discourse of acceptable behaviour, thus shaping 'gendered subjectivities'. The quotidian notions of respectable and decent behaviour were also used as 'discursive weaponry' by landlords and neighbours to determine who belonged and who did not to the neighbourhood (Vera-Sanso 2006).

It was believed by landlords and neighbours that single men would rip apart the place and single women would indulge in promiscuous activities. Singlism took the form of curiosity, unsolicited advice or downright hostility, but it was greater in the case of single women because it was assumed that they came from conservative families and would have a 'wild phase' when away from home. This is also indicative of the presumption that women should be restricted to a private domain and their relocation to another city is often perceived as entering the public space both literally (as working women) and symbolically (since they have moved away from their hometown and family). The feminine and the local are often associated with each other, and it is believed that women lead more local lives than men, that is, most women tend to be geographically less mobile and lead more circumscribed lives (Massey 1994). However, this pattern started getting dismantled because of new economic, social and political forces and is unsettling for the proponents of the dominant social order. There is a realignment that takes place in response to the changing global realities—roles are allocated and boundaries get dissolved (Ibid.). One can look at these urban villages and the possibilities they offer in the larger context of global economic forces that have allowed large-scale migration of the urban middle class to metropolitan cities. However, many of these urban villages have neither a gated structure providing security nor formal RWAs that can be approached in case of any grievances. Thus, the nature of social interactions between neighbours and single tenants in these neighbourhoods remain quite minimal. Despite so many attempts to make space for themselves within the neighbourhood, many of our respondents pointed out that seeking and getting help from landlords and neighbours were not easy.

Furthermore, there is an aestheticisation of power relations and exclusion. When searching for an accommodation, Abhilasha was once told by a landlady, '*Humein toh MNC wale boys chahiye, beta bura mat maanna, par ladkiyon ke saath problem ho sakta hai*' (We are looking for boys who work in MNCs. Do not feel bad *beta* [lit. for boys but in Delhi often used for both boys and girls to display affection] but there can be problems with girls). Anupam also shared his experience with the landlord: 'No girls, no drinks, no parties, no pan chewing, no loud music, payment between 1st and 7th of the month.' The presence of single men and women is seen as hampering the aesthetic and community values of these neighbourhoods, which are ostensibly only for families that reproduce the dominant social order. Home and neighbourhood are a result of wider culturally specific forces that play a significant role in delineating what is socially acceptable within a particular space, no matter how much that space has been altered by the global processes (Ibid.). They are, thus, a result of conscious design, planning and struggle, but they are also the 'materialization of inherent antagonisms, exclusions, unarticulated racism [singlism in our case], and reactions to global complexity as a threat to "the local"' (Duncan and Duncan 2004: 3–4). Duncan and Duncan argue how globalisation has created, on the one hand, a fear of placelessness and, on the other, a desire to belong, resulting in a kind of 'reterritorialization and search for traditional values' (Ibid.: 5). This can be seen in our study where the landlords who invariably belong to the same community try to make earnest attempts to keep a check on their tenants and make them conform.

Living in such a hostile and alienating social environment then also gives rise to insecurity and anxieties. Most of our respondents, especially women, were forced to make compromises on security to gain access to rental housing. For instance, Arpita shared, 'The one thing I've compromised on for getting this house is lax security. So, I take my own precautions and lock the doors and windows at night.' Similar kinds of concerns were also shown by other female respondents. Rhia pointed out that she sleeps with a knife under her mattress and convinced her landlady to get an iron gate fixed for security. This is not a concern that a single male tenant in the opposite flat has. Prerna also shared that safety was one of her primary considerations while looking for a house, but even when she found a flat in a gated locality, the guards/security team were partial towards 'regular residents' (those living with families) and did not look favourably at 'bachelors'. There was a difference between her and her parents' relationship with their respective neighbourhoods. She said,

> My parents are more at ease in their society, just more naturally comfortable with asking for what they think their house as part of that society deserves. Living as 'bachelors', we tend to hold back on making demands. To be fair, we haven't really needed to.

Thus, given how single tenants are made to feel that they are *not* a part of the society, a feeling that gets so deeply ingrained, they find themselves incapable of demanding their dues as residents of a locality.

Experiential narratives of our respondents revealed that because of both subtle and overt discrimination, singles devise various mechanisms to get access to accommodation. Although, through their tactics they may manage to operate 'within the enemy's field of vision', these very tactics might secretly configure their perceptions, everyday practices and conditions of social life (De Certeau 1988: 37, 97). Our respondents either pretended to be married or engaged, didn't disclose their sexualities (as pointed out by a respondent who identifies as gay) or invited their parents while moving in to give the impression that a family would be staying or specifically looked for houses where the landlord didn't stay or simply agreed to everything outlined in the rent agreement (to bypass it later). Satyajit, who used to stay in Kishangarh before moving to Greater Noida, pointed out, 'My current housing society has no allowance for bachelors but I managed to sneak in. There are several ways to outsmart the system and they are employed whenever needed.' He shared that when he was interviewed by the RWA members, he told them that his father will be staying with him. Niharika pointed out,

> Well, on paper we aren't allowed to smoke or drink on the premises. We can't have men over after 10 pm (not even male family members). However, our broker was quick to tell us that this was just a written formality for the housing society authorities and RWA. We were told that as long as we're not loud and disturbing or creating trouble for our neighbours, we can do what we want.

These 'ways of operating' do not come across as a complete negation of what was/is expected of them. Rather, they can be seen as an attempt to appropriate societal acceptability by claiming to be a part of a normative set-up and use them to 'manufacture respectability' (Phadke 2007). For instance, in one case, two of our respondents who were dating convinced their potential landlord that they were married and the woman had a job that required a lot of travelling. This was done mainly to make sure that the woman, who was from Delhi itself, could visit whenever she liked and could stay for a few days without the landlord objecting to it. They are now married and stay in a gated colony in Kalkaji.

Social acceptability by manufacturing respectability through various tactics has been the predominant form of negotiation that our respondents engaged in, which led them to adhere to societal norms and conventions to access an already established space. It is noteworthy that the process does not end once access to rental accommodation is achieved; rather, it becomes more rigorous and may take the form of self-censorship thereafter. Abhijeet, a thirty-year-old respondent from Chinsurah, West Bengal, pointed out,

> There were no explicit behavioural codes in the housing society, but I made a conscious effort to behave in a certain way. For instance, I keep the volume of the music low so that there are no complaints from the neighbours about single people being noisy.

Similar sentiments were echoed by Arianla who very consciously made sure that she does not disturb her landlord: 'I always try to behave myself, restrict guests and late nights for the first four or five months in a new place.' The urge to manufacture respectability is more urgent when one has just moved to a new neighbourhood. These responses show how single tenants are consciously trying to not fit into the stereotype about single people, which is that they are rowdy, noisy, irresponsible, promiscuous, insolent and inconsiderate. They also pointed out that noise made by children in the neighbourhood, which might be a problem for single people or those who are childless, isn't seen as a problem, but it is assumed that single men and women will be noisy, and hence seen as a nuisance for the neighborhood. The attempts by our respondents to recede in the background or be invisible is indicated in their inability to complain about the noise of children, which might be music to their parents' ears but not to a tenant's. On the other hand, the complain about loud music played in the homes of these tenants is identified as *legitimate* by others in the neighbourhood.

While both male and female respondents mentioned that they were conscious of the noise they make, many female respondents pointed out that they behaved in a *respectable* way adhering to the norms of *family conformity*, such as not having many male friends at home, smoking outdoors and buying condoms or liquor from stores away from their place or being careful of what they wear outside. This shows how the attempt to shape and reshape neighbourhood identities constructs 'gendered subjectivities'. These 'ways of operating' of single women are what De Certeau calls the 'art of the weak' (1988), but they also inadvertently end up reproducing hegemonic constructs of ideal womanhood. When our single female respondents entertained at home, they admitted to playing an ideal hostess and being assisted by their other female guests while the men relaxed and did not contribute to household chores. They may be able to resist marriage but their everyday ways of living and behaving might be embedded in the confines of 'ideal' femininity that they may have internalised over a period of time.

Interestingly, these single tenants often resist normative codes of behaviour by trying to *un-belong* in the neighbourhood. To un-belong, they resort to minimising their interactions with their neighbours. For instance, Arianla shared, 'I hardly know who lives in the house next door/across the road, so there is no question of neighbours forming a support system. Like me, most of my neighbours are renters who are just temporary residents, so there is hardly any interaction.' Kavya mentioned that the only time she turns to her neighbours for support is when she is locked out of her house and cannot reach her landlord. Neighbours also avoid getting involved, unless she has stayed in a place for long and 'won their trust'. The urge to embrace the temporary and transient or the refusal to 'settle' is evident in the response by Satyajit who considered his home and neighbourhood 'a temporary abode'.

From the responses of single tenants, *un-belonging* can be conceptualised as the inability to belong *because of the rampant singlism* in their attempts to establish a home or refusal to belong/or feel a part of the normative set-up that emphasises 'settling down'. Single tenants lack belonging in their inhabited neighbourhoods not only because of the biases against them but also due to their refusal to belong, as they were not allowed to 'be' or exist on their own terms. For them, home and neighbourhood are elusive concepts, always in the state of becoming and unbecoming and imagined as placeless, ephemeral, transient spaces as against the fixity often associated with them. This un-belonging is often paralleled with another kind of belonging that transcends geography and territoriality. Single tenants referred to their large circle of friends and acquaintances as their support system, which was more approachable and personal than the neighbourhood in which they resided. Few earlier studies (Keller 1968; McClenahan 1929, 1945; Sweetzer 1941) have argued that 'geographical' neighbourhoods can be transcended because of the wider network of attachments and associations made possible by transport, communication, lifestyles and so on.[7] The notion of a placeless or non-geographical neighbourhood forged by single tenants is a domain for future research, and it requires more in-depth engagement and analysis, which is beyond the scope of this chapter.

Conclusion

From the above discussion, one can clearly see how singles are seen as deviant and subjected to discrimination in their efforts to access and maintain rental housing. Singlism often pushes them to the margins. This can largely be seen as a result of a process where social relations, power dynamics and spatial organisation are intricately linked to each other. For most of our respondents, locality, cleanliness, safety and distance from the workplace were key considerations in their search for rented accommodation, but many a time they had to compromise on them owing to the constraints they faced in finding an accommodation. It was the bias against single tenants that made them compromise and stay in urban villages that thrive on rent economy and are heterogeneous in terms of social composition but not necessarily tolerant of heterogeneity when it comes to values and norms.

In a few cases, moving away was an escape from constantly adhering to *respectable* and *decent* behaviours in and around the parental home. It is what motivated the shift to urban spaces. Hence, the tragic irony of the need to 'manufacture respectability' to access rental housing indicates the sorry predicament of single tenants. What is interesting to note is that this may not necessarily be perceived as a problem by every single person, and they may act according to what is expected of them, often adhering to societal norms and conventions. While there are some who might question norms, albeit in limited ways, there are others who reject the idea completely. But as our study shows, they

7 This new state of affairs is called a 'personal neighbourhood', which is 'spatially discontinuous and compositionally unique' (Sweetzer 1941: 42), a shift from 'a neighbouring of place to a neighbouring of taste' (Keller 1968: 61) and 'contact clusters' with friends and support systems scattered all across the city (Riemer 1951).

might not be able to do so because of the power dynamics between the tenants (both men and women, but more in the case of women) and the landlords or between the outsiders (tenants) and the insiders (resident neighbours).

Although the neighbourhood is defined as a space-based community, an analysis of single tenants' negotiation with their neighbourhoods indicates how their relationship with their neighbours is marred by suspicion, hostility, caution, interference, but more often, indifference. The inability of the neighbours to understand the unconventional choice (of being single) and lifestyles of single tenants or to avoid being probed about their lives was cited as the most common reason behind the refusal to interact with neighbours. When asked about their support systems, most of them mentioned their close friends and colleagues, thus transcending the geographical neighbourhood. Fluid geographies are shaped by and in turn shape fluid identities. 'Progressive geographies' can be created by de-territorialisation or the creation of fluid, proliferating and heterogenous spaces and by resisting the urge to essentialise, naturalise and ghettoise identity (Duncan 1996). The focus on the predicament of single women and men and rental housing enable us to see the political nature of space and how, despite or perhaps due to globalisation, geographies/spaces are still struggling with fluid identities. The lived experiences of our respondents raise serious doubts about the 'progressive geographies' discussed by Duncan. Although places like Kishangarh and Munirka opened their doors to singles, the struggle to gain access to rental housing and the manoeuvring to maintain that access indicate the contrary pulls of re-territorialisation and de-territorialisation. By employing tactics such as lying that their parents would be staying with them or pretending to be married to their friends or live-in partners, our respondents' 'ways of operating' enabled the possibilities of entering spaces that would have otherwise been denied to them. But these tactics also lay bare the strategies of hegemonic forces and institutions that govern their ways of entering, living in or inhabiting a space. An analysis of the responses indicates that the bias is greater in case of single women, perhaps because of the association of feminine with the local, which when dissociated leads to concern and caution among proponents of the dominant order.

A realignment of geographical space also leads to realignment in social relations where existing roles and boundaries are dissolved or reworked. The entry of singles in urban villages because of global socioeconomic forces has led to a similar kind of realignment where these places are sites of an interesting dynamic between an earnest attempt to recreate the *mohallā* on the one hand and the creation of a heterogeneous space because of the dependence on rent economy on the other hand. The heterogeneity of the neighbourhood does not translate into acceptance of alternative/unconventional ways of living and being, leading to *un-belonging* in the neighbourhoods by those who may find themselves at the margins.

References

Bell, R.M. and V. Yans. 2007. 'Introduction'. In *Women on Their Own: Interdisciplinary Perspectives on Being Single,* edited by R.M. Bell and V. Yans, pp. 1–15. New Burnswick, New Jersey and London: Rutgers University Press.

Betancur, J.J. and J.L. Smith. 2016. *Claiming Neighbourhood: New Ways of Understanding Urban Change.* Urbana: University of Illinois Press.

Blunt, A. and R. Dowling. 2006. *Home.* London: Routledge.

Castells, M. 1977. *The Housing Question: A Marxist Approach.* London: Routledge.

Chanda, I. 2017. *Selfing the City: Single Women Migrants and Their Lives in Kolkata.* New Delhi: Sage Publications and Kolkatta: Stree.

Chatterjee, P. 1993. *The Nation and Its Fragments: Colonial and Postcolonial Histories.* Princeton, NJ: Princeton University Press.

De Certeau, M. 1988. *The Practice of Everyday life.* Berkeley: University of California Press.

De Neve, G. and H. Donner. 2006. 'Space, Place and Globalisation: Revisiting the Urban Neighbourhood in India'. In *The Meaning of the Local: Politics of Place in Urban India,* edited by Geert de Neve and Henrike Donner, pp. 1–20. London: Routledge/Cavendish.

De Paulo, B. and W. Morris. 2005. 'Singles in Society and Science'. *Psychological Inquiry,* Vol. 16, Nos 2–3, pp. 57–83.

Donner, H. 2006. 'The Politics of Gender, Class and Community in a Central Calcutta Neighbourhood'. In *The Meaning of the Local: Politics of Place in Urban India,* edited by Geert de Neve and Henrike Donner, pp. 141–158. London: Routledge/Cavendish.

Duncan, N. 1996. 'Renegotiating Gender and Sexuality in Public and Private Spaces'. In *Body Space: Destabilizing Geographies of Gender and Sexuality,* edited by Nancy Duncan, pp. 127–144. London: Routledge.

Duncan, J.S. and N. Duncan. 2004. *Landscapes of Privilege: The Politics of the Aesthetic in an American Suburb*. New York: Routledge.

Drydakis N. 2011. 'Ethnic Discrimination in the Greek Housing Market'. *Journal of Population Economics*, Vol. 24, No. 4, pp. 1235–1255.

Gans, H. 1962. *The Urban Villagers: Group and Class in the Life of Italian–Americans*. New York: Free Press of Glencoe.

Gordon, Tuula. 1994. *Single Women: On the Margins?* London: The Macmillan Press Limited.

Harvey, D. 1989. *The Condition of Postmodernity: An Enquiry into the Origins of Cultural Change*. Oxford: Blackwell.

Jackson, P. and S. Smith. 1981. *Social Interaction and Ethnic Segregation*. Cambridge: Academic Press.

Jamil, G. 2017. *Accumulation by Segregation: Muslim Colonies in Delhi*. Delhi: Oxford University Press.

Keller, S. 1968. *The Urban Neighbourhood: A Sociological Perspective*. New York: Random House.

Kurtulus, H. 2007. 'Global Flows and New Segregation in Istanbul: How Cloudy Class Identities Have Crystallised in Urban Space'. In *Globalising Cities: Inequality and Segregation in Developing Countries,* edited by R.S. Sandhu and J. Sandhu, pp. 65–86. Jaipur: Rawat Publications.

Lahad, K. 2012. 'Singlehood, Waiting and the Sociology of Time'. *Sociological Forum,* Vol. 27, No. 1, pp. 163–86.

Lefebvre, H. 1991. *The Production of Space*. Translated by D.N. Smith. Oxford: Blackwell.

Massey, D. 1994. *Space, Place and Gender*. Minneapolis: University of Minnesota Press.

McClenahan, B.A. 1929. *The Changing Urban Neighbourhood*. Los Angeles: University of Southern California.

———. 1945. 'The Communality: The Urban Substitute for the Traditional Community'. *Sociology and Social Research,* Vol. 30, pp. 364–374.

Okely, J. 1996. *Own or Other Culture*. London: Routledge.

Pati, S. 2017. 'Accumulation by Possession: The Social Processes of Rent Seeking in Urban Delhi'. In *Accumulation in Post-Colonial Capitalism,* edited by I.K. Mitra et al., pp. 93–108. Singapore: Springer.

Peach, C., V. Robinson and S. Smith. 1981. *Ethnic Segregation in Cities*. London: Croom Helm.

Phadke, S. 2007. 'Dangerous Liaisons: Women and Men: Risk and Reputation in Mumbai'. *Economic and Political Weekly*, Vol. 42, No. 17, pp. 1510–1518.

Prakash, G. 2002. 'The Urban Turn'. In *Sarai Reader 02: The Cities of Everyday Life,* edited by R. Vasudevan et al. New Delhi: Rainbow Publishers.

Raju, S. 1980. 'The Social Meaning of Urban Neighbourhood in India'. *Ekistics,* Vol. 47, No. 283, pp. 286–289.

Raju, S. and K.L. Dutt. 2011. *Doing Gender, Doing Geography: Emerging Research in India*. New Delhi: Routledge.

Rao, M.S.A. 1992. *Urban Sociology in India*. Delhi: Orient Longman.

Ranade, S. 2007. 'The Way She Moves: Mapping the Everyday Production of Gender-Space'. *Economic and Political Weekly*, Vol. 42, No. 17, pp. 1519–1526.

Riemer, S. 1951. 'Villagers in Metropolis'. In *British Journal of Sociology*, Vol. 2, pp. 31–43.

Robinson, J. 2006. *Ordinary Cities: Between Modernity and Development.* London: Routledge.

Sandhu, R. 2003. *Urbanisation in India: Sociological Perspectives*. New Delhi: Sage Publications.

Sibley, D. 1995. *Geographies of Exclusion: Society and Difference in the West.* London: Routledge.

Simon, B.L. 1987. *Never Married Women.* Temple University Press.

Soni, A. 2000. 'Urban Conquest of Outer Delhi: Beneficiaries, Intermediaries and Victims: The Case of the Mehrauli Countryside'. In *Delhi: Urban Space and Human Destinies,* edited by V. Dupont, E. Tarlo and D. Vidal, pp. 75–94. New Delhi: Manohar Publications.

Sopher, D. 1964. 'Landscapes and Seasons: Man and Nature in India'. *Landscape*, Vol. 13 (Spring), pp. 14–19.

Srivastava, S. 2015. *Entangled Urbanism: Slum, Gated Community, and Shopping Mall in Delhi and Gurgaon*. Delhi: Oxford University Press.

Sweetzer, F. 1941. Neighborhood Acquaintance and Association. Unpublished PhD thesis: Columbia University, USA.

Taylor, A. 2012. *Single Women in Popular Culture: The Limits of Postfeminism.* New York: Palgrave Macmillan.

Thrift, N. and A. Amin (eds). 1987. *Class and Space: The Marking of Urban Society.* London: Routledge and Kegan Paul.

Vera-Sanso, P. 2006. 'Conformity and Contestation: Social Heterogeneity in South Indian Settlements'. In *The Meaning of the Local: Politics of Place in Urban India,* edited by Geert de Neve and Henrike Donner, pp. 182–205. London: Routledge/Cavendish.

Young, I.M. 1990. *Justice and the Politics of Difference.* Princeton, NJ: Princeton University Press.

9

Paros and *Parosan*: Spatial Affectivity and Gendered Neighbourhood in South Asia

Sadan Jha

Impression

> Yet space is not something that faces man. It is neither an external object nor an inner experience. It is not that there are men, and over and above them space.... To say that mortals are is to say that in dwelling they persist through spaces by virtue of their stay among things and locations.... The relationship between man and space is none other than dwelling, strictly thought and spoken. (Heidegger 1971: 154–155).

> This is a space of loose ends and missing links. (Massey 2005: 12)

From where does the edge of a *mohallā* begin? The question gains relevance in urban landscapes of innumerable small towns and cities staged upon unbound neighbourhoods in India. Unlike *pols* of Ahmedabad (Doshi 1974) with their cul de sacs and walled *mohallās* of old Delhi, there are numerous unbound *mohallās*, particularly in north Indian small towns, having fuzzy boundaries. But, does the question of edge get resolved with a pointer towards the fuzziness of these *mohallā* boundaries? I hesitate to conclude in haste. Let me take an experiential route.

I grew up spending my childhood and adolescence in Darbhanga, a small yet prominent town of north Bihar. This was in the decades of the 1980s and 1990s. When asked, where did you live in Darbhanga? My response has always been: '*in* Banglagrah'. However, if inquisitiveness deepened with a follow-up question, the response would acquire a descriptive flavour:

> Well! While coming from Kadirabad side (from the direction of the bus station, or when you come by road from Patna, the state capital), don't turn *inside* the Banglagarh from *Neem gaachh/Neem chowk*. Instead, stay on the main road and a little further from the *Neem chowk*, ours was the second house on the right hand side. When you come from the direction of the Tower chowk, the central shopping vista of the city, this means, a little before *Neem chowk*. The house was adjacent to a *chuna-balu* [sand and lime; building construction material] and a small *sonar* [goldsmith] shop.

We never identified ourselves as living *inside* Banglagarh. The residents who lived *inside* Banglagarh never recognised us in that way either. Yet, for both of us—our family and those living *inside* Banglagarh—as well as for the town-dwellers, we lived in Banglagarh. Does this spatial location of our house qualify us to have lived at the edge of a *mohallā*? My emphatic response would be a 'no'.

Oh! Then one can guess that there were two or more segregated sections of Banglagarh, a *mohallā* split in its inside and the outside. Those familiar with spaces of Indian towns and cities would agree that such a binary of inside and outside often leaves a number of questions unanswered, instead of solving them. My answer would once again take recourse in the experiential and the descriptive. For me, there was no outside; there were no parameters *in* Banglagarh. However, as mentioned earlier, there was definitely an *inside* Banglagarh, the one when you turn inside from that *Neem chowk* which had a couple of tea and pan shops, a cycle repair shop and a washer man's shop.

Those living *inside* never considered us as their *parosi* (neighbours). Similarly, we never behaved with them as our neighbours. Thus, in this context, we can say that our house had a neighbourhood, a *mohallā* called Banglagarh with certain landmarks namely *chuna-balu* shop, *sonar* shop and a *kachhā rāstā* (unconstructed road) going inside and our house was at the confluence, where this *kachhā rāstā* used to meet the *pakka* main road. This *kachhā rāstā*, I caution the readers, must not be confused with another parallel track—the *kharanjā* (brick-lane) one going inside Banglagarh that I have mentioned a few times before. Ours was a different *gali* (lane).

The idea behind this micro-detail of space is not to trap you in a maze of spatial markers. This detail is narrated to bring home an argument that in various unbound settings of a *mohallā*, there exists no edge. To have an edge is to presuppose the existence of a unit, to conceive a *mohallā* as a unit. A subsequent question follows. What is the need for asking the question of edge, then?

The purpose is to move beyond the bounded and segregated idea of neighbourhoods—largely coming from one specific discursive trajectory, from the Western experiences of post-industrial town planning—or its other, the unbounded-ness of *mohallās*. In either case, our approach remains tied to the frames of territoriality. Instead, I wish to place another term *paros* as crucial in the socio-spatial make-up of the idea of neighbourhood in the lived experience of south Asian cityscapes.

Paros can be translated as 'in the neighbourhood'. It is a spatial term. However, *paros*, unlike neighbourhood is not scalar. It is fundamentally relational, therefore, keeps changing its locations and shifts its centre and its edges. In this way, the term is essentially determined by spatial subjectivities and bypasses certain distantiation, scaling or different other types of spatial fixities with which the idea of a neighbourhood or a *mohallā* as a unit is conceived. *Paros* cannot be quantified and labelled in any uniform logic. It eludes the possibility of objectively referring to space in the language of universality. *Paros* is about spatial proximity. One cannot say that one lives in x or y *paros*. One can only say that s/he lives in the *paros* of x house or the *paros* of y family.

Paros is not an independent referent or cannot be narrated without documenting who belonged to that space. *Mohallās* or other types of neighbourhoods can be emptied of their people, their social relationships and their lived experiences, and can be planted as a problem area on the desk of a town planner, the state or as study units for scholars—for example, Girnigaon for Raj Narayan Chandavarkar or *Pol* for Harish Doshi (Chandavarkar 2009; Doshi 1974; see Editorial Introduction to this volume). However, a *paros* cannot be studied bereft of its sociality. By asking the question of edge, my contention is that neighbourhood is neither a scalar concept nor a social space having a singular and universal meaning. It is *paros* and its relationality which makes a neighbourhood social and completes the equation of neighbourhood as socio-spatial in nature.

Deliberating upon *paros* and *parosan* (female neighbour), this chapter offers a critique of the existing discourse on the neighbourhood as a scalar spatial unit. I argue that a focus on paros allows us to engage with the subjectivities, the experiential dynamics of social-spatial relationship which unit-based understanding of neighbourhood cannot allow. The core idea of the chapter is to harp upon this potentiality of *paros* to problematise the spatial moorings of the urban experience in a South Asian milieu. To achieve this objective, the chapter locates the affectivity of *paros* in the problematique of urban experience, as it comes down to us in and through its genealogy. On the one hand, these two segments of the chapter—namely a deliberation on *paros* and its location in the genealogy of urban experience—make it pertinent to pay closer attention to the category of urban experience itself from phenomenological perspectives. On the other hand, we find that a discussion on *paros* cannot be meaningful without taking into account the people, namely *parosi* and *parosan* (male and female neighbours, respectively), who inhabit in a *paros*. The later section of the chapter then moves towards these figures and in particular, the study, analytically privileges *parosan*. Such an analytical tactic, then allows us to engender the space of the neighbourhood and also leads to the specificities in which feminisation of space allows us new facets of spatial experience in South Asian urban landscapes.

The Ubiquitous yet Ignored *Paros*

If *paros* is what enables the space of the neighbourhood and its social groundings, then the figure of a *parosi* is central to the making of the social world of a *paros* and by extension of the neighbourhood. Unfortunately, just as *paros* has remained unacknowledged in the discourse on neighbourhoods, the figure of a *parosi* too has eluded the attention of scholars.

In the absence of scholarly attention to *paros* and *parosi*, we are left speculating about etymological roots, genealogical trajectories or historically shifting dimensions of these terms. In Sanskrit, we have various terms to denote a neighbour and neighbourhood—*prativesh* and *prativasin* (*drishti he prativeshini kshanamihapyasmdgrihe dasyasi*) (Apte 1957–1959: 1078); *Praativeshya* (*nirantargrihavaasi*) (Ibid.: 1128); *anantara* (Ibid.: 74) and *anuveshya* (Ibid.: 108) are noteworthy for their meanings as next-door neighbour or spatial proximity of residential spaces. In these Sanskrit words, which are made up by adding *upsarga*, meaning prefixes, such as 'prati' in *prativeshya*, 'an' in a*nanatra* and 'anu' in a*nuveshya*, suggest that neighbourhood and neighbours are conceptualised in terms of an extension of, or proximity to, one's own living spaces/houses. Unlike, this Sanskrit vocabulary, *paros* in all probability has a *desaj* trajectory—in terms of roots, words are classified into four categories in Hindi: *tatsam* (having Sanskrit roots), *tadbhav* (Sanskrit roots but are in circulation in slightly altered forms), *desaj* (having indigenous roots in different vernacular languages and linguistic traditions) and *videsaj* (imports from 'foreign' languages like *mohallā* that has Arabic roots). *Paros* comes down to us from Saurseni Prakrit roots. *Desaj*, or vernacular roots of *paros* and *parosi*, adds onto linguistic layers in this search. Yet, it can be safely deducted that the term was in circulation in the medieval period as we get a reference of it from the epic *Ramacharitmanas* of *Tulsidas* when he composed *Basi kusang chāhat kushal Tulsi! Ye man soch! Mahimā ghati samudra ki Rāvan baso paros* (Tulsi! Who can get good in the company of evils, the greatness of the ocean diminished as Ravan settled in its neighbourhood [the water became salty] (Fallon 1879 [1989]: 932). We also have similar couplets from Rahim when he says, '*Basi Kusang Chāhat kushal yah rahim jiya sos, mahima ghati Samudra ki Rāvan basyo paros*' (One should not desire well-being in the company of bad people, the greatness of the ocean diminished as Rāvan settled in its neighbourhood). Here, the spatial proximity is clearly delineated and is achieved not merely by adding a prefix, but we have a separate word itself describing the spatial proximity or co-inhabitation of a shared space. This sharing of space comes clearly when in John Shakespear's *Dictionary*, a neighbour means *hum sāyā*, *parosi* and *hamjavār* (Shakespear 1849: 2339).

Javaar is a spatial word and Fallon registers it as vicinity (*aaspaas*; Fallon, 1879 [1989]: 486). We often find it in hyphenated usages and tied along with the word *gaaon* (village) like *gaaon-javaar*. One may speculate that such hyphenation suggests that it is not a synonym of the village and therefore the vicinity of *javaar* is not a rural space. If *javaar* is not rural (most likely, it is one of those layers which mediate between the rural and urban), *hum-javaar* implies someone who shares common space within that vicinity/*javaar*. In this scheme, *hum-javaar* and *parosi* acquires non-rural connotations. What is also noteworthy is the word *hum-saayaa* for a neighbour, as mentioned earlier. In many ways, *hum-saayaa* contains a sense of being an extension of the self, neighbour as an extended self. Does this make a *paros* harmonious and homogeneous vicinity where similar people reside? Certainly not! Had this been the reality there would be no yearning: *aa parosan mujh si ho* (Come neighbour, be like me! This is a proverb used to when bad men strive to corrupt the innocent and good (Fallon 1879 [1989]: 359). The yearning, in this case, is particularly for a female neighbour by another woman, the housewife.

We will return to the figure of a *parosan* or *parosin* (woman neighbour) a little later. Here, let us stay a little longer with the space of *paros* itself. If neighbourhood as a unit is premised as a scalar (Appadurai 1997), *paros* has to be conceived as an affective-spatial term. Also, if this term has affectivity fundamentally inherent into its spatial connotations (as we have seen in *hum-saayaa* as a spatial extension of the self), the task at hand is less oriented towards acquiring a definitional understanding of *paros* or how to define the affective in the making of a *paros*. Instead, I ask the question, how to approach this affective space? For this reason, I wish to rely on phenomenological insights and argue for a need to re-orient our scholarly apparatus towards the experiential narratives so that we can engage with the affective-spatial inter-twinning in the making of a *paros*. This is essentially an urban question, a question of the urban experience.

Space of Affectivity

Spaces are produced and consumed. And, spaces are experienced. While the first two (i.e., production and consumption) are quite closely correlated with each other, the third experience may have a different and distinguished trajectory both in terms of social practices as well as in terms of discursive engagements. Yet, by no means, do I wish to suggest that experiencing the space can take us into an isolated terrain, a romantic world that can yield a purist notion of life unhampered by forces and structures that are responsible for the production and consumption of spaces. Far from such a purist impression of the experience, I would prefer to embed experience within a frame which will have strong bearings upon the contingencies of both production and consumption. This is to acknowledge the historical processes in and through which space comes to us. This is also to emphasise that the frame suggested here does not look at the question of experience in a romantic fashion. My perspectives on experience are informed by scholarship on the question of experience in feminism and the concept of 'lived experience' in Dalit Studies (Scott 1991: 773–797; Haraway 1988: 575–599; Guru and Sarukkai 2012). In this discussion on the experiential, feminist and Dalit epistemic interventions are crucial for their critique of the universalising discourse of knowledge and science and their insistence on the power dynamics. Such an emphasis upon the power or the politics of knowledge needs to be kept in mind, here, as we do not intend to treat spaces as ignorant of this power dynamics that go into the making of their knowledge.

While proximity has always been recognised as a key aspect in the neighbourhood discourse, I contend that the proximity is dealt with in an unproblematic and innocent manner as giving shape to spatial intimacy in the neighbourhood. These innocent usages have then contributed significantly in framing neighbourhoods as a little oasis of social and communal harmony in an otherwise violent city. For instance, in the Indian context, we have utopian imaginations assigned to neighbourhoods by way of their names when we find cities dotted with Adarsh Nagar, Model Town (more anchored in the history of planning), Gandhi Dham, Gokul Dham, and so on. This brief discussion is by way of a disclaimer that by affective spaces, I do not intend to mean neighbourhood as an affectionate space bereft of its violence and politics, a little island of harmony and social cohesion in an otherwise alienating urban landscape.

Drawing upon phenomenology, affective space here means immersed spaces, situated-ness of human bodies and their embedding which allow us new ways of looking at the linkage between social and the spatial. In many ways, this boils down to the question of belonging as primarily a spatial question and vice versa (the question of space as essentially a located one and not merely as abstract, quantified or scalar). Therefore, I argue that even when all these three categories (production, consumption and experience) overlap with each other, only the experience as a trope can engage with the openness, eccentricities and strange charm of dwelling that Heidegger forcefully brought before us in his deliberation on *Building, Dwelling, Thinking*, as we saw in the impression at the beginning of this chapter. Without privileging dwelling, it is not possible to address the question of affective-space of a *paros*. Ironically, the scholarship on neighbourhoods in the South Asian context has largely ignored the question of dwelling or this spatial affectivity. Before moving ahead, it is also important to remember that in Heidegger's dwelling, affectivity would be necessarily about the immersion of human experience and space in such a way that the question of space as 'external object or inner experience' becomes redundant.

This is a reminder that I intend to distinguish the experience of space from its discursive sibling—the production of space. This is neither to conceive of space as a priori nor as an inert container that experience can then colonise and make alive. Building upon Henry Lefebvre, it would be fallacious to argue that there is space and then there are social structures and practices. He argues that the 'production process and product present themselves as two inseparable aspects, not as two separable ideas' (Lefebvre 1991: 37). Lefebvre has emphatically propounded that '(Social) space is a (social) product' and further claimed that 'the space thus produced also serves as a tool of thought and action; that in addition to being a means of production, it is also a means of control, and hence of domination, of power; yet that, as such escapes in part from those who would make use of it' (Lefebvre 1991: 26). To harp upon this difference is also not an excuse to go back to the category of 'lived experience'. Lefebvre writes, 'Like all social practice, spatial practice is lived directly before it is conceptualised; but the speculative primacy of the conceived over the lived causes practice to disappear along with life, and so does very little to the "unconscious" level of lived experience *per se*' (Ibid.: 34).

The production presupposes a process and an outcome, some kind of finality is engrained whenever we speak about it. The space with all its complexities and dynamism gets frozen in its stillness, no matter how momentary it may be. Space acquires the form of a commodity endowed with exchange value and occasionally, as an exception, stretched to a fetish. Experience, on the other hand, allows one to remain humble before such a grand orchestration of the production. As a human being, here, one is grounded in her/his innate limitations. Doreen Massey is quite insightful here. Having argued that space is a product of relations and is characterised in multiplicity, Massey writes,

> These are not the relations of a coherent, closed system within which, as they say, everything is (already) related to everything else. Space can never be that complete simultaneity in which all interconnections have been established, and in which everywhere is already linked with everywhere else. (Massey 2005: 11–12)

The field of urban experience—the subject of our immediate concern as we intend to excavate the *paros* and *parosi* essentially in the urban landscape—is vast, amorphous and full of ambiguity. Just as a city is a place of the unexpected, its experiences also lead us to uncanny, irresolvable and unfathomed alleys. However, these lanes are neither hidden nor unexplored. A good number of scholars, litterateurs and urban theorists have squarely addressed the question of the urban experience. David Harvey grounds his claims when he writes that 'the testing of theory depends upon confrontation with experience' and that '[the] "restless analyst" is open to the unpredictable collision of experience and imagination' (Harvey 1985: XV).

For Harvey, experience is both a testing lab for the theory about capitalism as well as an object of theory itself. He follows Lefebvre when the later claims that capitalism has survived into the 20th century through the production of space and adds that it has been an increasingly urbanised space that has been produced. Thus, in Harvey, we find an entwined deployment of the urban experience—at one level as a resource to understand the complexities of capitalism and at another, a unique form, a particular type of consciousness that is shaped by capitalism. We need to keep in mind that while Harvey shows concern towards experience, he does 'not intend that it [urban experience] be considered a theoretically specific object of analysis separate from what Capitalism is about' (Harvey 1985: XVIII). In Harvey's formulation, all three—urban experience, capitalism and urban process—are inseparable. For him, the city is a place of mystery, the site of the unexpected, full of agitations and ferments, of multiple liberties, opportunities and alienations (Ibid.: 250). In that scheme, urban experience and its mysteries and circles of alienations are crucially structured along the axis of money, time, space and labour relations. He demonstrates how these are enmeshed together where 'the path between the historical and geographical grounding of experience and the rigours of theory construction is hard to ignore' (Ibid.: XVI).

In highlighting the role of money, time, space and labour, Harvey draws a lot of insights from Georg Simmel who has argued that 'the psychological foundation, upon which the metropolitan individuality is erected, is the intensification of emotional life due to the swift and continuous shift of external and internal stimuli' (Simmel 1950: 411). Simmel has drawn our attention to the de-humanised psychological profile of individuals in a metropolis. What emerges forcefully is the figure of an alienated, regimented and objectified self that is devoid of irrational, spontaneous and subjective selfhood in the environment of a city.

The pessimism of Simmel and his formulation of the regimented and calculated self acquires another dark layer of war-torn Europe in Walter Benjamin where experience does not come wrapped with new properties. In Benjamin, it is unavailable, lost and destroyed. He talks about the wealth of ideas as opposed to poverty of human experience, physical experience by hunger and moral experience by ruling powers (Benjamin 1999: 732). A caveat must be put here that unlike the other two, Benjamin is concerned about experience in general and is not particularly reflecting only on its urban variant. These formulations have decisively influenced how city life has been theorised and written about in the last century. Benjamin's tiny human figure dwarfed in the jungle of concrete or Simmel's alienated punctual individual in the maze of a crowd rushing mechanically from home to work and Harvey's conflation of historical time into urban spatiality and in turn shaping the contours of capitalism are stereotypes that continue to shape our understanding of what we call urban experience. However, the question remains—from what vantage point should we see such figures, landscapes, processes and their experiences?

Addressing this fundamental dimension of approach, Michel de Certeau privileges practices over representations and streets overlooking down from above. He advocates for the ordinary, the walk and the figure of the walker *Wandersmanner* and allows us to recover the unregulated, non-regimented and subjective selves of the city, experiences that were lost in Simmel and Benjamin. Just as the street and the act of walking, respectively, function as a vantage point and a strategy of looking at the city for De Certeau, neighbourhood and its in-between-ness allows us to engage with subjectivities and sensibilities called the urban experience.

At another level, we find that just as city and capital collude in producing a field, which is barren of subjectivities and experiential dynamics, we also find similar coming together of modern science and knowledge where 'the expropriation of experience was implicit in the founding project of modern science' (Agamben 1993: 17). By 'referring knowledge and experience to a single subject', modern science has reduced experience as a mere resource for knowledge-building and thereby denied its autonomy (Ibid.: 19). This is towards producing a universal language of knowledge and its truth claims—something that has been questioned from various perspectives in the last sixty-seventy years. Thus, for scholars working under the overarching frame of gender studies, instead of universal claims of science and knowledge, the claims are articulated along with the logic of 'limited locations' and 'embodied objectivity'. Donna Haraway states that the 'feminist objectivity is about limited location and situated knowledge, not about transcendence and splitting of subject and object' (Haraway 1988: 583). Articulated around the question of caste and lived experience of untouchability in the Indian context, the question acquires both political as well as epistemological dimensions (Guru and Sarukkai 2012). Lived experience in Guru's framework is determined by the lack of choice and entails regimes of sufferings both along historical as well as geographical (spatial) trajectories. An important epistemic and political question raised in this context is, who has the right to own and who has the right to represent this lived experience?

The right to own experience, then also becomes deeply ethical. The argument can be further extended from who has the right to own experience to who has the right to own her/his life as life cannot be separated from lived experience. In such an extension, the right to own life presupposes the right to live and represent lived experience with dignity. In the current study of urban experience, such a formulation can be safely translated into the right to live in the city with dignity and can be extended ultimately to who belongs to the city? It is at this level that the question of belongingness or attachment—that is the core of spatial affectivity—remains no more confined to the psychological profiling of alienated individuals that Simmel identifies.

A focus on belongingness can also help us recover and analyse the imprecise, ambiguous and the emotional attachment that constitutes the field of urban experience. Its anthropology can develop an account of this emotional attachment with the space of a neighbourhood. Here, the spatial attachment comes before us in the form of longing. Longing lacks precision and definition but it is spatially immersed. Like the Benjaminian experience, it is unregulated and defies the calculated self that Simmel talks about. Belonging in this sense is similar to Heidegger's notion of dwelling. For him, 'dwelling itself is always like staying with things' (Heidegger 1975: 151).

Heidegger takes us into its complexities when he proposes that space is not something external to man 'nor an inner experience'. However, just like all types of human experience do not qualify for what Walter Benjamin considers experience or every experience is not lived experience in the framework of Guru, every relationship between man and space does not make a fitting example for dwelling. To make this distinction, Heidegger crucially introduces 'thinking' in the ambit of dwelling (Heidegger 1971: 160–161).

This relation between thinking and dwelling is hugely pertinent in our discussion on experience and belongingness. Thinking also distinguishes the Indian tradition of philosophy on experience from its Eurocentric counterparts. This is explained by Sundar Sarukkai who informs us,

> [that] commonly used terms for experience in Indian languages exhibit the intrinsic relatedness of experience and knowledge. In Tamil, one commonly used word for experience is *pattarivu* and in Bengali, it is *abhigyotā*. Both these words have explicit connotations of knowledge in them. Even in common parlance, it is difficult to find words for experience that do not have terms for knowledge, skill, or wisdom (like *arivu*) stitched into them. (Guru and Sarukkai 2012: 55)

Thus, we can safely argue that being in experience always presupposes an intrinsic presence of agency in human subject. Capitalising upon this genealogy, I would argue that this belongingness to the urban gets actualised and scripted in the affective spatiality of the *paros* or the neighbourhood. To elaborate this argument, let us pay attention to the following three narratives.

Three Figures from Neighbourhood

Nurur Rahman Khan is an architect in his mid-fifties, who lives in Dhaka (Khan 2013). For him to be termed as Dhakaite is an honour. He says, 'It's what Dhaka does to you: the city is powerful enough to make you want to be a part of it.' Born six years before the birth of Bangladesh as an independent country, he spent his few childhood years in Liverpool. However, it is Dhaka and particularly his own neighbourhood, Ramna, with which he loves to associate himself. In his words, 'It's what Dhaka does to you ...' Dhaka University, Bangla Academy and other academic institutions are located in this neighbourhood of Ramna. For him, the neighbourhood prompts social habits like discussion, thinking and debating. Instead of pubs and nightclubs, he and his friends socialise in a form known as *adda*. For Khan, 'conversations in these *adda* range over many topics and moods, from light to serious, covering daily affairs, friends, events, the past, politics, religion, art, music, nostalgia, common interests, work and study' (Khan 2013).

Khan no longer lives in Ramna but Dhanmondi, an upper-middle-class residential neighbourhood. The city of Dhaka has undergone massive changes. Khan complains that the city seems unable to extract itself from a morass of poor planning and politics. But the chaos requires Dhakaites 'to find our way around' and he still finds that exciting. I, as a researcher, ponder about his attachment with his old neighbourhood, about this chaos and how to make sense of this attachment. I also find that Nurur Rahman Khan is not alone.

Manharlal Chintaram Gandhi (name changed) is in his mid-eighties and now lives in Anand Mahal Road, Adajan (Surat, Gujarat) with his son and grandchildren in a large extended family. He was born in a poor *Ghanchi* family of Jhampa Bazar. His younger brother recounts, 'we were a community that struggled even for the basic human needs of food and shelter'. With a monthly family expenditure of two rupees and another one rupee going to the Jain Trust as house rent, everyday life was not easy in this family of eleven members. His father Chintaram (name changed) had a small grocery shop and was also involved in 'ill practices' like selling country liquor and smuggled Chinese firecrackers purchased in Daman and sold in Surat. Survival was difficult and at the age of twelve, Manharlal was sent to Rangoon (present-day Yangon), as the recent trend in his community at that time dictated. The late 1930s and early 1940s was a challenging period for the community. With the outbreak of World War II, Manharlal returned from Rangoon and began working as a labourer in a grocery store in Calcutta (present-day Kolkata). By 1945, he returned to Surat when his brothers started a family workshop in Surat making ribbon machines. With the success of the venture, the family moved from Jhampa Bazar to Amliran (another neighbourhood in what is now known as the old city or *Kot Vistaar* in Surat) and from Amliran to Anand Mahal Road at Adajan, when the city expanded in the 1970s. With a massive growth in the economy since the 1960s, the city offered the neo-middle and business class a way to move out of congested places like Amliran into the planned residential neighbourhood of Adajan on the other side of River Tapi.

Manharlal moved from Jhampa Bazar (Surat) to Rangoon and came back to Adajan (Surat) taking a detour via Calcutta and Amliran (Surat) in-between. The family retained their house in Amliran even after moving to the middle-class residential neighbourhood of Adajan. In 2010, we visited this empty house and met a few neighbours who looked up to this family with a sense of pride and respect.

On this canvas, we find that after his siesta, Manharlal visits his old home at Amliran every day and spends some time in the otherwise empty house and interacts with his neighbours there. It is this territory of bonding between individual and neighbourhood, between individual and old home, that forces me to look into the dynamics of attachment between people and their neighbourhood. Finally, I am persuaded to think about another figure, this time not an individual but the term, *Suratilala*.

In Surat, there is a cluster of communities identified as *Suratilala*. These communities reside in *Kot Vistaar*—roughly old city or walled city; now central zone in the administrative language. It may be worth noting that this figuration is less dependent upon caste or community-centric logic. The caste and communities must have been influential ingredients though. For example, one can safely presume that a Dalit might not be included in this figuration. But the figure is not defined by any specific caste. It is often referred to in connection with particular traits and lifestyle behaviours. For example, a *Suratilala*, even when he lives outside the *Kot Vistaar* area, would visit to his ancestral house or neighbourhood to celebrate Kite festival on the day of *Uttarayan* (mid-January when the sun changes its course in the orbit). So, in popular perception, *Kot Vistaar* as a space remains foundational to the figuration of *Suratilala* or speaking broadly in defining what is the essence of Surati-ness. Here, we need to bear in mind that a visit to *Kot Vistaar*—what takes a *Suratilala* to *Kot Vistaar* on customary occasions—is guided by festival time or a ritual calendar.

Even metaphorically we cannot just assume that a walled city (though no wall exists now) or the space of the social in the walled city can be seen as a place which lacks anonymity of social relationships.

We intuitively know that a walled city is not the opposite of an anonymous city. The question is not about the binary between the *Kot Vistaar* and the rest of the city. The challenge is how to conceptualise this space which circulates so prominently in the mind of people.

Summing up the relevance of these three narratives, we find that all three figures—*Dhakaite*, Manharlal and *Surtilala*—talk about the affection people have for their neighbourhoods. Is this affection pervasive? Is it innocent of micro-physics of social power? The response would be negative. This affection is gendered too. The unidirectional nature of this affection gets broken when we focus our attention on the relation between women and the neighbourhood. This is about engendering the neighbourhood.

Women and the Affective Space of Neighbourhoods

Jigna and her family live right next to Balaji Street in the vicinity of Chauta-Bhagal in *Kot Vistaar* area of Surat. Known as a traditional bazaar of *Chauta*, the crowded vicinity is centrally located and consists of shops and residences. There are six members in the family—her in-laws, her two children, her husband and Jigna herself. At the time of this research in 2010, the couple had decided to move to the City Light area, a planned spacious middle-class residential neighbourhood that came into existence in the early 2000s. However, within a couple of months of moving to a new neighbourhood, they began contemplating the idea of returning to their old neighbourhood at Bhagal. Jigna's in-laws felt nauseated in the planned neighbourhood of City Light. Her father-in-law would complain every day about the place saying that he could not go out for evening walks. Eventually, they came back to Bhagal. However, in contrast to male members of the family, Jigna condescendingly talks about Chauta and Bhagal. She said,

> I never go to Chauta to buy anything, I do not even like going for snacks or meeting friends there. Here, in Chauta, parking is such a nuisance. Everyone who comes to Chauta with a two-wheeler, parks here. For them, it is a commercial place, but we live here. A market is a nuisance for people who live inside it.

In a different conversational chord, her husband says,

> We have always loved sitting by the porch and watching the market transform, especially till Limda Chowk. It is wonderful to get everything right close to the house and moreover, it is trustworthy because we know all the sellers, not only them but their great grandfathers [laughs]. (Interviewed by Nishpriha Thakur [Jha and Thakur 2016; Jha 2018]

Her husband was born and brought up here. While male members of her family want to stay—even return to their old neighbourhood—the young wife feels she is stuck there. I argue that the difference of attachment along gender lines is not merely due to Jigna not being born here. To appreciate Jigna's yearning, it is required to factor in aspirational dynamics in the question of spatial affectivity. And, we find that Jigna is not alone in her desire to move out of a neighbourhood of the old city.

Pradeep Shirish *bhai* (name changed), a thirty-two-year-old man, has lived in Ghānchiseri (another neighbourhood in *Kot Vistaar*, Surat; Ghānchi is a caste also known as Modh Vanik) for generations. He says,

> Ghanchi women are very demanding. They want everything, they want a big house preferably in Adajan [a middle-class planned neighbourhood developed in late 1960s and located far away from the old city] or other posh residential areas. They want a government job or a well-set job, they want their husband to be rich, not even middle class. (Jha 2018)

Compelled by these factors, most of the Ghanchis started moving out to the newer sections of the city. Those who stay, look outside the community to get married.

The examples given here, one may legitimately argue, come from traditional neighbourhoods and therefore do not qualify for much of the conceptualisations of the post-Industrial, modern metropolitan urban characteristics, which we listed earlier in the chapter while referring to Simmel and Benjamin, among others. It must be clarified, at this point, that the objective behind this study is not to criticise concepts coming from the West by showing contrasting social-spatial realities from non-Western cities like that of Surat or Dhaka. The scholarship on experience and its relation with the urban has been referred solely to delineate genealogical trajectories of the category and to mobilise insights. Also, there is no attempt to produce any universal theory of spatial affectivity or how neighbourhood functions in the cities of the global South.

On the contrary, the idea is to deny the possibility of such a universal theory of the linkages between experience and the space of an urban neighbourhood. Traditional neighbourhoods in this scheme, then, must not be seen as traces from pre-Industrial, pre-Modern past but as socio-spatial constellations, which are not to be judged merely on the axis of the civilisational time. Yet, these examples can be found in cross-cultural locations. These are about how people are emotionally attached to their neighbourhoods. The question of gender further helps us in puncturing the possibility of a singular and authoritative understanding of how bodies and spaces are immersed in each other. The question of the gendered neighbourhood and aspirational narratives of women, coming from the field, demands that we turn our attention to the figure of a *parosan* (also written as *padosan*—female neighbour) in this last segment of the chapter.

Parosan

Parosan is a generic category. Unlike a housewife which draws its social meanings from home and the family, a *parosan* has certain publicness built into her. In many ways, a *parosan* is like a ubiquitous *bhābhi* (sister-in-law) or a non-descriptive aunty. At times, we even get the two (*parosan* and *bhabhi*) as a template conflated onto each other. This happens particularly in the zone of romance and lust. In that zone, the body of a *parosan* is scripted and designed to titillate along the lines of sadomasochism. At this terrain, the figure of a *parosan* connects the coordinates of a beautiful unmarried girl of the neighbourhood from the 1968 classic Bollywood film *Parosan* (starring Saira Banu, Kishore Kumar, Sunit Dutt and Mahmood) with Savita Bhabhi (a web graphic series started in 2008) (Guha 2008; Sreedhar and Baishya 2020). In this sense, there are certain shared commonalities between *parosan* and *bhabhi*, which make these figures as templates circulating among the public. Yet, unlike the public characters of Jane Jacobs, which are quite crucial in her treatment of neighbourhoods and which have far-reaching implications, particularly how a researcher can approach neighbourhoods, women neighbours in South Asia intuitively bring in certain conversational energy. Here, it may be an opportune moment to recall an earlier mentioned proverb, a wish—'come, neighbour, be like me!'

Is it about homogeneity and neighbourhood? At one level, the proverb strongly points in that direction. But, instead of venturing in that direction, my curiosities are towards this housewife, from the proverb, who aspires to homogeneity in fashioning her neighbourhood? Is it about sameness? Pierre Bourdieu has made us aware of the significance of difference that is produced and invoked whenever a social element wishes to assert her or his social status (Bourdeieu 1984). In Bourdieu's frame, all the social agencies from education to taste are geared towards producing this differentiation. Then, thinking from that perspective, is not this desire to have a *parosan like me* a camouflage, a certain kind of moral prescription? However, more than the message, it is this figure that keeps me occupied. This is a unique social category and we have not paid due attention to it in social sciences so far.

Unlike figures like *devrāni*, *nanad*, *bhaujai* or such kinship-based figures, a *parosan* may not necessarily pre-suppose such social ties. Scholars have documented how kinship and community tie crucially influence social relationship in neighbourhoods (Abraham 2018; Vatuk 1969). Yet, theoretically, it is quite possible that a *parosan* may not come before us ubiquitously in and through kinship and community network. This is particularly in a situation of multi-community neighbourhoods, making a *parosan* as one who draws her definitional contours only from her locatedness in the space of a *paros*.

A *parosan*, unlike *devrāni*, *jethāni* and others, is not someone who is part of the family and 'home'. She stands outside the 'home'. However, the linkages between women of the house and the *parosan* cannot be undermined either. In stereotypes, proverbs and folk sayings, these other figures (*devrāni* and *jethāni*) often come before us in competitiveness and camaraderie with a housewife in a joint family setting. In that realm, just as these figures of *jethāni*, *devrāni* and *nanad* provide a kinship rivalry or an embedded other for a housewife, the body of a *parosan* comes before us scribbled with markers of insecurity, mistrust and jealousy. Poems from *Gatha Sattsai*, a Prakrit text from the 1st century ce are titillating illustrative of such imageries:

> It is pitch dark outside,
> My husband left today,
> And the house is deserted.
> Please, neighbour, do keep watch:
> I don't want to be burgled.
>
> —Khuzoche and (Tieken 2014: 139)

> She shares my tears,
> Counts off each day,
> And grows as thin as I do,
> While my husband is away,
> Aunt, the concern my neighbour shows,
> Is quite extraordinary
>
> —(Ibid.: 140)

> As the woman from next door,
> Threw her arm around him,
> To welcome him home,
> The wife's face grew dark,
> Despite her husband's return.
>
> —(Ibid.: 152)

These are merely three poetic ramblings on the possible dangers of a female neighbour. There is an investment in sexuality capitalising upon the spatial proximity in these poems. These are subtly alarming and threatening to the figure of the wife. It is her spatial proximity, the presence of her body, which is the sole source of agony. It is this shared space, which generates the possibility of a promiscuous relationship. While in the first poem, a *parosan* is sending a covert invitation by way of an announcement of being alone in the night; in the second, the warmth, sharing of the pain of loneliness of a migrant wife by *parosan* raises an alarm bell in the mind of this housewife. In the third, this possible danger gets translated as a clear violation of a moral-ethical boundary when *parosan*, upon the return of her neighbour's migrant husband, openly expresses her joy and performs like the wife herself, by throwing her arm around him. In a sense, this completes the circle of a *parosi*—

in this particular case, a female neighbour or a *parosan*—as *hum sāyā*, as mentioned earlier, when we discussed the dictionary meaning of the term *parosi*. However, here, the presence of *hum sāyā* is neither desirable nor soothing one for the harmony of the space called *paros*.

Conclusion

Scholars following Judith Butler have helped us see the politics of gendered space through their analysis of the performativity of bodies in and through which the politics of the space functions. Taking insights from such a framework, these circulating bodies of a *parosan* not merely leads us towards dominant regimes of sexual morality but also allows us to venture in the direction of transgressive potentials embodied in this figure of a *parosan*. As a threat to the next-door housewife, *parosan* also becomes a personification of transgressive practices, threatening monogamous norms of neighbourhood space.

While the figure of *parosan* unleashes subversive energy, the mother figure, apparently believed to be generous, benevolent and protective, too subverts the very imagination of cartographic space of a neighbourhood. Here, I would like to show the figuration of a neighbourhood itself as a mother. This example comes from a traditional neighbourhood called *Mandvi ni Pol* from Ahmedabad (Figure 9.1). This is about *mohallā Mata*. Shifting the ground of analysis by prompting us to move away from treating social figures in neighbourhoods to social figures *as* neighbourhoods, in *mohallā Mata*, religiosity, spatial affectivity and gendered configuration of the neighbourhood all come together like an ethnographic puzzle. While *mohallā* is a widely circulating generic term for neighbourhood across India, in Gujarat, the words that we often come across are *pol*, *khancho* or *sheri* (literally *gali* or bye-lane) and not *mohallā*. However, this is not to say that the word *mohallo* is completely absent in Gujarati. This is only to suggest that *mohallo* is not a widely used word in Gujarati. In such a milieu, when none of the spatial markers coming from that neighbourhood even remotely hints towards the presence, let alone circulation, of the word *mohallā* for the space of neighbourhood, the very language of *mohallā Mata* is baffling.

Figure 9.1: ***Mohallā Mata, Mandvi ni Pol,*** **Ahmedabad, October 2019. Photo credit: author**

Is it a recent phenomenon drawing its semiotic strengths from another overarching figure of *Bharatmata*, the figuration of India as Mother nation? We do not know. Yet, speculatively one may not like to foreclose this analytic possibility either. This is a possibility where there may be considerable overlap between the conceptualisation of the space of a neighbourhood with that of a country. It seems some kind of spatial template in vogue. In both cases, there seems to be a process of sacralisation at work. This process makes the space of a neighbourhood sacred and immediately qualifies to be termed as ambiguous. To me, this also takes me to Michel Foucault's formulation when he drew our attention to the hidden presence of the sacred in our everyday life (Foucault 1986). It is here the affective space of a neighbourhood comes before as an enigma. However, it is certainly not *merely* a scalar concept, as we are made to believe. This is about the embeddedness of the social and spatial into each other, where the urban cannot be conceptualised without its *paros* and *parosan*, where the *paros* defies boundedness and precision and remains a space of loose ends to borrow the epitaph from Dorren Massey (mentioned in the beginning). This is where the landscape of the neighbourhood essentially becomes a dwelling in *paros* in the sense in which Heidegger talks about the concept of dwelling. It is an experience of living in the *paros* of a *parosan*.

References

Abraham, Janaki. 2018. 'The Lives of Others: The Production and Influence of Neighbourhood Cultures in Urban India'. In *Palgrave Handbook on Urban Ethnography,* edited by Italo Pardo and Giuliana B. Prato, pp. 95–111. Swtizerland: Palgrave Macmillan.

Agamben, Giorgio. 1993. *Infancy and History: Essays on the Destruction of Experience.* Translated by Liz Heron. Verso: London.

Appadurai, Arjun. 1997. 'The Production of Locality'. In *Modernity at Large: Cultural Dimensions of Globalization*, pp. 178–200. Delhi: Oxford University Press.

Apte, Vaman Shivaram. 1957–1959. *Revised and Enlarged Edition of Prin. V.S. Apte's 'The Practical Sanskrit English Dictionary'.* Poona: Prasad Prakashan. Available at Digital Dictionaries of South Asia, University of Chicago. Available at dsal.uchicago.edu/dictionaries/apte/ (accessed on 5 April 2020).

Benjamin, Walter. 1999. 'Experience and Poverty'. In *Selected Writings* 2 (1927–1934). Translated by Rodney Livingstone and others, edited by Michael W. Jennings, Howard Eiland and Gary Smith, pp. 730–735. Cambridge, MA: Belknap Press of Harvard University Press.

Bourdieu, Pierre. 1984. *Distinction: A Social Critique of the Judgement of Taste.* Translated by Richard Nice. Cambridge Massachusetts: Harvard University Press.

Chandavarkar, Rajnarayan. 2009. *History, Culture and the Indian City.* Cambridge: Cambridge University Press.

Doshi, Harish. 1974. Traditional Neighbourhood in a Modern City. Delhi: Abhinav Publication.

Fallon, S.W. 1879 [1989]. *New Hindustani–English Dictionary with Illustrations from Hindustani Literature and Folklore.* Benaras: Lazarus and Co., Trubner and Co., London/Delhi: Asian Educational Service.

Foucault, Michel and Jay Miskowiec. 1986. 'Of Other Spaces'. *Diacritics*, Vol. 16, No. 1, pp. 22–27.

Guha, Anastasia. 2008. 'The Beatitudes of a Bountiful Bhabhi'. *Tehalka*, 17 March. Available at http://old.tehalka.com/the-beatitudes-of-a-a-bountiful-bhabhi/ (accessed on 6 April 2020).

Guru, Gopal and Sundar Sarukkai (eds). 2012. *The Cracked Mirror: An Indian Debate on Experience and Theory*. Delhi: Oxford University Press.

Haraway, Donna. 1988. 'Situated Knowledge: The Science Question in Feminism and the Privilege of Partial Perspective'. *Feminist Studies*, Vol. 14, No. 3, pp. 575–599.

Harvey, David. 1985. 'Preface', *Consciousness and the Urban Experience: Studies in the History and Theory of Capitalist Urbanization*. Baltimore: John Hopkins Press.

Heidegger, Martin. 1975. 'Building Dwelling Thinking'. In *Poetry, Language, Thought*. Translated by Albert Hofstadter, pp. 145–161. New York: Harper Colophon Books.

Jha, Sadan. 2018. 'The Social Fabric of Surat'. Unpublished report submitted to ICSSR. Surat: Centre for Social Studies.

Jha, Sadan and Nishpriha Thakur. 2016. 'Ethnography of Trust and History as Circulating Commodities in Chauta Bazaar, Surat'. *History and Sociology of South Asia*, Vol. 10, No. 2, pp. 138–161.

Khan, Nurur Rahman. 2013. 'Creativity, Complexity and a Little Adda Everyday, in Dhaka, Bangladesh'. *Ideas.ted.com*. Available at https://ideas.ted.com/my-city-dhaka-bangladesh/ (accessed on 6 April 2012).

Khuzoche, Peter and Herman Tieken (eds and trans). 2014. *Gatha Satasai, Hala's Sattasai: Poems of Life and Love in Ancient India*. Delhi: Motilal Banarasidass.

Lefebvre, Henry. 1991. *The Production of Space*. Translated by Donald Nicholason-Smith, p. 37. MA: Blackwell.

Massey, Doreen. 2005. *For Space*. London: Sage Publications.

Sarukkai, Sundar. 2012. 'Understanding Experience'. In *The Cracked Mirror: An Indian Debate on Experience and Theory,* edited by Gopal Guru and Sundar Sarukkai. Delhi: Oxford University Press.

Scott, Joan W. 1991. 'The Evidence of Experience'. *Critical Inquiry*, Vol. 17, No. 4, pp. 773–797.

Shakespear, J. 1849. *A Dictionary of Hindustani and English and English and Hindustani*. London: Pelham Richardson.

Simmel, Georg. 1950. 'The Metropolis and the Mental Life'. In *The Sociology of Georg Simmel,* translated and edited by Kurt H. Wolff, pp. 409–424. New York: Free Press.

Sreedhar Mini, Darshana and Anirban K. Baishya. 2020. 'Transgressions in Toonland: Savita Bhabhi, Velamma and the Indian Adult Comic'. *Porn Studies*, Vol. 7, No. 1, pp. 115–131.

Vatuk, Sylvia. 1969. 'Reference, Address, and Fictive Kinship in Urban North India'. *Ethnology*, Vol. 8, No. 3 (July), pp. 255–272.

Part IV

A House in a Neighbourhood: Planning, History and Aspirations of Housing

10

Government Officer Housing Precincts in Urban Lucknow: A Construction of Urban Exclusivity through Occupation-defined Neighbourhoods

Sonal Mithal

After Independence, Lucknow saw the establishment of public institutions on a large scale to cater to the new agenda of progress laid down in the First Five-Year Plan. That warranted setting up research facilities for agriculture (Sugarcane Research Institute), medicine (Central Drug Research Institute), aviation (Hindustan Aeronautics Limited) and waterworks (Hydelworks) as well as the establishment of a housing board to provide new housing solutions for new India. The employees of these public sector projects live in precincts exclusively designed for their needs. These precincts are closer to their workplace and are low-density residential neighbourhoods. The housing units are also designed in accordance with the hierarchy of the employee. The quality of construction is good and amenities are well laid out. The presence of such precincts forms a large component of the urban landscape of Lucknow—to the extent that they have tended to marginalise the residential precincts that are not for public sector employees until neoliberal policies started to govern approaches to urban landscaping. This chapter considers these precincts as a neighbourhood typology and discusses the dynamics of exclusivity and gentrification formalised by the state and the pre-neoliberalisation markets through architectural design, town-planning parameters and land policy frameworks.

Further, this chapter discusses how regulations applicable to the British cantonment have largely informed the post-Independence town-planning schemes for the public servant housing precincts such as the ones listed above. For this, the chapter draws upon previous research that argues that much of the post-colonial Lucknow residential landscape derives its form, organisation and zoning regulations from the colonial cantonment—implying a continuity of colonial imagery emerging from a latent internalisation of colonial planning principles in Independent India's town-planning schemes.

The chapter deliberates upon why architectural design practice in India considers active occupational and economic segregation as a normalised practice of creating neighbourhoods? To inquire about this, the chapter addresses the following questions: (a) How did government officers housing precincts continue the European ideals of organisation, hierarchy and segregation? (b) What was the desirable urban lifestyle that the architectural design emulated? and (c) To what extent were these precincts conceived as self-sustainable units and functioned as isolated microcosms?

Why Lucknow?

Government employees form a significant share of the working population of Lucknow, and hence it follows that the residential precincts for these employees also contribute significantly to the landscape. As seen in the map (Map 10.1), such residential precincts are mostly close to the cantonment and the Civil Lines of the British period, and also proximate to the present-day administrative offices. The layout of these precincts reflects a planning template informed by Western modernist planning principles. Interestingly, these precincts are called colonies. The accompanying map of Lucknow highlighting these precincts[1] has been prepared by typing the word 'colony' into Google Maps (Map 10.1).

1 The following government officers residential neighbourhoods have been mapped: Agriculture Development Officer (ADO) Colony, Badshah Nagar Government Colony, Bank Colony, Bank of India Colony, Bankers Institute of Rural Development (BIRD) Colony, Butler Colony, Canal Colony, Cantonment, Central Armed Police Forces (CAPF) Colony, Central Institute of Medicinal and Aromatic Plants (CIMAP) Colony, Central Power House Colony, Civil Services Institute (CSI) Colony, Council of Scientific and Industrial Research (CSIR) Colony, Crime Investigation Department

The search results have been cross-checked to verify whether they are government employee housing precincts, which almost ninety per cent of them were. Historian Veena Talwar-Oldenburg notes that the word 'colony' was often used instead of *mohallā* during British presence in Lucknow. River Bank Colony is an example of one such neighbourhood that was developed during the British period. After Independence, the term 'colony' was retained in addition to the word *nagar* which means city to name the upcoming neighbourhoods. The term 'colony' refers to a group of people of one nationality or race living in a foreign place; it may also refer to a place where a group of people with the same occupation or interest live together. According to the Oxford Online Dictionary, in India, it has come to refer to as a housing estate or residential community, especially one originally constructed by an employer for its workers. It follows from this observation that the natives saw the colonizers as the one living in colonies which denoted organisation and discipline, and also status. This observation suggests that the government employee

---

(CID) Colony, Dalibagh Government Colony, Defence Colony, Dilkusha Colony, Doorsanchar Colony, Electricity Department Colony, Forest Colony, Geological Survey of India (GSI) Colony, Government Press Colony, Government Railway Police (GRP) Lines, Havelock Lines, Hindustan Aeronautics Limited (HAL) Colony, Hudson Lines, Hydel Officers' Colony, Income Tax Colony, Indian Council of Agricultural Research-Central Institute for Subtropical Horticulture (ICAR-CISH) Colony, Indian Council of Agricultural Research-Indian Institute of Sugarcane Research (ICAR-IISR) Colony, Indian Revenue Service (IRS) Officers' Apartments, Irrigation Department Colony, Jal Nigam Colony, Jal Vayu Vihar, Kaisarbagh Officers' Colony, Laplace Colony, Lawrence Terrace Colony, LKS Colony, Lucknow Development Authority (LDA) Colony, Mepta Golf Course, National Bank for Agriculture and Rural Development (NABARD) Colony, National Botanical Research Institute (NBRI) Colony, New Railway Colony, Paper Mill Colony, Police Colony, Police Lines, Police Radio Colony, Post and Telegraph Colony, Post Office Colony, Pradeshik Armed Constabulary (PAC) Colony, Pradeshiya Industrial and Investment Corporation of Uttar Pradesh (PICUP) Limited Colony, Radio Colony, Railway Colony, Rajkiya Colony, Rajya Sampatti Colony, Research Designs and Standards Organisation (RDSO) Colony, Reserve Bank of India (RBI) Colony, River Bank Colony, Sainik Nagar Colony, Secretariat Colony, State Bank of India (SBI) Officers' Colony, State Bank of India (SBI) Staff Colony, Tikait Rai Government Colony, Transport Nagar, Uttar Pradesh Power Corporation Limited (UPPCL) Colony, Uttar Pradesh Rajkiya Nirman Nigam (UPRNN) Residential Colony, Uttar Pradesh Rajya Setu Colony Van Nigam Colony and Wireless Radio Colony. The total land area of these precincts is approximately 39.68 square kilometres.

housing precincts were more susceptible to be termed as colonies than their civilian (non-government) counterparts. The continuity of the term is, hence, an indicator to the aspiration of the colony for the new elite of Independent India. Urban elite here is referred to as those urban, educated individuals who were practitioners of law, medicine, or education, who had access to worthy positions in the government. They were committed to social reforms, modernisation and development. Their imagination for the new India was informed by British methods. However, having enjoyed the privilege of proximity to the erstwhile colonial power they too were vehicles of social segregation—except that they visualised themselves as part of the higher strata of the society. Their position enabled them to exercise their vision through the second tier of professionals, such as the town planners, who they would have employed for the designing and layout of their own housing precincts.

Defining Neighbourhood

This chapter uses the 'neighbourhood unit' as proposed by Clarence Perry, an American urban planner and sociologist to refer to the neighbourhood. In 1929, Perry published a monograph, *The Neighborhood Unit, a Scheme for Arrangement for the Family-Life Community*, which diagrammatically proposed an ideal layout for a neighbourhood. Based on the population size, this model provided specific guidelines for the spatial distribution of residences, community services, streets and businesses (Map 10.2). Perry conceptualised neighbourhoods as a response to the fast-moving traffic facilitated by the freeways of the United States, to create residential precincts that would be self-sufficient and hence avoid any conflict between walkability to urban amenities and the ever-present freeways. The concept intended to allow people, especially children, to be able to safely walk to nearby playgrounds and other amenities; however, it was integrated into mainstream planning efforts as a framework for designers and planners to envisage urban centres as a composition of smaller suburbs. Thus, the neighbourhood became an identifiable tool,

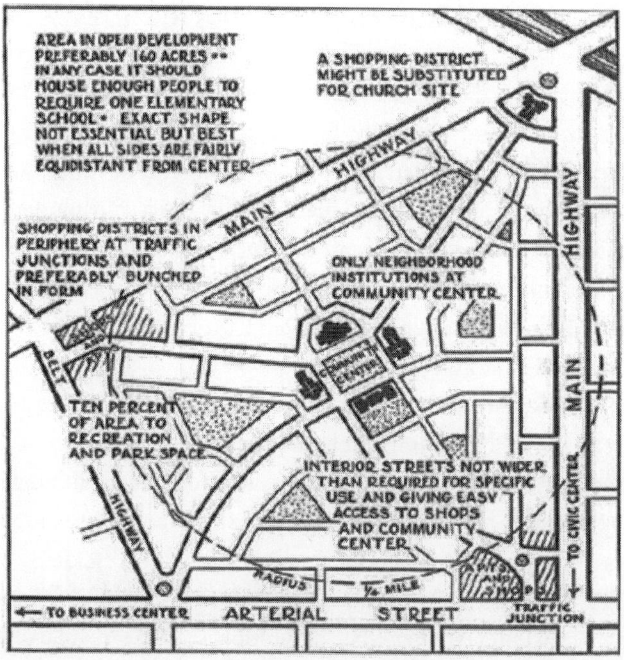

Map 10.2: A diagram of Clarence Perry's Neighbourhood Unit, illustrating the spatiality of the core principles of the concept. Map credit: Perry [1998] 1929, *New York Regional Survey*, Vol. 7

almost formulaic in nature for urban planning to provide community-centric self-contained residential precincts. Perry's neighbourhood unit has the following key design principles:

- School is the centre of the neighbourhood—a quarter to half-mile walk from the residential unit, without any arterial road crossing that walk.
- Large play area near the school that could also be used by the entire community.
- The periphery of the neighbourhood is defined by roads.
- Peripheral roads also discourage traffic through the neighbourhood.
- Local shopping areas near the periphery of the neighbourhood, to further exclude vehicular traffic to the shopping areas.
- At least 10 per cent of land left open for play and community interaction and open space.

Civil Lines to Housing Colonies

Post-Independence Indian town planners adapted through internalisation and translated into indigenous 'colonies' the neighbourhood unit of Perry. Otto Königsberger and Albert Mayer—German and American town planners in India during the post-Independence period and responsible for designs of new towns such as Jamshedpur and parts of Bangalore are two such examples. This chapter will also discuss how the elite favoured an emulation and an unquestioned continuity of the cantonment and Civil Lines typology in the design of their own residential precincts. The Civil Lines typology represented a deliberate improvement upon the unhygienic and chaotic Indian precincts with its broad and regular streets lined with houses set back within large plots. The potential of the neighbourhood as a secular, egalitarian and efficient unit appealed to Nehru's socialist vision. Additionally, the neighbourhood unit shared several characteristics with the Civil Lines typology such as building setbacks, regular and wide roads, open spaces and a certain spatial and visual discipline. However, it used smaller plots than the Civil Lines and hence was spatially economic too. Perry's vision of the neighbourhood unit to house people of a similar social background was contradictory to Nehru's idea of residential precincts. It was this advocacy of social and economic homogeneity and a foregrounding of the nuclear heteronormative family as a household unit that convinced even the Indian elites to adopt this model of town planning in the subsequent residential precincts. Racial segregation in the West is equated with class and caste segregation in India—the manner in which the neighbourhood unit furthered an agenda of exclusivity for the urban elite in the West (Harris 2012) translated smoothly to the agenda of exclusivity within the Indian context as well for precisely the same reason. Urban designer and spatial planner Sanjeev Vidyarthi argues that the acceptance of neighbourhood unit among the pioneering planners and their clients to housing different social groups demonstrates their belief that 'neighbourhood units would have a civilizing effect on the residents, a majority of whom were recent immigrants from villages or the historical quarters of Indian cities' (Vidyarthi 2015: 20).

History of Planning in Lucknow: Extracts of Exclusion

After the 1857 mutiny and despite their victory, the British acknowledged lack of hygienic conditions, safety and ease of movement as biggest threats to their assertive presence in Lucknow. To address those concerns, the British administration employed Robert Cornelius Napier—a military engineer—to reshape city to make it defensible, safe and sanitised for the British. Napier envisioned a new road layout connecting the city's prominent areas and dividing the city into five distinct segments. With the coming of Napier, there was the insistence on building houses, following approval from the municipal representative. Frontage was prioritised to discourage encroachments and encourage a controlled urban appearance (Map 10.3).

Later in 1916, the Municipal Board invited Scottish town planner Patrick Geddes for further advice on town planning. Geddes undertook a series of surveys through which he observed that the roads proposed by Napier were too wide for the context, and recommended reducing the width to follow the old pattern of development. He published a detailed critique of Napier's bye-laws restricting the layout and facades of urban built form. Subsequently in 1920, the Lucknow Improvement Trust was formed, which began the task of laying a new city. Cantonment was created for the military and the Civil Lines was created for the European non-military community comprising civil servants, traders, shopkeepers and school teachers. This residential area, together with the cantonment and railway station, was 'New Lucknow'. Security, health and racial prestige were the dominant justifiers for the segregation which further contributed to the creation of the Cantonment's Act of 1924. This act codified delimitation of cantonment, nuisance control, sanitation and public health, street and public control, water supply and drainage, apart from other matters which were more social and moral in nature. The physical form of cantonment and later townships provided spacious exclusive residential areas, segregated from the Indian population, by building free zones. Historian, geographer, town planner Robert Home argues

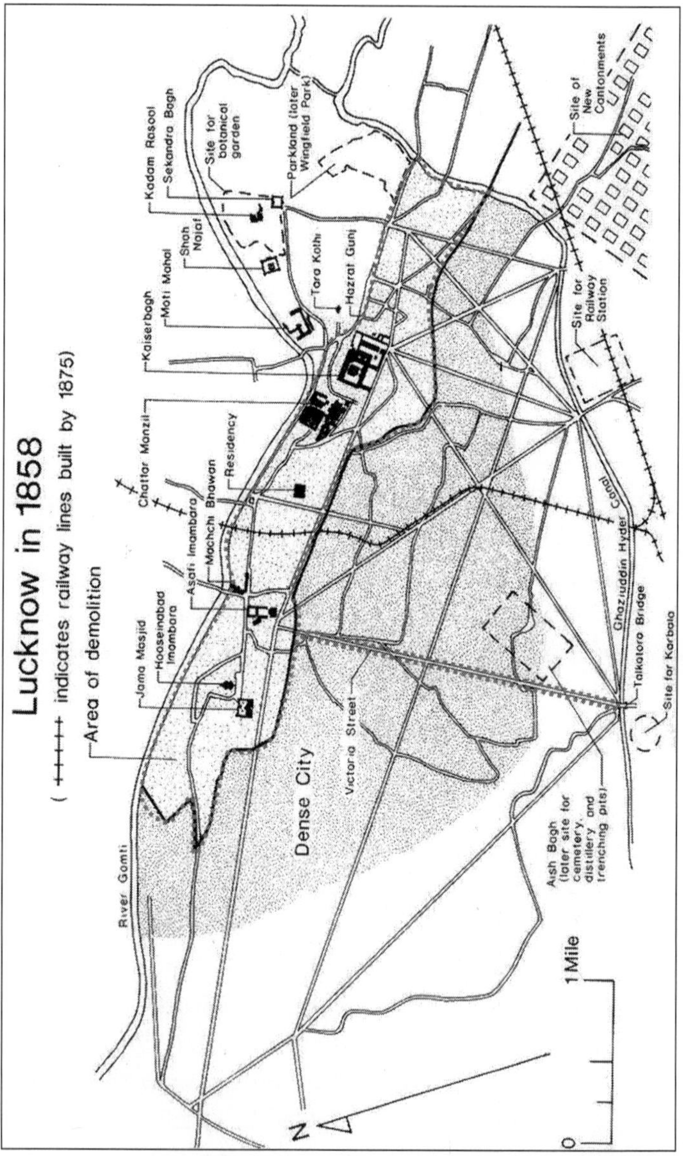

Map 10.3: Robert Napier's post-mutiny proposal for Lucknow, 1858.
Map credit: adapted by the author from Oldenburg (1984: 32).

that in many cities including Lucknow, British colonisers consciously exercised law and policy to exercise spatial separation based on race to reinforce unequal power relations and highlight cultural differences (Home 2014: 75). He traces the process of translating cantonment clause to township rules, but there has been a dearth of study on the post-Independence townships per se.

The Development Plan for Lucknow 1955 published by the Institute of Town Planners, India (ITPI) was prepared for a projected total population of 7,50,000—a number estimated for the next two decades based on past census data. The plan clearly assumes a nuclear heteronormative family of five as a basic household unit and breaks down the housing requirements as a percentage of total residential units into six categories: (a) 5 per cent to be two single and double bungalows per acre, (b) 5 per cent to be four single or double family houses per acre, (c) 10 per cent to be ten single-family houses per acre, (d) 50 per cent to be eight two-family houses per acre, (e) 20 per cent to be six three-family to five-family houses per acre and (f) 10 per cent to be six four-family to six-family houses per acre (ITPI 1955: 23) The officers' residential neighbourhoods followed the same typologies ranging from approximately 15 persons per acre to a maximum of 150 persons per acre. The intention was to keep the residential density low in order to accommodate further inevitable development with the growth in population (Figure 10.1). In keeping with the neighbourhood unit spatial distribution recommendation, the Lucknow Development Plan provided for the following: (a) playing fields and playgrounds within a one-mile radius, (b) wide green margins along major thoroughfares for pedestrians and (c) green belts to separate residential precincts from industrial ones.

Post-Independence Indian town planners insisted on careful research and methodical data collection that would represent India's varied socioeconomic conditions pragmatically to propose town-planning standards specific to India. At the same time, while acknowledging the absence of any such information at a regional scale, they approved adopting 'workable standards of general nature based on [...] the experience gained in other progressive countries so as to enable the planners [in curbing] further deterioration and unhealthy

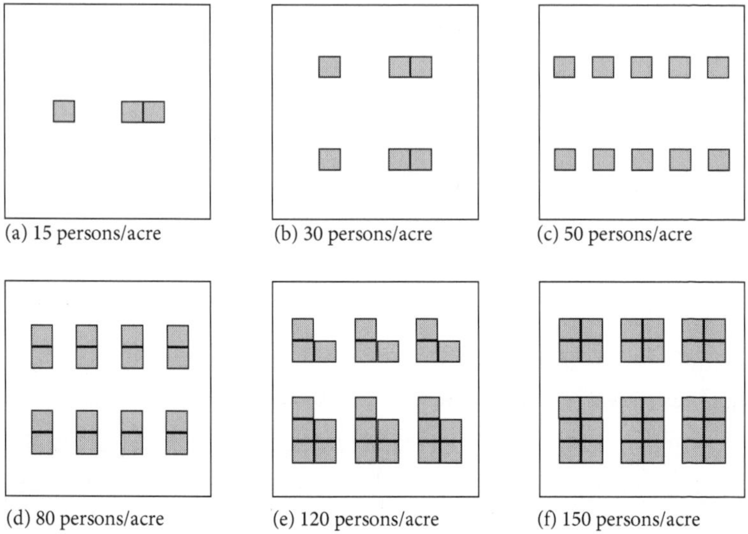

Figure 10.1: 1955 Lucknow Development Plan residential categories. Image credit: author

growth of [Indian cities...]' (ITPI 1956: 23). Figure 10.1 suggests that in 1955, the allotted area was one acre for sixty-four people. This is too low in comparison to the present-day approximately minimum density of 245 persons per acre.[2] The densities are incomparable. However, it is important to underscore the discretion of the Lucknow town planners in 1955 to have 'proposed open[ing] up the residential zones for development gradually [...] so as to prevent sporadic development which becomes unmanageable at reasonable cost' (ITPI 1955: 24). This foresight has become more relevant in the present-day neoliberal context when the Lucknow Development Authority (LDA) has revised the permissible residential density for existing residential neighbourhoods to 245 persons per acre; and has the option of using land in these sparsely built neighbourhoods to create more housing

2 The present-day minimum density is based on clause 8.3.1 of the Lucknow Master Plan 2031 prepared by the Lucknow Development Authority, which permits a revised minimum residential density of 600 persons per hectare in already built neighbourhoods, and 400 persons per hectare in new and upcoming neighborhoods.

(LDA 2031: 54). While the rest of the city—which had a similar density in 1955—has adapted to accommodate the changing residential densities accorded by the neoliberal policies, the government housing precincts have been slow, rather insulated from any such effects.

In Vidyarthi's view, the concept of the neighbourhood unit was 'formally accepted' by the town planners of Independent India at the fourth conference of ITPI held at Lucknow in 1955. He goes on to share the 'land use table recommended by the ITPI for a residential neighbourhood of 10000 population', drawing similarities between it and Perry's design principles (Vidyarthi 2015: 32). In outlining the similarities, Vidyarthi points to the mechanisms that facilitated an absolute abstraction of the neighbourhood unit into an Indian model. He attributes 'legitimacy of rational precision', and the possibility to 'collapse the design concept into mathematical formulation', as the key to Indianising the neighborhood unit concept—'spatially and spiritually removed from Perry's conception' (Ibid. 2015: 33). The recommendations follow the neighbourhood unit through their insistence of providing primary schools with accompanying playgrounds to be part of the neighbourhood, and secondary schools with accompanying playgrounds to be within one mile (ITPI 1956: 23).

Oldenburg's work describing the colonial undertaking for locating the cantonment soon after the mutiny can be used to develop an argument for further demonstrating that the post-Independence town planners used the same logic. First, the way cantonment was cited on the very green Dilkhusha and adjoining villages without any negotiation with the lawful owners are similar to the post-Independence socialist ideology of the new government. It allotted the areas near the cantonment and the civil lines to its own housing enclaves. Second, the spatial arrangements in the cantonment were in exact contradiction with the layout of the old city. This became the new desirable norm for the new elite. Third, the cantonment received the municipal subsidy, and hence, it was technically part of the city. However, the British conveniently considered it outside the municipal limits exempting it from all tax obligations. Similarly, even in Independent India today, the cantonment is outside the municipal limits of Lucknow (Map 10.4).

Oldenburg further cites the municipal committee report to show that the construction rules tended to favour Indian individuals with resources or power, who were willing to construct dwellings in the bungalow style of the Civil Lines, rather than the courtyard-style house, which was adjudged ill-designed and poorly ventilated. This is clear evidence of slow and steady eradication of the courtyard-style house rendering it selectively permissible, and hence, undesirable. This is also evidence of the assertion for the normalisation of morally higher, and culturally superior bungalow typology, which would soon become an accepted house type in Independent India. Such normalisation is evident in engineer and town planner Raghunath Deshpande's (1943) assertion in his *Modern Ideal Homes for India*, a series of illustrated books that provided directions for design and construction of a house during the 1930s, and well into the 1960s. In the 1939 version, which he wrote after his return from a world tour, he curated a set of house designs that combined American, English, German, Danish, Swiss, French and Japanese's features and Indianised them. Deshpande served as a member of the National Housing Sub-Committee of the National Planning Committee too. Hence, the plausibility of his work having an influence on the national housing policies is quite high. The National Planning Committee (NPC)[3] recommended that 'urban housing is to be regarded as a public utility service, the responsibility for which primarily rests with the State. [...] Definite standards for various types of unit house accommodation shall be laid down by the appropriate authority'. (NPC 1940: 64). Given Deshpande's extensive outlining of 'ideal' home designs, that might have played a major role in the formulation of approvable standards for various unit types.

Deshpande's (1943) work is a fair representation of the aspirational typology of the new urban elite. His house type consists of components

3 The National Planning Committee was set up in 1939 for the purpose of formulating development plans and economic planning in sectors such as education, agriculture, industry, science and housing. Jawaharlal Nehru was the chairman of the committee and continued to hold that position after Independence too through which the Five Year Plans were launched.

such as the veranda, drawing room, dining room, kitchen, bedroom, dressing room, lady's apartment, storeroom, prayer room, bathroom, staircase, comfort room, guest room, children's room, toilet and garage. He gives a detailed description of the criteria for space allocation for each of these components. Those criteria can be seen in almost all government housing schemes. The criteria are flexible to accommodate a small house as well as a big house without compromising the connotation of the word 'home'.

Home is described—beyond just a house—to not just provide shelter but also function as a centre of social life and a place of health, comfort, and happiness for its residents. By that logic, it upholds the morality of a heteronormative lifestyle (Map 10.5). The daily routine of a family is cleanly classified into a set of activities which can be performed in specific locations of the house. For example, the veranda has a definitive purpose for having morning tea and breakfast; dining room for family meals could be combined with the adjacent drawing room for small parties; and courtyard or garden for festivals. Afternoon tea is to be had in the drawing-room, while children's home tuition to be performed in either the front

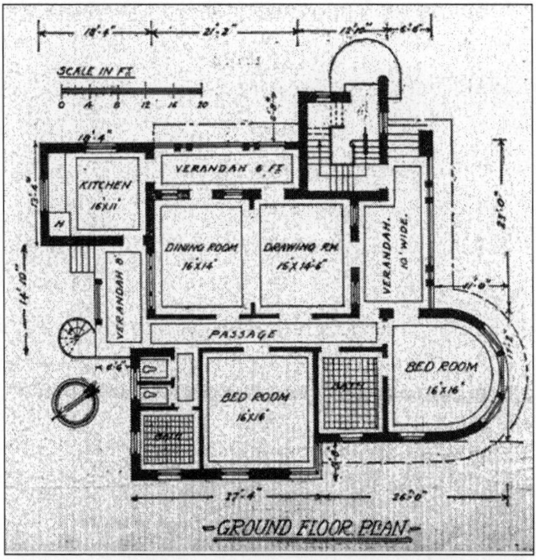

Map 10.5: House layout curated by Deshpande.
Map credit: Deshpande (1943: 311)

veranda or dining room. Homework and serious reading are to be done in the library, but in case of a small house, could be done in the bedroom. Even thinking is considered a distinct activity which could be done in the library or the bedroom depending on the size of the house. Drawing room or lounge is meant for listening to the radio, the rear veranda is for boys' handicrafts, while girls' music and needlework could be done in the dining room or lounge. Deshpande recommends separate makeup rooms in large houses but insists on the mere presence of a looking glass in small houses. Casual short-time visitors are confined to the front veranda but may be invited into the drawing-room, based on the status of the visitor. Guests could also be invited into the library in larger houses. The yard adjacent to the dining room or kitchen is meant for drying clothes. He recommends two entrances for all houses—one from the front veranda, and one from the kitchen or back veranda to function as a separate entrance for the servants.

The emphasis is on uni-functionality, immovability, imposing presence and hierarchical labelling. Each room has a strictly defined role corresponding to one or another of the various functions of a family unit. Even the furniture is placed in a way that it captures a regular chronology of action. To borrow from sociologist Jean Baudrillard's *System* of *Objects*—his doctoral dissertation under Henri Lefebvre, Roland Barthes and Pierre Bourdieu—'within this private space each room its own furniture and takes on a symbolic dignity' (Baudrillard 2008 [1968]: 18). In that significance, the primary purpose is to personify human relationship captive to the moral dimension.

The emphasis on the recommended location of the garage indicates the growing importance of visual markers of status in the emerging urbanscape. Deshpande convinces his readers of the pointlessness of the garage in a corner of the backyard likening that to the redundant horse stables. Instead, he argues that the garage be integrated with the house to avoid inconvenience during rains. Also, the proximity of the garage to the kitchen would facilitate easy and smooth delivery of grocery shopping into the interiors. Additionally, 'one can look to its and cars upkeep much better', and hence it should be visible. The emphasis on the garage location and its visibility points to an integration of the automobile with the family unit.

His descriptions and arguments align with the romanticist picturesque landscape genre of painting patronised by the 18th-century European bourgeoisie. To remain in accordance with the 'modern trends in the civilised countries', Deshpande advises the front yard just enough to provide a sufficient foreground and a good setting for the building; while the backyard to be more elaborate for family use. These yards were also meant to grow vegetables such as greens, beans, pumpkins, snake-gourd, creepers and so on for healthy nutrition of the family. Similarly, lawns were to be provided, not only for outdoor enjoyment and as children's play area, but also as an object of the pride of the family. The use of boundary wall hedges, lotus fancies, shrubberies were encouraged to maintain privacy from neighbours. The lawn was also treated as a tool for providing an appearance of exclusivity to the house from its surroundings. These advice suggest the aspirations of the urban elite to acquire and maintain exclusivity. However, the popularity of these ideas also indicates the commonness—and hence the non-exclusivity—of exclusivity among the residents.

Deshpande's (1943) work has the potential of influencing the types of house plans that were approved for construction at the local town planning level. It is also possible that the types of house layouts that were approved might have aligned with his inventory.

Organisation, Hierarchy, and Segregation in Housing Colonies

Typically, in an employee precinct, the residence of the director, or the chief, would have a bungalow typology surrounded by green lawns on all sides, thus intentionally enclosing it and separating it from the rest of the residents. Such precincts are governed by byelaws that do not permit parking and vending on its tree-lined streets. The floor plans of the houses are derivative of the colonial bungalow although the elevations no longer carry any features of colonial architectural ornamentation. The town planners and architects produced a number of standardised housing models dominated by the concepts of efficiency, minimum costs and rapid installation.

Such colonies or neighbourhoods have fostered a system of spatial segregation—between the government employees and non-government employees at the urban level, and among the government employees themselves at the neighbourhood level. These neighbourhoods are defined and bounded by peripheral roads and comprise various categories of housing to correspond with the rank and income of the employee. Urban demographer Veronique Dupont cites Asok Mitra who qualifies this phenomenon of residential segregation based on employment in government and the resultant urbanscape as 'salaried apartheid'. This segregation and its equation with the British residential pattern formalised in colonial India have already been underscored by various scholars in studies on Delhi. Such studies have made a case for the socio-spatial hierarchy established in the distance of residence from the administrative centre—for example, the Viceregal Palace of British India or the Rashtrapati Bhawan of Independent India. Other studies, including that by Dupont, have also pointed out that 'the spatial organization of housing estates built for government employees after Independence can be read as a revival of the traditional pattern of spatial and residential segregation based on caste origin, and applied here to the rank and status in the administrative service' (Dupont 2004: 160).

Having lived most of their professional lives in state-provided housing, these employees choose to later live in apartment blocks or co-operative societies that have a similar demographic profile.

> The associations are formed on the basis of professional affiliation: lawyers of the Supreme Court, employees from the same press group, or the same institute, officers from the police, high rank government officers, or teachers from the same university, for instance. The founding group is then in a position to exert control on the selection of new buyers, while the owners renting out their flats apply a screening process on the prospective tenants. This system of co-optation and selection ensure a social and professional homogeneity of the residents of the same complex of apartment blocks, and hence leads to further exclusion. (Ibid.)

Lucknow neighbourhoods such as Indira Nagar, Gomati Nagar and Mahanagar are some such examples that have created isolated precincts within larger urban schemes where retired employees of a similar organisation stay together.

Conclusion

It has been seen that much of the post-Independence residential landscape of Lucknow derives its form, organisation and zoning regulations from the colonial cantonment and Civil Lines implying a continuity of colonial imagery emerging from a latent internalisation of colonial planning principles in Independent India's town-planning schemes. These precincts stand in stark contrast with the rest of the city which has been allowed to give in to development pressures seen in high density, high rise skyline dotted with shrinking green spaces. Neoliberal policies and agendas have seen an upsurge of gated communities, but that has had little to no impact on these enclaves—making them even more exclusive and desirable residential addresses among the urban elite.

References

Bartholomew, John et al. 1893. 'Lucknow and Its Environs'. In *The Constable's 1893 Hand Atlas of India*. Available at http://www.columbia.edu/itc/mealac/pitchett/00maplinks/colonial/constable1893/xlucknowmap.jpg (accessed on 26 August 2019).

Baudrillard, Jean. 2008 [1968]. *System of Objects*. New Delhi: Navayana.

Deshpande, Raghunath. 1943. *Modern Ideal Homes for India*. Poona: United Book Corporation.

Dupont, Venorique. 2004. 'Socio-Spatial Differentiation and Residential Segregation in Delhi: A Question of Scale?' *Geoforum*, Vol. 35, pp. 157–175.

Harris, Dianne. 2013. *Little White Houses*. Minneapolis: University of Minnesota Press.

Home, Robert. 2014. 'Shaping Cities of the Global South: Legal Histories of Planning and Colonialism'. In *The Routledge Handbook on Cities of the Global South*, edited by Susan Parnell and Sophie Oldfield, pp. 75–85. New York: Routledge.

Hosagrahar, Jyoti. 2005. *Indigenous Modernities: Negotiating Architecture and Urbanism*. New York: Routledge.

Institute of Town Planners, India (ITPI). 1955. 'Development Plan for Lucknow'. *Journal of the Institute of Town Planners, India*, July, pp. 18–26.

———. 1956. 'Autumn Planning Seminar and State Planning Officials' Conference at Lucknow'. *Journal of the Institute of Town Planners, India*, January–April, pp. 23–28.

Joshi, Ashutosh. 2008. *Town Planning Regeneration of Cities by Joshi*. New Delhi: New India Publishing Agency.

———. 1976. *Colonial Urban Development: Cultural, Social Power and Environment*. New York: Routledge.

King, Anthony. 2016. *Writing the Global City: Globalisation, Postcolonialism and the Urban*. New York: Routledge.

Lucknow Development Authority (LDA). 2016. *Lucknow Master Plan 2031*.

National Planning Committee (NPC) Number 2. 1940. *Proceedings and Other Particulars relating to the National Planning Committee*. Bombay: National Planning Committee.

Oldenburg, Veena Talwar. 1984. *The Making of Colonial Lucknow 1856–1877*. NJ: Princeton University Press.

Perry, Clarence. 1998 [1929]. *The Neighborhood Unit: From the Regional Survey of New York and Its Environs*, Vol. VII. London: Routledge/Thoemmes Press.

Vidyarthi, Sanjeev. 2015. *One Idea, Many Plans: An American City Design Concept in Independent India*. New York: Routledge.

11

Neighbourhoods in Space–Time: A Case of House Prices and Latent Aspirations

Yugank Goyal and Harini Shah*

This chapter looks at the neighbourhood as a spatial and temporal category through the prism of its individual units' prices. Neighbourhood in this project is understood to act as an intermediary, which cushions or absorbs the shock between the interiority of a home and the anonymity of a city. This conceptualisation, in tune with the introduction chapter in this book, helps us view the neighbourhood as a socio-spatial construction between home and city. The two ends of this continuum, mediated by neighbourhood become important to understand the design and philosophy, in which neighbourhoods get formed, evolve and get (proverbially) destroyed. In other words, just like the functional aspect of an intermediary rests crucially on the two players she (dis)connects, so is the neighbourhood's socio-spatial presence heavily dependent on the house and the city.

At the same time, the concept of time value of money affords a temporal aspect to the socio-spatial dimension of the neighbourhood. One can imagine a space–time continuum. On the spatial side, the neighbourhood's expanse starts right outside one's home and stretch until the unfamiliar city is triggered. On the temporal spectrum, one's dwelling in the neighbourhood over time, predicated on the factor of cost of its use and occupation comes to mind. If we have a house purchased or have it on rent, our presence there signifies how the capital invested in it sticks through time—the bigger the capital, the longer the temporal association. This invokes the idea of the discount factor, namely, how do we view the future. Such an analytical category infuses a temporal

* The authors would like to thank Prasen Kundru for his research assistance.

dimension in understanding neighbourhoods, which are a collection of individual residences, and so how expensive a neighbourhood is, is linearly correlated with the prices of the houses in it.

In this chapter, we want to excavate the 'capital' silences buried under the house, as one foundational ingredient of the neighbourhood. And specifically, we will draw the meaning of neighbourhoods in a function of house prices. The reason house price is an interesting parameter is because it captures aspirational aspects of modernity. Therefore, it is a unique window to study how such an aspiration self-selects people into certain social categories, which in turn, lead to the formation of a certain character of neighbourhoods. Using house prices to study neighbourhood contributes not only to the discourse on the socio-spatial understanding of neighbourhoods but also pushes the frontier of knowledge on housing as an analytical tool to study people's aspirations as locked in time.

We estimate the ratio between the price of the house and annual rent. This ratio (house price divided by annual rent) gives us the number of years one would need to pay the rent to roughly justify the purchase of the same house. This is then an analytical keyhole to view the aspirational lock-in of preference. In other words, whether people are choosing to buy or rent a house is a decision embedded in—in addition to the cultural construct of societal preferences—evolution and formation of a certain type of neighbourhood. The neighbourhood then surrounds the question, namely, why do we buy houses as opposed to renting one? Or the other way round.

This question, in its simplistic formulation, captures some of the most fundamental assumptions of how modernity has interplayed with human nature. The answer to this question also wraps itself in various apparatuses of accomplishments, as much as in varying equipment of misery. The answer offers us a new lens to imagine a neighbourhood formation, alteration and dissolution. Yet, the question has attracted little scholarly scrutiny. And like most unchallenged viewpoints, this may well be hinged on—however solidly held—invisible, and therefore (unchallenged) assumptions. If one relies on understanding humans as temporally plural beings and investigates the role of socio-legal frameworks to assert and reify structures of modernity that dilute the temporal self-view of humans when they make their choice, one will not be surprised upon this intellectual journey to arrive at neighbourhoods.

There are three strands the chapter takes upon. First, it explains the relevance of locating house prices in relation to neighbourhoods for understanding the temporal dimensions of neighbourhoods. A flip side of the question is to what extent neighbourhoods are constructed out of this parameter (of price–rent ratio). Second, it explains the price–rent ratio to analyse house prices and studies this parameter in select cities in India. Third, it opens up the qualitative judgements over select neighbourhoods in Delhi, where data was collected from, to inform contours of neighbourhoods that were *co-produced* as a result of house and rental prices there.

Neighbourhoods Constructed Out of the Prices of Homes That Inhabit It

In an urban agglomeration, human cohabitation starts with a home and evolves from a neighbourhood to a city. The neighbourhood then is an intermediary step, a bridge if you will, connecting the familiarity of a home and the anonymity of the city. There is a necessity for this bridge because the promise of modernity directs our desire to be part of an interiority that is home into experiencing the exteriority of our workplace. From the familiar homes, we move to the unfamiliar and anonymous city, guiding ourselves through the bridge. The everyday anxiety of exiting from the neighbourhood and 'hitting the road' to be in office on time in the morning, is only matched by a comforting feeling of entering the same neighbourhood, and halting to fetch fruits 'round the corner', the same evening. In some sense, it is the extension of homes, opening up into the diverging mobilities of our everydayness of work lives, and at the same time, the reservoir-like collection of the returning global mobilities—a type of intersection of complex flows of the global and the local (Savage et al. 2005).

Neighbourhoods operate as independently managed city units, where many municipal functions can be absorbed by its constituent members. In many ways, therefore, neighbourhoods are unique sites to observe decentralised, democratic participation of a range of community decision making.[1] These rules render a processual interaction with members of the community offering a relational expression of a neighbourhood (Massey 1994). All of this makes the neighbourhood a cultural phenomenon as much as spatial.

The sociocultural aspect of a neighbourhood enables us to harvest many economic impulses necessary for developing new layers in its study. If Whyte's (1993) vibrant ethnography of Italian streets or Jacob's (1997) study of American cities in the 1960s is to be admired, one cannot help but recognise neighbourhood as a frame through which one can understand the contested social mobility relating to class and status. These underlying structures of class and status are directly manifested in the residence one possesses, and how it is located. There is considerable literature on how neighbourhood leads to the 'neighbourhood effect', which in turn is manifested in social exclusion (Bauder 2002), or its determinants for social capital (Forrest and Kearns 2001). For these concepts, the materiality of class comes into the picture, more clearly visible in the houses that form and is formed by the 'type' of neighbourhood. Martin Heidegger, in his seminal chapter 'Building Dwelling Thinking', reminds us that etymologically, neighbour means 'the near dweller, he who dwells nearby' (Heidegger 1971: 147), and in doing so, asserts that dwelling is an 'active process of accomplishment rather than a given' (Bissel 2013). These ideas centralise not just the house, but the class and capital of neighbourhood, which gets reflected in how expensive a constituent house in a neighbourhood is. In Galster's (2001) conceptualisation of neighbourhood, land usage and the cluster of residence are the conceptual hinges tying neighbourhood with idiosyncrasies like, inter alia, price of constituent units (even if figurative) and consumption.

These ideas centralise house prices, as prime tools to produce neighbourhoods, and in turn produce themselves. Estimating house price is tricky because it involves assessing a diverse set of idiosyncratic factors. Hedonic pricing models are often used in these cases, where

1 See for example Taylor (2003), Bailey and Pill (2011), Zerah (2007), Lama-Reval (2007), Coelho and Vekat (2009).

house price is regressed on a range of inherent attributes,[2] in which prices are explained through type (flat/plot), age, floor, job and recreational facility accessibility, physical characteristics and most importantly, neighbourhood characteristics, which includes its social and economic characteristics (Tse 2002). That is why aspects of housing markets and that of urban regeneration depend on each other (Kauko 2009). Just as neighbourhood characteristics are crucial for determining housing prices, the same house prices can also lead to certain neighbourhood characteristics to emerge. Because a range of attributes that go in estimating house prices are rather homogenous (location, the physicality of the house, age, distances, etc.), a convergence in house prices will likely dilute the heterogeneity of neighbourhoods. Tiebout (1956) had recognised these inter- and intra-neighbourhood differences and predicted that households with similar interests will form somewhat homogenous neighbourhoods. Building on this work, more recently, Lynch and Rasmussen (2004) showed that income can be the singular factor which can incentivise households demanding high-quality services to exclude low-income households from the neighbourhoods.

The interplay of income and neighbourhoods gets mediated through the pricing of the constituent units of a neighbourhood, namely houses. These prices fluctuate between the binaries of purchase price and rent price. So, in analytical terms, rent or price, both become a floating signifier of what type of income levels are exhibited in a neighbourhood and consequently the neighbourhood type. Prices or rentals, therefore, inform a substantive aspect of a neighbourhood. The ongoing discourse on neighbourhood segregation, or gated societies, that dots the greener pastures of buzzing metropolis in emerging economies makes the practical dimension of 'being' in a neighbourhood. In other words, if I want to live in a neighbourhood, the price of living is predominantly determined by the price of living—either rental or purchase price. So the design, scope and aspiration of a neighbourhood suddenly appear out of other spatial–temporal characteristics when we observe how expensive is it to live there.

2 Informed by Himmelberg (2005), Freeman (1979), Kain and Quigley (1970).

In many ways, therefore, house prices themselves can form certain neighbourhoods and vice versa. This co-production of house prices and neighbourhoods can be valuable to advance our understanding of neighbourhoods, both spatially and temporally. Spatially because that would become part of the house attributes (location and physical features). Temporally because house purchase is a long-term investment. And so, the decision to buy a house captures within it, the time–value view of the buyer. I will buy an exorbitantly priced house because I think the purchase is justified over time (note that this also sheds light on my own aspiration measured against time). Simply put, it offers a unique window into the discount rates of people. The discount rate is the time value of anything. It is the estimate of how important the future is to me. Anything that has a long-term implication affects our brains differently—for some, the future is far too distant to be worried about today. For another, it is rather close and therefore she must be careful in her decisions. A smoker has a high discount rate of the future. She values her present time far more than the future one.

But how do we know if the price of the house is 'exorbitant?' There is no absolute scale against which one can benchmark house prices as high or low. We exploit a unique parameter for this, namely the price–rent ratio. If we divide the price of the house with the annual rent it will earn on a sublet, we will get the approximate number of years one needs to rent it out for, to justify its purchase. Consider the value is, say, 25. This would mean that if I were to rent it out for 25 years or so, it makes more sense for me to buy the house than rent it. Alternatively, if the value is 80, then I'd rather be staying in here for 80 years at least to justify the purchase. The question at the heart of our study is, if people indeed choose to buy a house with a large price–rent ratio, what does it tell us about the aspirational (temporal) aspect of the house purchase specifically, and that of the neighbourhood, generally. Such an exercise, in addition to throwing fresh fodder for research on the temporal aspect of neighbourhoods, will also help us re-imagine the continuously churning socioeconomic designs of a neighbourhood.

Price–Rent Ratio: An Indicator of Aspiration and Temporal[3]

Price–rent ratio is crucial to understanding the true return to housing over time, as it estimates the expectations of market participants about future capital gains to housing (Davis et al. 2008). If one suppresses rent by subsidised rented housing, the value will shoot up, thereby reducing incentives for people to buy the house (Chen 1996). On the other hand, the high price of the house encourages people to rent out the property. This is visible in many 'expensive' cities in the world. The premia on the house purchase rely significantly on this parameter (Campbell et al. 2009). Price–rent ratio carries within it, an ability to estimate future returns and rent growth, where the future returns encompassing expected real interest rates and expected risk premium over a risk-free rate (Engsted and Pedersen 2015; Kishor and Morley 2010). While studies on price–rent ratios abound for countries like the US (Cochrane 2011; Gallin 2008), data and studies on developing country contexts are entirely missing.

Even though research shows that an increase in ratio signifies a future increase in returns, many confounding puzzles exist—the increase in the ratio can also be attributed to the suppression in rentals rather than increase in house prices, and second, predictive patterns may also depend on the values being real or nominal (Engsted and Pedersen 2015). Inflation will perhaps push rentals and house prices differently. Yet, despite all these diverging results, price–rent ratio must conceal within it, a very strong estimate of how people view their future.

This also means, if the value of price–rent ratio is, say 40, its price is far higher than that with a price–rent ratio of 20, or its rents are highly suppressed compared to the other. Since rental values and house price values move synchronously (expensive houses also draw higher rents), one can say with some sense of certainty, other things constant, a

3 This section relies considerably on Goyal (2020).

higher price–rent ratio means the house prices are inflated, irrationally. Price–rent ratios capture within them, a rational tool to decide a smarter choice between renting or buying.

So when we have a high price–rent ratio, and people are still buying the houses, there can be two economic reasons. First, I have a considerable surplus and disposable capital. Second, and more importantly, I am looking into a distant future, and reasonably sure my decision to buy is justified—I will be able to make up for it, very soon. This, therefore, puts undue stress on evolving a particular type of aspiration. Such an aspiration is built out of the ingredients of modernity. This modernity promises you that a house purchase is a 'worthy' decision, and therefore, you end up carving out aspirations with a blind belief in this promise of modernity. You carry on with your work harbouring a hope that one day, you will 'buy' a house—may be the same house you are living in. The high price–rent ratio may not justify the purchase at all, but you are immune to that constraint. Aspirations, over time, become overtime. And this forces you to accept any type of hardship, as long as your aspiration of 'owning a house' comes true.

Homeownership is a construct of owning a place in a specific neighbourhood. House prices and neighbourhood characteristics, as discussed previously, are co-producing each other. So the motivation of this aspirational thinking is often fuelled by the impulse of 'being part of' a neighbourhood. Neighbourhoods in many cities of India are categorised as high-income-group (HIG) society, middle-income-group (MIG) society and low-income-group (LIG) society. The house prices decrease in this order. And these are government housing projects, with official nomenclature. Is not the force of aspiration evolving a neighbourhood as it evolves a house price? The prices of houses correlate with the aspiration projects of modernity, and builders exploit these very sensitivities in people, calling them out for a 'Page 3 living', 'your dream home', 'home cutoff and yet within your city', 'luxurious abode' and even 'living with no neighbours on your floor'!

A look at a bank's loan-disbursing branch is also a powerful lens to observe this house–neighbourhood aspiration. The sight is a phenomenological instruction into this overarching 'social self-becoming' in practice. One observes a number of young couples with their little children wandering about, waiting in line carrying several file-folders and documents that assert their identity, obligations and proof of what they had to part with to fulfil an obligation. They are all expressionless. The other side of the counters, full of un-eager bank employees offering a series of necessary congratulatory, dry smiles when paperwork verification is over. The handshake between them confirms a loan is disbursed, a dream being traded and a so-called aspiration being fulfilled. The couple drags its child out, with the same expressionless face, but dragging a smile as well.

Surely, there is a cultural reason to purchase such a house as well. And that is a social norm to buy the house. This cultural norm is high in India, and one might say that this affects people's aspiration too. Various studies have shown that for many cultures, homeownership has a value-laden heaviness, India included (Proxenos 2002). But cultural preferences may not compel you to make an economically disastrous choice. Indeed, for most liquidity-constrained Indians, purchasing an expensive home is akin to bondage. Whatever the importance of culture, paying capacity is a strong influencer in these type of cases.

Let us try to exhibit what we found. We did an extensive online study from rental and real estate transaction websites, to find out the prices and rentals in select neighbourhoods for five Indian metropolitan cities—Mumbai, Delhi, Hyderabad, Chennai and Bangalore. The houses were categorised into standalone homes with ownership to land and apartment in high-rise buildings with no ownership to land. Adjusted for the area (to get per unit area prices), we also saw both the rich and poor areas of the cities. We then divided the prices and annual rents per unit area in these neighbourhoods. The results, displayed in Figure 11.1, are interesting.

The price–rent ratio in Indian cities goes through the 'roof', proverbially speaking. For independent bungalows, some places in Delhi have a ratio beyond 100! The x-axis moves from expensive to inexpensive areas in terms of real estate, generally considered. And yet, one observes how high the ratio is even in poor localities. Keeping Delhi aside, even the remaining cities exhibit an average ratio of around 40. This average is only slightly lower in case of apartments. Not only are house prices in India insanely high, but there is also little

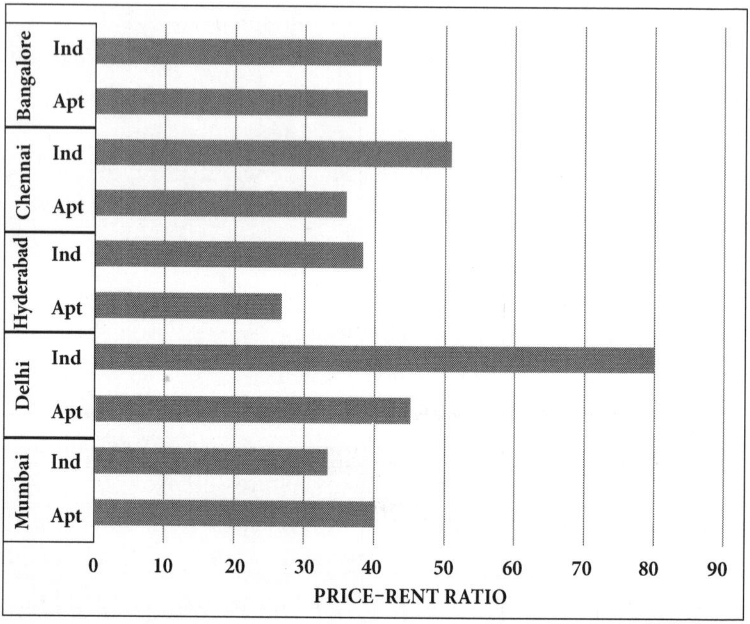

Figure 11.1: Price–rent ratio in five cities in India. 'Apt' denotes flats in apartments; 'Ind' denotes independent houses/bungalows. Image credit: authors

correlation between house prices as compared to the average incomes in these places.

Indian price–rent ratio is enormously high. For most societies, research has shown price–rent ratio of 20 is where the average lies. In fact, for many, 15 is considered to be the value of the ratio of a place where one is better off buying a house. In the US, for example, NYC, Honolulu, San Francisco and Boston command high house prices with the price–rent ratio at 34, 30, 28 and 27, respectively (Andreevska 2019). Even Washington DC is considered to have high house prices and its price–rent ratio is 22 (Ibid.). In fact, analysts recommend that if price–rent ratio is higher than 15, you would rather buy it than rent it (Alford 2010). This is because if you buy a house with a high ratio you will need a higher increase in the house price in coming years to justify the price you have paid for it. Places with irrationally inflated values of house prices will also have high levels of price–rent ratios. Conversely, if the ratio is high, the house prices would be artificially inflated.

With irrationally inflated house prices, neighbourhoods in India suddenly adopt a temporal dimension too. This, therefore, adds to the imagination of a neighbourhood, beyond its spatial aspect. And since the temporal dimension is most certainly captured in house prices, which in turn depends on income, it opens up a range of questions not merely on the exclusionary makeup of a neighbourhood, invoking both its social and economic mapping, but also the inaccessibility of neighbourhood from an aspirational point of view. This time–space stamp of a neighbourhood is most visible in developing countries where the price–rent ratio is often 'depressingly' high.

Another point is in order here, which further explains the temporal aspect of a neighbourhood. People view time differently. At the risk of sounding Orientalist, one may claim that Western societies look at time linearly, while those in the east, like Indians, understand it cyclically. For the former, time is a limited resource and people structure their lives around deadlines. In a country like India, deadlines are often looked at as targets, which compete with, tasks at hand. It must be putting strain on the relationship (Pant 2016). Be that as it may, one would imagine, people to behave in their own cultural contexts. These contexts are often used to understand the absence of benchmarks across large-scale societies where the cultural meaning of time keeps changing. This is true not just of culture, but of any group analytically differentiated from another. So time moves differently for my grandmother than it does for me. Children do not have the same discount rates as adults have; just as Germans don't have the same discount rates as Chinese, Chen (2013) discusses how different languages contain discount rates sensitivities of different cultures within them. A few years ago, one of us was to fly to Doha for an international conference. A few days before the trip, the organisers sent a list of cultural 'dos and don'ts' for Qatar. One of its suggestions was as follows, 'If someone is late, please do not get offended. It does not mean disrespect here. It only means this person was having better time elsewhere!'

But this is changing and as a consequence, time is losing its plurality. It is changing because people in India, buying houses and, therefore, staking claims in certain neighbourhoods are divorced from reality in so many ways and adopting homogeneous ways of life. The impact of local contexts and spatial organisation of housing has a good deal to influence such choices, but we still find the lack of wide divergence in ratios across cities, across poor and rich neighbourhoods within cities. People in Delhi look at the future in the same way as those in Mumbai or Hyderabad look, and even those within Delhi or Mumbai. The design of economic imperatives has led to a strong homogenising attitude amongst people of various cultures to consider their time value of aspirations, similar to anyone possessed by similar economic imperatives. These imperatives are shaped by modernity and get manifested in the society through the existence of modern institutions like banks, the insurance industry and their modern tools like interest rates, predictive models and probability distribution patterns that define the scope of such tools. Neighbourhoods dance to the tune of these models and borrow a similar pattern across societies. A rich neighbourhood behaves like another rich one, in another part of the country. And so does a poor one. Spontaneity is lost. An order, a routine sets in. And this foundational feature of modernity infects everything, including neighbourhoods.

This means a neighbourhood must also be evolving in order, a routine. Their evolution would also be following a certain trajectory. The planning model of Clarence Perry's (1998 [1929]) neighbourhood unit which offered a functional and self-contained design of neighbourhoods, continued to be used to order and organise new residential communities, and therefore evolved a certain type of neighbourhood. What house prices do, is that they draw some homogeneity between neighbourhoods benchmarked against income levels, on these very neighbourhood units. This is then, assuming a different type of evolution of neighbourhood, predicated upon how the time value of money is shaping and reshaping the 'level' of our neighbourhoods. Time has lost its plurality, leading to a disappointing convergence from the cherished goal of humanity to diversify its methods to flourish. The dominant institutions of modernity are forcing a homogenised value system of time, which is predominantly driven by Western conceptions. The strange ways in which modernity acts is to keep filling the container of culture with its own fluid until a point comes when the drinker begins to like it. It may be an acquired taste, so to speak. And with time as an ingredient, a differing taste for everyone, and yet, the same taste for those having big containers and same for those having small ones. This time is the taste of neighbourhoods.

And herein lies the proposition. Modernity is using time as a mould to construct homogenous entities, and neighbourhoods are one of the tools through which these entities are emerging. Neighbourhoods are making all efforts to push up the prices of their constituting housing units. These prices rub off each other. Prices in a neighbourhood move synchronously. House price increases do not affect individual homes alone. Price increase is most impacted by neighbourhood effects, so it is about how expensive a neighbourhood is. This is what is generally discussed in real estate transactions—not how expensive an individual house is.

Delhi: Its P-R Ratio and the Spatiality of Neighbourhood

There is a spontaneity associated with a neighbourhood. Indeed, in most places, neighbourhoods evolve organically, where an inchoate fashion governs the emergence of the human congregation in a permanent manner (Mumford 1954). This morphology has now co-exited with the 20th century residential planning and development, where architectural planning and cultural evolution go hand in hand with varying emphasis (Filian and Hammond 2003). In fact, neighbourhood sociology as a subfield of urban sociology studying local communities has been quite prominent (Wellman and Leighton 1979). But the organic nature of their emergence and evolution is a powerful phenomenon. They construct themselves through the social interaction of people, and, therefore, are essentially, socially designed. People in a neighbourhood produce and implement implicit rules of the game and institutions of that neighbourhood.

Prices dominate these rules extensively. The space–time trajectory of neighbourhood evolution is now heavily dependent on the pricing of its real estate component. Since that, in turn, is dependent on average income levels in the neighbourhood, it is really the economic class which lends characteristics to modern neighbourhoods. This way, organic evolution has become rather homogeneous. Neighbourhoods are now a function of a consistent pattern of preference, which is predicated chiefly on the average incomes manifested in house prices. And once this pattern of preference begins appearing, it colours every constituent neighbourhood within it.

The study of these neighbourhoods was not done in the same vigour as that of their price–rent ratio. And so the description of these neighbourhoods will be hugely alloyed with our own subjectivities. While at one level, such subjectivities themselves are evidence to exactly the type of discourse our work aims to trigger, at another, these are nothing more than stereotypical with an unintelligently bold brush used to paint the picture of the world around me. While an independent view may be lurking around the corner waiting to be discovered, this part reconciles with some honesty at the cost of independence. At the cost of imposing a subjective, stereotypical and incomplete view, let's take a closer look at Delhi, and the neighbourhoods studied in our empirical work. We looked at five residential areas, namely, Greater Kailash (GK), Lajpat Nagar, Defence Colony, Vikaspuri and Jahangirpuri. The first two are in South Delhi, Defence Colony somewhere in between the centre and south, and the last two in west and north, respectively. The first three residential areas colloquially fall under what Delhi citizens often refer to as 'posh' areas. Vikaspuri is aspiringly posh, and Jahangirpuri is nowhere close.

Posh is an emotive category, signifying guilt of elitism, so brazen and ceremonious that it is used more as an aspirational value, rather than an accomplishment. It is like when you achieve it, you don't want to use it because it separates you of the rest of the world. But you carry it in your head. It is a constant reminder of your achievements, even though ironically, educated circles would find it too exclusionary to use it. And exactly by the same token, the non-elites use it as an unhinged indicator of their aspirations. According to some, 'POSH' stood for 'port out, starboard home', which are a reference to certain cabins on ships travelling between England and India. These cabins did not face direct sunlight and hence were cooler. These were mostly occupied by aristocratic and rich travellers. Despite there being no evidence to it, these areas being cooler in Delhi, due to green cover, strike a chord.

GK is home to some of the most affluent people in Delhi (including politicians, businessmen, even those associated with Bollywood) and is highly coveted in both commercial (it has some of the most prime commercial markets with numerous international brands and retail stores) and residential categories. It has two parts—GK-1 and GK-2. These were developed in the 1960s by private developers as an extension to the existing Kailash Colony, and even today represent a vast area beyond just what goes by the name of GK-1 and GK-2, absorbing various surrounding slums and creating all kinds of governance complexities (Bhandari 2016).

Lajpat Nagar, again separated into four zones, has a slightly different makeup. It was established in the 1950s and catered mostly to refugees coming from Pakistan during Partition. Refugees who were living in camps in central Delhi were allotted lands in Lajpat Nagar. The area was named after one of India's prominent freedom fighters, Lala Lajpat Rai. Earlier, the plots were tiny, constructed like barracks. This is perhaps the reason why Lajpat Nagar neighbourhood is more cramped than GK. There are multi-storey buildings. The market is massive and attracts people from all walks of society, not just the affluent ones. The area has remained predominantly Punjabi, exhibiting its character in many Bollywood movies too. But this is a noisier, more informal space compared to GK.

Defence Colony is closer to GK in its character. This colony was also built in the 1960s, but as the name suggests, it was built for the veterans of Indian Armed Forces (mainly those who had travelled to India from Pakistan after Partition). Again, the place is an 'expensive' neighbourhood. It is also closer to the centre of Delhi. Over time, it has become a hub for expensive lawyers, expats, and affluent politicians and businessmen. The Defence Colony market is again, 'posh', for lack of a better word that can convey the same meaning.

Vikaspuri is a much younger, planned neighbourhood, which was established by the government in the 1980s. Falling in the western part of Delhi and quite distant from the power centres of Central or South Delhi, it is mostly home to affluent Punjabi businessmen, and this is reflected in its suburban residential living. In the last two decades, it has considerably swelled in population and is constantly managing the class-diverging population from villages adjoining it, which were not zoned in by the government in this neighbourhood.

Jahangirpuri is a nondescript neighbourhood in north Delhi. It is an area with a vast majority of the population belonging to the lower economic class, and unless someone undertakes a primary survey, it is difficult to draw up a socioeconomic picture of this neighbourhood, with any sense of confidence. Adjoining the largest vegetable wholesale market of Delhi called Azadpur, it has a contemporary image of a neighbourhood dotted with small workshops, household factories and commercial establishments which fall under the small-scale sector.

When we look at the price–rent ratio in these neighbourhoods given in Figure 11.2, we find that Defence Colony has the highest values, both of independent bungalows as well as apartment flats. Closely following it is GK. Next in line is Vikaspuri, very closely followed by Lajpat Nagar, with Jahangirpuri at the very end. What's noteworthy is the evolution of Vikaspuri, which was a suburban neighbourhood but now 'boasts' of a higher price–rent ratio than Lajpat Nagar.

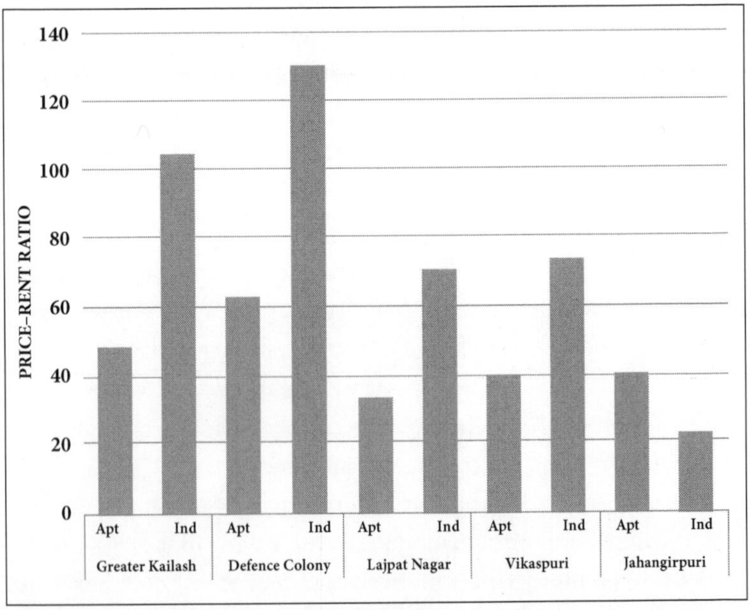

Figure 11.2: Price–rent ratio in five neighbourhoods in Delhi. 'Apt' denotes flats in apartments; 'Ind' denotes independent houses/ bungalows. Image credit: authors

The neighbourhoods with high-income levels also carry a high price–rent ratios, and the makeup of these neighbourhoods reflect the character of 'posh-ness' alongside. Indeed, each of these neighbourhoods has evolved spatially, but an interesting aspect is that of their temporal evolution. Refugee colonies have become affluent neighbourhoods, and those that were developed recently, despite being inferior in their connectivity, have emerged as 'formidable' neighbourhoods in terms of influence.

But the most interesting thing is that in terms of aspiration, Jahangurpuri is no less. Despite being predominantly occupied by people from lower economic classes, its price–rent ratio is as high as 40, for flats and apartments. Even in Jahangirpuri, prices are irrationally inflated, and yet people want to buy them. Another aspect is that perhaps rentals are highly depressed here. The low values for independent houses here is an anomaly, and this may be related to higher prices of rentals in independent houses. But for this, more research is needed. Be that as it may, it is certain that house prices are irrationally high. Low rentals indicate lower willingness of people to live in these neighbourhoods, and that should pull the prices down. But that is not happening. Modernity's promise has suppressed people's discount rate for house purchase, even in poor neighbourhoods like Jahangirpuri. That this neighbourhood is pressured to evolve like Vikaspuri cannot be doubted. Whether that will happen is a matter of time and another set of correlated variables.

There are two more facets of neighbourhoods in Delhi that we want to draw attention here. First, the increasing affluence of neighbourhoods manifested in price–rent ratios, is also directly correlated with how isolated the neighbours themselves are. In other words, the richer the neighbourhood, the more individualistic and private its members are, with greater independent living exhibited. Mediocre neighbourhoods have far closer-knit societies, with some form of community engagements and interactions. Here, neighbours know each other and keep an eye on everything. The higher up the price–rent ladder one goes, the lower one falls on the collectivistic scale of societies.

The other thing is about the uncomfortable irony in the act of purchase of housing even in these 'posh' colonies. These areas have a very high price of land; in fact, exceedingly high—by one estimate, builder floors and independent villas can be priced at anything between 60 million rupees and 250 million rupees. And yet, the public infrastructure in the city is crumbling. Delhi has one of the world's worst pollution problems, it has frustrating traffic, public services are non-existent if one compares with New York or Hong Kong, and the law and order perception is declining every year. In its race to become a world-class city, Delhi is unable to meet basic standards of community living. In its race to build broad roads for cars, it has become an unwalkable city. And in its race to become a city for the rich, it is hardly able to qualify as a decent city to survive in, even for the middle class. The neighbourhood evolution is the poster-child of this imagination.

So what did we get finally, from this economic sojourn into our socio-spatial designs of living in Delhi? We would wager two things. First, neighbourhoods are crystallised through class-distinctions, and that is captured in their price–rent ratio. This distinction pushes them to evolve into assuming certain characteristics which further feeds into the price–rent ratio. Second, affluent neighbourhoods are homogeneous and that becomes an aspirational model to emulate. The ordinary culture of neighbourhoods in Delhi (or other cities in India) reflect a certain sense of drive towards elitism. This may come at a great cost to embedded values and community-level projects which now one no longer witnesses in the isolated worlds these neighbourhoods have developed into. However, one cannot say with certainty, how costly is that.

Conclusion

The presence of neighbourhoods has had a consistent spatial and temporal element. Spatially, because neighbourhood as a fundamental cohabiting block of cities exists throughout the world, in every city without fail. And it keeps changing, altering its boundaries, swelling up or thinning down. In fact, a city does not exist without the concept of neighbourhood integrated both on its physical map, as well as in the social psychology of people. It is ingrained in the urban social fabric of city dwellers everywhere in the world. Temporally, because neighbourhoods have existed throughout human evolution. Indeed, archaeological records of most of the world's oldest cities have evidence of social neighbourhoods as units of agglomerations (Spence 1992).

How people lived in neighbourhoods—and not cities per se—during medieval times has been a matter of vibrant interest amongst scholars quite vividly (Marcus 1989; Heng 1999; Smail 2000).

There is another dimension to the temporal aspect that is not constrained to a linear view of the historical significance of neighbourhoods. And, that is how neighbourhoods and their aspirations change in time, or more importantly, are expected to change over time. It is this aspect which we made an effort to dissect. And in return, it exposed us to a range of aspirational impulses embedded within the pains of house purchases in India, perhaps symptomatic of the mute absorption of modernity in an epistemically violent endeavour.

Overall, the use of price–rent ratio guided us to traverse the aspirational path of the neighbourhood, over time (and not just space). Since price–rent ratio captures within it, an irrationality of future aspirations in 'owning' a house, it makes a sincere noise about the foundations of economic makeup of the neighbourhood. The need to be in a neighbourhood swiftly transforms into wanting to be in that neighbourhood. This transition is embedded within the manner in which the type of inhabitants the neighbourhood attracts or detracts. The price–rent ratio is a simple variable that allows us to recognise the transition dynamically. If I know the price–rent ratio to be high, I will take cognizance of the aspirational element of the neighbourhood. Whether the aspiration is drawn out of the external environment or is endogenously chiselled, is a matter of empirics. One may also use the variable to push the understanding of neighbourhood as a cushion between familiarity to anonymity. If the neighbourhood's aspirational capacity is opened up, then the meaning of familiarity and anonymity may get recalibrated. This, of course, requires further exploration but the price–rent ratio offers a glimpse into such conceptual compulsions.

This chapter sheds light on the temporal plurality of today's times in a fast-growing 'urban' world (of India) that justifies an idiosyncratic investment of houses. It exposes the assumptions of modernity that underlie these decisions and builds claims of rationality in them. Questions of alternative conceptions of ethics that can be woven around these assumptions to reimagine an alternative social order (read neighbourhood) become starkly posed. Further, if neighbourhoods also have a temporal transition, this study ventures into the direction of what makes these transitions towards homogeneity of the neighbourhoods. In doing that therefore, the chapter advances a dynamic view of neighbourhoods, in addition to the spatial one.

References

Alford, P. 2010. 'Rent Ratio Tells You Whether Renting Or Buying Is the Better Deal'. *Forbes*, 2 November. Available at https://www.forbes.com/sites/greatspeculations/2010/11/02/rent-ratio-tells-you-whether-renting-or-buying-is-the-better-deal/#ce81aece9d08 (accessed on 30 March 2020).

Andreevska, D. 2019. 'US Price to Rent Ratio Reviewed by City 2019'. Available at https://rentberry.com/blog/price-to-rent-by-city (accessed on 30 March 2020).

Bailey, N. and M. Pill. 2011. 'The Continuing Popularity of the Neighbourhood and Neighbourhood Governance in the Transition from the "Big State" to the "Big Society" Paradigm'. *Environment and Planning C: Government and Policy*, Vol. 29, No. 5, pp. 927–942.

Bauder, H. 2002. 'Neighbourhood Effects and Cultural Exclusion'. *Urban Studies*, Vol. 39, No. 1, pp. 85–93.

Bhandari, L. 2016. 'Delhi's Greater Kailash Constituency Highlights Complexity of Urban Governance'. *Business Standard*, 17 October. Available at https://www.business-standard.com/article/economy-policy/delhi-s-greater-kailash-constituency-highlights-complexity-of-urban-governance-116101600805_1.html (accessed on 30 March 2020).

Bissel, D. 2013. 'Pointless Mobilities: Rethinking Proximity through the Loops of Neighbourhood'. *Urban Studies*, Vol. 8, No. 3, pp. 349–367.

Campbell, S.D., M.A. Davis, J. Gallin and R.F. Martin. 2009. 'What Moves Housing Markets: A Variance Decomposition of the Rent–Price Ratio'. *Journal of Urban Economics*, Vol. 66, No. 2, pp. 90–102.

Chen, A. 1996. 'China's Urban Housing Reform: Price–Rent Ratio and Market Equilibrium'. *Urban Studies*, Vol. 33, No. 7, pp. 1077–1092.

Chen, M.K. 2013. 'The Effect of Language on Economic Behavior: Evidence from Savings Rates, Health Behaviors, and Retirement Assets'. *American Economic Review*, Vol. 103, No. 2, pp. 690–731.

Cochrane, J.H. 2011. 'Discount Rates (Presidential address)'. *Journal of Finance*, Vol. 66, No. 4, pp. 1047–1108.

Coelho, K. and T. Venkat. 2009. 'The Politics of Civil Society: Neighbourhood Associationism in Chennai'. *Economic and Political Weekly*, Vol. 44, Nos 26–27, pp. 358–367.

Davis, M.A., A. Lehnert and R.F. Martin. 2008. 'The Rent-Price Ratio for the Aggregate Stock of Owner-occupied Housing'. *Review of Income and Wealth*, Vol. 54, No. 2, pp. 279–284.

Engsted, T. and T.Q. Pedersen. 2015. 'Predicting Returns and Rent Growth in the Housing Market Using the Rent–Price Ratio: Evidence from the OECD Countries'. *Journal of International Money and Finance*, Vol. 53, pp. 257–275.

Filion, P. and K. Hammond. 2003. 'Neighbourhood Land Use and Performance: The Evolution of Neighbourhood Morphology over the 20th Century'. *Environment and Planning B: Planning and Design*, Vol. 30, No. 2, pp. 271–296.

Forrest, R. and A. Kearns. 2001. 'Social Cohesion, Social Capital and the Neighbourhood'. *Urban Studies,* Vol. 38, No. 12, pp. 2125–2143.

Freeman, A.M. 1979. 'The Hedonic Price Approach to Measuring Demand for Neighbourhood Characteristics'. In *Studies in Urban Economics,* edited by D. Segal, pp. 52–77. New York: Academic Press.

Gallin, J. 2008. 'The Long-run Relationship Between House Prices and Rents'. *Real Estate Econ.*, Vol. 36, pp. 635–658.

Galster, G. 2001. 'On the Nature of Neighbourhood'. *Urban Studies*, Vol. 38, No. 12, pp. 2111–2124.

Goyal, Yugank. 2020. 'Of Modernity, House Prices and Suspending Singularity of Time'. *Journal of Human Values (forthcoming).*

Heidegger, M. 1971. 'Building Dwelling Thinking'. In *Poetry, Language, Thought,* edited by M. Heidegger, pp. 145–161. New York, NY: Harper and Row.

Heng, C.K. 1999. *Cities of Aristocrats and Bureaucrats: The Development of Medieval Chinese Cityscapes.* Honolulu: University of Hawai'i Press.

Himmelberg, C., C. Mayer and T. Sinai. 2005. 'Assessing High House Prices: Bubbles, Fundamentals and Misperceptions'. *Journal of Economic Perspectives*, Vol. 19, No. 4, pp. 67–92.

Kain, J.F. and J.M. Quigley. 1970. 'Measuring the Value of Housing Quality'. *Journal of the American Statistical Association*, Vol. 45, pp. 532–548.

Kauko, T. 2009. 'Policy Impact and House Price Development at the Neighbourhood Level: A Comparison of Four Urban Regeneration Areas Using the Concept of "Artificial" Value Creation'. *European Planning Studies*, Vol. 17, No. 1, pp. 85–107.

Kishor, N.K. and J. Morley. 2010. 'What Moves the Price–rent Ratio: A Latent Variable Approach'. Working paper, University of Wisconsin-Milwaukee. Available at https://www.isid.ac.in/~pu/conference/dec_10_conf/Papers/KundanKishor.pdf (accessed on 30 March 2020).

Lama-Rewal, S.T. 2007. 'Neighbourhood Associations and Local Democracy: Delhi Municipal Elections'. *Economic and Political Weekly*, Vol. 42, No. 47, pp. 51–60.

Lynch, A. and D. Rasmussen. 2004. 'Proximity, Neighbourhood and the Efficacy of Exclusion'. *Urban Studies*, Vol. 41, No. 2, pp. 285–298.

Marcus, A. 1989. *The Middle East on the Eve of Modernity: Aleppo in the Eighteenth Century*. New York: Columbia University Press.

Massey, D. 1994. 'Power-geometry and a Progressive Sense of Place'. In *Travellers' Tales: Narratives of Home and Displacement,* edited by G. Robertson, M. Mash, L. Tickner, J. Bird, B. Curtis and T. Putnam, pp. 75–85. London: Routledge.

Mumford, L. 1954. 'The Neighborhood and the Neighborhood Unit'. *Town Planning Review*, Vol. 24, pp. 256–270.

Pant, B. 2016. 'Different Cultures See Deadlines Differently'. *Harvard Business Review,* 23 May.

Perry, C. 1929 [1998]. *The Neighbourhood Unit.* Reprinted. London: Routledge/Thoemmes.

Proxenos, S. 2002. 'Homeownership Rates: A Global Perspective'. *Housing Finance International*, Vol. 17, No. 2, pp. 3–7.

Savage, M., G. Bagnall and B. Longhurst. 2005. *Globalization and Belonging*. London: Sage Publications.

Smail, D.L. 2000. *Imaginary Cartographies: Possession and Identity in Late Medieval Marseille*. Ithaca, NY: Cornell University Press.

Spence, M.W. 1992. 'Tlailotlacan, a Zapotec Enclave in Teotihuacan'. In *Art, Ideology, and the City of Teotihuacan,* edited by J.C. Berlo, pp. 59–88. Washington DC: Dumbarton Oaks.

Taylor, M. 2003. 'Neighbourhood Governance: Holy Grail or Poisoned Chalice?' *Local Economy*, Vol. 18, No. 3, pp. 190–195.

Tiebout, C. 1956. 'A Pure Theory of Local Expenditure'. *Journal of Political Economy*, Vol. 64, No. 4, pp. 416–424.

Tse, R.Y.C. 2002. 'Estimating Neighbourhood Effects in House Prices: Towards a New Hedonic Model Approach'. *Urban Studies*, Vol. 39, No. 7, pp. 1165–1180.

Wellman, B. and B. Leighton. 1979. 'Networks, Neighbourhoods and Communities: Approaches to the Study of the Community Question'. *Urban Affairs Quarterly*, Vol. 14, No. 3, pp. 363–390.

Zérah, M. 2007. 'Middle Class Neighbourhood Associations as Political Players in Mumbai'. *Economic and Political Weekly*, Vol. 42, No. 47, pp. 61–68.

12

Whose Neighbourhood Is It Anyway: A Spatial History of Urban Patna

Sheema Fatima

Contemporary writing in urban studies has dealt substantially with the spatial transformation of our cities in recent years. The question of 'gentrification' (Ghertner 2011) and 'urban restructuring' in the face of shifting terrains of urban politics (Shatkin 2014) defines a large part of this scholarship. The urban frontier, thus, encompasses within it a spectrum of state- and market-led mechanisms of capturing land both of judicial and quasi-judicial nature for 'greenfield urban development' (Kennedy and Sood 2016). The practice of acquiring land through both formal and informal techniques as discussed in this chapter is not a recent phenomenon and has been endorsed by the state in colonial and postcolonial cities. Historically, it has been state practices that have determined spatial restructuring (Fernandes 2004), often at the expense of subaltern groups. When I say 'state', I include within its analytical division the private social identities of the individuals (Harriss-White 2015), represented by caste, religion, gender and region, who as officials, politicians and the people themselves have the power to influence the decision-making process. In the case of Bihar, I borrow from O.J. Frödin (2012) that one needs a relational understanding to be able to conceptualise state. He argues, '[institutions] exist in so far as they are systematically activated in social relations' (Ibid.: 14). And the real-world outcomes of negotiations between the state and its varied social realities had clear spatial implications in Patna's built form.

This chapter looks at the spatial history through the concept of neighbourhood formation and ideology of urban planning, which metamorphosed into a process of accommodation and adjustment through exemptions and exceptions (Gururani 2013) over the years in India. The concept of neighbourhood formation originated from Ebenezer Howard's model of Garden City in the 19th century and was used for slum clearance in the industrial town of London (Hall 2014). The term neighbourhood in the planning domain was used by Clarence Perry in the early 1920s in her work 'City Planning for Neighborhood Life' (Perry 1929). The Western models of land-use planning and master plan had a planned conception of neighbourhoods. It complimented the Nehruvian ideals of development and growth in a newly Independent India (Vidyarthi 2010). Spatial planning approach was imagined to be an ideal one for inclusive development, building houses in a planned manner for all income and social groups and a site for learning the virtues of cleanliness and hygiene for those coming from the countryside. We will see later in the chapter how cities like Patna continued with this vision of neighbourhood while preparing the master plan and how it influenced the spatial form of the city. The imagined inclusive space had different size housing units for each income group. Spatially, the placement of each income category within that neighbourhood was hierarchical. The emphasis of the Second Five-Year Plan (1956–1961) on the preparation of a master plan for urban centres in the country was a step towards the fulfilment of this imagination. Subsequently, the Third Five-Year Plan (1961–1966) identified control of land values through the public acquisition of land and defining tolerable minimum standards for housing and other services as one of the key areas of concerns. The formation of Delhi Development Authority (DDA) in 1957 was an early template for this exercise and for other states to emulate. It undertook large-scale land acquisition for implementing the master plan and marked the initiation of the state's near-monopoly over the development of new neighbourhoods and housing in Delhi (Vidyarthi 2014). This mechanism was implemented in other states through an Urban Improvement Trust.

In the case of large metropolitan Indian cities, institutions such as Improvement Trusts kept their colonial characteristics (Rao 2013) of privilege and power over urban development and expansion alive in post-Independent India. Separate and independent from the municipal body, an Improvement Trust's elite imagination of a neighbourhood was equally encouraged by bureaucratic officials who headed it and endorsed by town planners educated in American universities and engaged in preparing master plans across the country (Vidyarthi 2014). Improvement Trusts mostly focused on Middle Income Group housing, and in the given scenario was considered to be an adequate response to the demand for planned urban growth and housing (Commission 1983). In India, one of the early proponents of the concept of 'neighbourhood' was Le Corbusier who designed Chandigarh. Writing about Le Corbusier's plan for Chandigarh, Hall (2014) points out the complete failure of its built form in being able to create a sense of neighbourhood; rather, it remained segregated based on income and civil ranks. Over the years, slums proliferated on the margins of these neighbourhoods and were often evicted since they didn't conform to the ideals of the grand master plan vision. Associated with the concept of neighbourhood in case of Chandigarh was the idea of 'city beautiful' given by the first planner of the city, Albert Mayer. This concept of 'city beautiful' remained ingrained in the urban planning mechanism of our cities in the years to come and provided justification for encroachment drives. In fact, one could see it become synonymous with slum clearance.

For this chapter, neighbourhood is defined as a formal spatial unit which was created by the public sector housing project undertaken by Improvement Trusts and housing department in the capital city of Patna. Land acquisition for these projects was directly undertaken by the government, and units under each economic category were identified. Based on this, the allocation was announced and processed for Economically Weaker Section (EWS), Low Income Group (LIG), Middle Income Group (MIG) and High Income Group (HIG). The master plan prepared by the Patna Improvement Trust proposed housing projects to fulfil its imperative of neighbourhood spatial planning. For the city of Jaipur, Vidyarthi (2014) shows master planning as a powerful tool used by the ruling elite for their own benefit in collaboration with the local-level bureaucrats and political functionaries. The Patna master plan made in 1962 by the Improvement Trust identifies neighbourhood planning as its first imperative and clearance of slums as the second imperative. Later in the chapter, I argue that although the logic of the first drew from the second imperative, it was only the component of social housing which was fulfilled. It leads to my second proposition that a state-initiated land acquisition did not prevent speculation over the years and encouraged encroachment of various kinds. The bureaucrats and higher officials of Improvement Trusts, as demonstrated by Jones (1974), acted as crony builders and appropriated land by allocating the land for housing cooperatives and at the same time, relegating slums housing as a secondary concern. In the course of mapping the spatial history of neighbourhood formation, we will moreover analyse the micro-political interactions in the city of Patna and the deviations carried out by embedded actors to be able to fulfil their specific requirement (Sundaresan 2017).

The chapter began with a background of the city and the state politics which influenced decision making in relation to allocation and allotments. The following section gives a historical outline of the creation of the 'new capital' of Patna by the Imperial government. One can draw parallels between the colonial mechanisms of building the capital city with the manner in which Improvement Trust functioned in Independent India. The third section elaborates on the making of the Patna Improvement Trust, preparation of the master plan and its undertaking of grand housing projects. The last section looks at the slum-related development work done by the Improvement Trust and how it was implemented as a separate disjointed project rather than an integrated social housing scheme. The politicisation of decision making and project implementation by the Improvement Trust will be explained through certain specific housing projects that it undertook. This work for all analytical purposes limits itself to the tenure of the Patna Improvement Trust which lasted till 1972.

Patna: The City and Its Politics

Urban politics in the city of Patna was determined by the impermanent nature of state politics that influenced its spatial history. The impermanence was largely due to caste allegiance and took a particularly volatile and precarious shape in Bihar in the years to come. Although the Zamindari Abolition Act, 1951 claimed to balance out the skewed distribution of agricultural land in rural Bihar in Independent India, in reality, it further accentuated the classification of zamindars as tenant landlords, tenants and sub-tenants in the middle, and agricultural labourers at the lowest rung (Timberg 1982). These categories later formed the plebian group, and over the years percolated down into the state machinery for privileges of patronage or became brokers and middle-men. The ruling Congress Party during the 1960s controlled the state administration through people belonging to the upper caste landed aristocracy. An overwhelming majority of bureaucrats, technocrats and professionals belonged to this category (Das 1992). The result of the alliance by the nationalist state with the landed elites and other dominant classes in the state encouraged development and consolidation of systems of exploitation by new national institutions (Damodaran 1993: 373). The second general elections in India were held in February 1967 and the first non-Congress majoritarian government through alliances was formed in Bihar. A clear polarisation between the 'upper' and 'middle'—also known as 'forward' and 'backward' caste in the state—(Prasad 1976) became visible henceforth. It was the beginning of a long period of instability and the people of Bihar experienced thirteen governments, three president's rule and a national emergency from 1967 to 1980 (Kumar 2009). It was primarily an outcome of political manoeuvring and opportunism based on caste equations leading to unstable governments. These coalitions were not necessarily on ideological or party basis but provided ample opportunities to all caste groups that capitalised on every possible situation to gain access to power (Jain 1989). Even though it meant temporary control of government offices, it was enough to facilitate access for family and group interests (Frankel 1990). An explicit categorisation of caste made it an enabler in the bargaining process for patronage, lobbying and bribery in everyday life of the state. The state was being defined through experiences of transfers, allotments, allocations and approvals of both judicial and quasi-judicial nature. For example, the Aiyar Commission inquiry against ministers who were in government from 1946 to 1967 and the Mudholkar Commission of inquiry implicated thirteen out of the fourteen ministers for abuse of their official positions. Several of these abuses of powers were done in the ministry of local self-government and urban development. Under the given circumstances, negotiation and decision making determined by state politics had far-reaching spatial implications on the city of Patna in the years to come.

If we look at the physical layout of the precolonial city of Patna, the eastern side comprised the old city. Some of the prominent neighbourhoods on the eastern side were Mansurganj, Maroofganj and the world-renowned Harmandir—the birthplace of Guru Govind Singh. Central Patna consisted of neighbourhoods that had developed as a fringe to the old city, starting from Bankipore and beyond, including Sabzibagh, Mahendru, Bakerganj and Patna market as important residential areas, intercepted with pockets of slum and dilapidated houses. The New Capital Area started from Gandhi Maidan and beyond. The population of Patna grew from 27.43 per cent in 1941–1951 to 45.31 per cent in 1951–1961 (Shanker 2001). In the decade from 1951 to 1961, the rural population in the state grew by 17.64 per cent while the urban population increased by 50 per cent (Karna 1981). This big jump was due to a large influx of migrants from East Bengal at the time of Partition and migrants from other districts working in the government offices in the city. It experienced in-migration by the landed class of rural Bihar to Patna who invested money in the property (Das 1992). If we look within the state, southern Bihar was more urbanised compared to northern Bihar which, historically, has been at a disadvantage due to frequent floodings in the region and resulting high dependence on the agricultural sector. This led to poor development of urban centres with higher administrative and institutional functions in its subregions. As a consequence, the dependency on Patna, the capital city of Bihar, for higher-order functions remains very high till date.

Provincial to New Capital

The history of urbanisation in colonial India is largely reduced to accounts of insanitary towns and failing municipal improvement projects due to financial austerity (Mann 2007). Often these 'failures' (Kishore 2015) were followed by elaborate expansion in the regulatory powers of the colonial bureaucracy giving the municipality leverage to alienate itself from the inner core of the city at the expense of newly developing areas. Patna City Municipality was established in 1864. Several efforts for sanitary and water-supply projects proved unsuccessful due to financial constraints and lack of expert handling. Suffice to say that by the beginning of the 20th century, the municipality was 'regularly in debt' (Boyk 2015: 27) due to frequent plague outbreaks and famine conditions in the city.[1] The Province of Bihar and Orissa was created in 1912 bifurcating it from Bengal Presidency. The agitation of 'Bihar for Biharis' (Chakravartty, 2013) was spearheaded by upper-caste Brahmans and Kayasthas equipped with English education. They benefited by getting government jobs and other administrative positions created in the new capital of the province. The British continued with its practice[2] of building a new capital on the remains of the old (Roberts 2013).

The New Capital Area was laid out west of Boring Road on a ring and radial road pattern along a central axis, King George Avenue, highlighted by the Old Secretariat and the Raj Bhawan (*Patna Master Plan* 1962: 47). J.F. Munnings[3] was appointed as the consulting architect for the new province. He emphasised that the fundamental feature underlying the planning of this city was zoning (Munnings 1919). He headed the design and planning[4] of the New Capital area of Bankipore that included the Government House, officers residence, a guesthouse at Chajjubagh, professors quarters, executive engineers residence and the commissioner's house. Government houses with electricity and water were planned in double rows with service roads—

1 It was due to famine that the iconic Golghar was constructed in 1764 but never severed its intended purpose (Brown 2005).

2 For example, in case of Lahore, the colonial government believed that it is far easier to build unhindered outside the native town (Glover 2008).

3 Joseph Fearis Munnings was appointed as an architect to the Government of Eastern Bengal in 1909. In the beginning, he was the only qualified architect for the province of Bengal and Orissa. He is attributed with the designing of several other buildings in the state like the commissioner's residence in Ranchi and Muzaffarpur among several others. In the beginning, he was the only qualified architect and could therefore be credited for designing all the buildings in the city during his time. He remained the consulting architect of the province from 1912 to 1918.

4 The article 'Town Planning in Bihar' published on 31 January 1915 in *The Express* raised the question if Patrick Geddes expertise would be utilised for building the new capital area. However, by that time, the layout plan had been completed and construction work had started.

where the sewer lines were laid—in between. Near the service roads, servant quarters, stables and motor garages were also built. The Anglo-Indian assistant's quarter was provided with a fenced compound because they liked to maintain a garden; it was presumed that Indian clerks who have *zanana*[5] enclosures would seldom care to maintain a garden, 'though they can be given permission if the natives can convince the government if they wish to do so'.[6] The spatial layout of the capital city maintained the hierarchical residential segregation in its built form. The *Patna Gazetteer* of 1924 while describing the new capital areas evidently brought out this stark reality. It began with the section to the east of Digha railway line which had the High Court and clerks' quarters, the water tower, the post and the Telegraph office, the Hardinge Park and the market. The part on the west of the Digha railway line comprised the Government House, the secretariat, council chamber, the principal official residences and the electric powerhouse. A third section on the south of the main railway had clerks' quarters, an English high school, a dispensary and a police outpost. It goes on to describe the grandeur of the central avenue and notes, 'the designers of the capital laying out the roads have kept in mind the necessity of modern transport. Its roads have no dangerous turnings caused by old encroachments. The roads are 150 feet wide' (Omalley 1924).

The coming up of New Capital Area was the beginning of complete neglect of Patna City municipality. Grants meant for sanitary and water supply for the Old City was regularly diversified to New Capital Area projects. The Patna Improvement Trust with the formation of the new province, intended to open up congested areas and widen the road in the eastern part of the city (Ibid.). It was proposed that some of the most insanitary *bastis*[7] like Bankipore were to be demolished and resettled. In 1916, the land was acquired by the Patna Improvement Trust in Muharrampur, Kadam Kuan and Pirthipur for housing the families displaced from these slums. However, the Improvement Trust in provincial urban centres like Patna acted as patronage centres with

5 Part of the house in the Indian subcontinent reserved for the women of the household.

6 Honourable Mr Stanley in the Vidhan Sabha on 4 March 1918.

7 Slum in colloquial language.

too many members being nominated from the elite class of the city. Their priorities did not stretch beyond the opening of roads and actual construction work undertaken was negligible. Therefore, the proposed slum improvement and decongestion scheme remained incomplete. The purpose of the colonial administration was easily fulfilled by the Patna Administrative Committee to monitor the construction of the New Capital Area leaving the Improvement Trust irrelevant. On the other hand, any demand by councillors from Patna City Municipality was dismissed and reprimanded for having an 'illusion of the inexhaustible purse of government'.[8] The new capital area was envisaged as a planned and sanitised space from the local presence. However, this spatial segregation was not clear in terms of the 'white town' and the 'black town' (Brown 2005). The native wealthy and the aristocratic population was well-taken care off. By the early 20th century, Patna city municipality was on the verge of bankruptcy, severely affecting the sanitary conditions in the city. In a question raised in the assembly by Ganesh Datta Singh about the poor maintenance of the ghats along River Ganga, the local self-government (LSG) minister M.G. Hallet said, '[T]he honorable member is in a better position to talk about it, because I don't live in that municipality.'[9] The expression characteristic of the imperial tone depicts the indifference towards the inner city administered by the Patna City Municipality. In the years to come, ministers from the inner city would only raise questions[10] related to the poor sanitary conditions without any relief. We see this characteristic of the Imperial government to acquire land and plan an unhindered social–spatial neighbourhood, evidently segregated from the old city and creating a 'modern city' (Glover 2008), across undivided India. In the next section, we will understand the implications of this practice by the colonial government of circumventing the problems of the existing city and building a new neighbourhood. The ruling elite in post-colonial Bihar managed to extend this practice

8 Bihar and Orissa in 1918–1919 (Superintendent, Government Printing, Bihar and Orissa, 1920).

9 15 February 1923.

10 In a house debate on 29 January 1926, Babu Gur Sahay Lal and Babu Rajandhari Sinha raised questions about the poor sanitary condition in Patna City Municipality and that no work was being taken up due to the poor coordination within the municipality.

further—from the site where the colonial government had built New Capital Area in Patna. The dream of Greater Patna began from the immediate vicinity of that site.

New Capital Area and the Plan of Greater Patna

During a question hour session in the Vidhan Sabha, Mr Burhanuddin Khan, an MLA, asked: '[T]he people of Patna have been very much oppressed by the bite of mosquitoes. What measure does the government intend to take?' To this, the minister Bindodananda Jha replied,[11] '[T]he scheme of Greater Patna, costing a huge sum, the execution of which alone will save the people of Patna from mosquitoes.' Post-independence, the foremost concerns of urban local bodies was simply urban expansion and clearing of slums and slum-like condition in the core city of Patna. The villages on the west of New Capital Area were announced and demarcated as Greater Patna. It was imagined as the panacea of all the woes being suffered by the people in the city, particularly the congested Old City. The plan envisaged Greater Patna and planned for hundred years with 80 feet wide roads and open spaces based on neighbourhood principles. It divided the new city into three sections with each of them catering to a population of 5,000–15,000. The proposed housing typology was detached, semi-detached, terrace type and flats. The notification for land acquisition for Greater Patna was published in the *Gazetteer* on 13 September 1944. It was severely opposed by the villagers of Mainpura, Khurji and others up to Digha and Danapur. In total, seventy-four villages had to be acquired. The villagers, on the other hand, argued that post-war reconstruction did not mean effacement of their villages and rather the government should pay attention to reconstruction and development work. The government, however, wanted to control speculation in land prices and hence property rates in the city. It reassured the people that this notification would curb the presence of middlemen, and owners would directly benefit at the time of acquisition. It was claimed to be

11 The Bihar Legislative Assembly Debates, 3 July 1946.

a preliminary notification[12] and the villages identified for notification were deftly marked as 'plague spots' to justify their acquisition. The farmers organised under Patna Kisan Sabha protested[13] against this categorisation and criticised the government for underplaying the fact that these were highly arable and cultivable land.

The Patna Improvement Trust was established in 1952. The primary responsibility of the Trust was to prepare the *Patna Master Plan* for removal of over-crowding, slum clearance and urban obsolesce, develop residential areas on neighbourhood principles and make provisions for integrated infrastructural development (*Patna Master Plan* 1962). The *Patna Master Plan* was prepared by the Trust in 1962 and notified by the government in 1967 (Map 12.1). It was the Patna Improvement Trust that had the power to acquire land on behalf of the government for the development of housing projects and integrated infrastructure. It meant that even though the land for Greater Patna was acquired at the beginning of 1950 for clearance of slums and planned neighbourhood development, the institutional mechanisms for it was developed much later. The master plan took a decade to be prepared and duly approved, and in that one decade, elite capturing of prime land and construction of housing cooperatives had already been completed in different parts of the city. In the following sections, I deal in detail with a few of these housing projects to demonstrate the everyday corrosive practices of the state and the bureaucracy to make such spatial capturing possible.

Elite Capturing of Greater Patna

The land acquired under Greater Patna, as can be seen in Map 12.2, was the immediate extension of colonial Patna. The first-ever formal housing colony was quickly formed by the ICS officers, people from the judiciary and the landed elites leading to the formation of the Patliputra Housing Co-operative Society—the name very much claiming the historical Patliputra in a city in Independent India.

---

12 'Present notification only preliminary', *Searchlight*, Patna edition, 14 October 1944.

13 'Land acquisition in Machuatoli: Kisan deputation to wait on ministers', *Searchlight*, Patna edition, 28 November 1952.

Map 12.1: New Capital Area outgrowth. Map credit: Patna Improvement Trust Master Plan, 1962

Patliputra Housing Co-operative Society was established in 1953. It was exclusively meant for government officials. A total of 26.2 acres of land was acquired in villages of Mainpura and Digha in November 1955 for the same. Lying on the north-west of Bankipur area, a concentrated effort was made to acquire prime land extending beyond the New Capital Area, as can be seen in Map 12.2.

During the time of its construction, there were reports of preferential treatment being given in the allotment of cement for the construction of houses under the pre-war regulatory sanctions. Between April and December 1957, cement was allotted mostly to officials many of whom were ICS and IAS officers among several other officers and ministers. Expressing his anguish in the state assembly, MLA Jogendra Prasad Srivastava charged the government[14] for favouring government servants that led to black marketing of cement in the state. Patliputra Housing Co-operative Society received a loan from the Housing Board for its construction and maintained its independence both from the Patna Municipal Corporation and Patna Improvement Trust. Any attempt to include it within the municipal corporation was strongly resisted. It was alleged that high officials residing in the area did not want to be part of the municipal boundary and pay taxes.[15] The Patliputra Housing Co-operative Society, therefore, at the very beginning provided an achievable mechanism for elite capturing of land and funds by the Housing Board and the Improvement Trust.

The *Bihar State Housing Board Annual Report, 1973* notes that 'largely the Housing Cooperatives formed by the influential senior government officials benefited from these projects who benefited from the state machinery in easing the process of land acquisition and being easily able to access housing loan'.

The Srikrishnanagar Housing Scheme, named after the first chief minister of Bihar, was developed as a planned neighbourhood for LIG housing. By notifying villages of Mainpura, Rajapur, Dujra and Dhakhanpura, a total area of 407.85 acres was acquired under the Greater Patna proposal. In 1962, Srikrishnanagar Housing Scheme was allotted

14 *Civic Affairs*, January 1958, pp. 51–54.

15 Bhola Prasad Singh, March 1964, Vidhan Sabha.

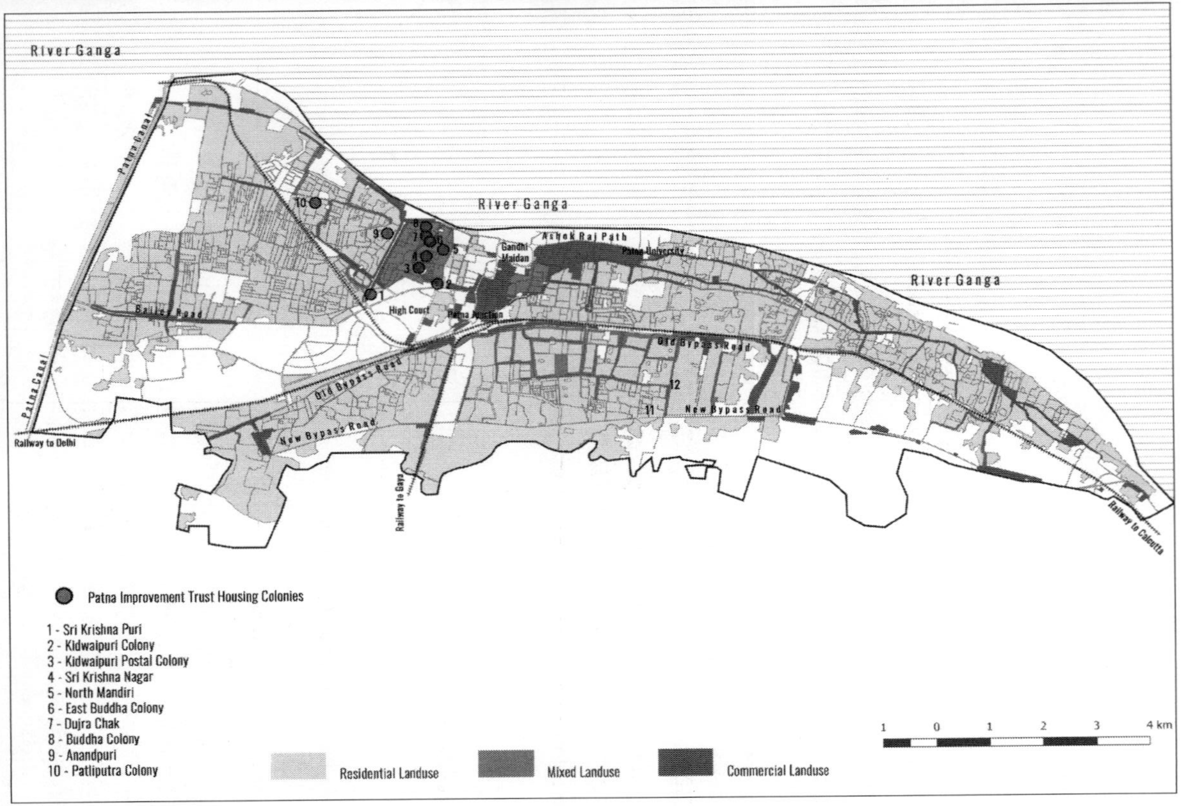

Map 12.2: Housing colonies made by Patna Improvement Trust. Map credit: author

65.26 acres of land from this acquisition and 179 plots were exclusively marked for LIG housing. But the housing board allotted 127 plots to HIG and MIG housing at the beginning of the scheme. And the LIG housing units ended up being much beyond the reach of the intended buyers. Charges of corruption and poor quality of work within a year led to an uproar in the assembly.[16] There were reports of houses being built with mud walls rather than cement.[17] This provided justification for the work to be stopped by the government and land to be sold directly to MIGs and HIGs by the Housing Board. There was also news[18] of plots of bigger size being sold directly by the housing board to HIGs, and in few cases, land meant for public parks were converted into residential land. Speaking about the Sri Krishnagar housing project, Satish—one of the residents whose father was its founding member—says, 'After the initial construction of some 130 houses for LIG category, influential people started coming in this area and soon government changed the land use and allotted MIG plots.' Though Patna Improvement Trust failed in the Srikrishnanagar Housing Scheme, it continued designing 60–80 feet broad roads and demarcating plots towards Boring Road on the western side and Mandiri on the north for selling to MIG and HIG housing schemes in future.

The second housing scheme carved out was a plot of 8.72 acres for the Postal Co-operative Society in 1958. The land was acquired exclusively for this society as a LIG housing scheme. Out of the original demand for ten acres, they were allotted only 8.72 acres of land and after the final disbursement, a mere 5.45 acre was released. The housing board demanded a betterment fee for the construction of a 40 feet wide road before finalising the work. In hindsight, this negotiation and coercion was to save land from LIG allotment in the heart of the city. Satish recalls,

> It paved way for allocation of 3.27 acres of land to Adarsh society. The society had forty-one members and four others plots in the

16 'Srikrishna Nagar or Controversy Nagar', *Searchlight*, Patna edition, 3 March 1964.

17 'Enquiry into Srikrishnanagar colony buildings', *Searchlight*, Patna edition, 25 December 1960.

18 'Our housing colonies: Department is yet muddling through', *Searchlight*, Patna edition, 3 March 1964.

> same society were allocated to other influential people in the city on the discretion of the Housing Board and recommendation from politicians. The Housing Board gave the land on [a] ninety-nine-year lease but for Adarsh society—a housing co-operative of mainly Patna High courts judges and employees—it was transferred with full ownership. Almost all the allocations were done from 1965 to 1970 and were sold at arbitrary prices[19] as there was no systematic categorization and demarcation of land by the Housing Department.

Explaining the implication of this arbitrariness, Satish also says, 'Today if we take out all the land deeds in Srikrishnanagar we can find at least five types of arbitrary rules. It was changed for anyone and anytime.' The original LIG residents of Srikrishnanagar formed an association in 2010 but not everyone agreed to be part of it 'because people are not willing to share the original papers'. As per the original layout, the housing scheme was planned as a closed campus with a boundary wall. In reality, it was never constructed but exists in the files of the housing board. Members of the association complained that even after repeated reminders, the Bihar State Housing Board is reluctant to share the original layout of the Srikrishnanagar scheme.

The selective mechanism of negotiation and regulation was possible because of active political patronage. By the time several of Patna Improvement Trust's housing projects and neighbourhoods had fully developed, state politics had become volatile and offices and positions of power were openly used for seeking and distributing patronage (Frankel 1990).

Encroaching Planned Neighbourhoods

In this section, we look at the housing schemes undertaken by the Patna Improvement Trust and the efforts it made to invigorate the concept of neighbourhood in the city of Patna. It developed two new colonies—Rajendarnagar in central Patna and Sri Krishnapuri on the western side. The rationale for both these settlements were to clear slum pockets from the inner city. The 1962 master plan underlines that its first imperative

19 Bihar State Housing Board, Minutes of the 28th Meeting, 31 March 1974.

is to maintain Patna as the centre of administration. Confirming to the nationalistic agenda, the *Patna Master Plan* (1962) defined one of its imperative as 'to provide for a balanced development of the human intellect along with proper physical growth'. The city planners envisaged Patna city as the fountainhead of human thoughts and repository of the nation's cultural achievements. Therefore, it was imagined that the city is not only a place to live but a place of learning, cultural activities for all age groups and all classes of people. A series of public land acquisition in the 1960s in the new capital area—rationalised based on the master plan—was undertaken to design integrated neighbourhoods in the city. The master plan was approved in 1967 but it failed in getting detailed plans and estimates for particular schemes approved by the government,[20] providing procedural loopholes and ambiguities. It led to frequent instances of mismanagement and delay and were taken advantage off by the department heads and their subordinates. For example, till 1963, residential and commercial plots were auctioned in case of more than one applicant which was advantageous to comparatively wealthy people leading to public resentment. In later years, this practice was abandoned. It was easier for the power close to the *Sachivalaya*[21] who systematically organised themselves as co-operative housing societies and benefited from the state-initiated housing schemes and plot allocation. There were also the *Parviwalas*[22] whose caste relations and access to power made it possible for them to get an allotment. For example, the LSG minister Satyendra Narain Sinha,[23] through the executive officer of

---

20 In twenty-four such instances, expenditures had been made in anticipation of future approval. Often the letter had been sent to the department two to eleven years ago. Schemes and tenders remained for approval with the LSG department for years.

21 A colloquial word to signify clerks and junior officers employed in the government offices who had unhindered access to information and files.

22 In 'Patna the unplanned city' by R. Naryan. As noted by the author, '*Parviwalas*' in Hindi means patronage or recommendation. Article published in *Hindustan Times*, Patna edition, 17 September 1971.

23 There were allegations made that allocations for construction of a swimming pool in Srikrishnapuri and materials sanctioned for the same were diverted for the construction of the minister's wife's house. Officers of Patna Improvement Trust were personally supervising the construction of the house. He also utilised the services of slum officer of the Trust for private work.

Patna Improvement Trust Kameshwar Deo, got allotments for his relations, caste-men and friends in the land acquired for Rajendernagar and Sri Krishnapuri.[24] Materials sanctioned for construction of social infrastructure were diverted for the construction of the minister's house on Boring Road. Several such instances and local politics ensured that the bureaucrats and higher officials in the state government had a free hand in optimising land and public resources for their own benefits. We discuss a few more cases to understand the deviations from the norm in the everyday materiality of urban Patna benefiting the elite actors.

Political and Friendly Collusions

The second large project for the Patna Improvement Trust was Shrikrishnapuri Phase I proposed in the year 1962. The scheme was taken up for execution without government approval and 63.98 acres of land was acquired by the housing department and given to the Trust for construction of LIG houses. Contrary to the assurance given, plots were allotted to MIG and HIG by the Trust without a formal government approval.[25] Even so the government duly approved funds for the construction of these MIG houses in Srikrishnapuri.[26] In total, 158 plots were carved from which only eighty-two plots were given for LIG housing. The Patna Improvement Trust Enquiry Commission report confirms that land was allotted to officers from the Housing Department and the LSG Department. This proves that they had tactic support of the government, even if they claimed otherwise. Patna Improvement Trust also promised to allocate land for LIG housing in its phase II project but land acquisition for it was de-notified in late the 1960s stating paucity of funds and the precarious political conditions in the state. The inquiry commission goes on to note 'execution of these projects would have prevented the growth of slums on a large scale and

24 Report of T.L. Venkataraman Aiyar Commission of Inquiry, 5 February 1970.

25 When the file was sent to the government for approval, it didn't refuse rather directed Patna Improvement Trust to reduce the size of the plot. It implied approval of the government for the layout plan.

26 R.C. Sinha, Ex-chairman Patna Improvement Trust, in reply to the inquiry commission.

should have been persuaded but unfortunately the government has de-notified the land acquisition process for these two projects and the schemes came to an abrupt end'.

The land acquisition by the Patna Improvement Trust was part of the larger scheme of making a complete residential neighbourhood by acquiring land between Boring Road and Boring Canal Road, Patliputra Housing Colony and Patna Dinapur Road. As mentioned earlier, the rationale for land acquisition was said to be clearing of slum and urban obsolesce—both possible only through the development of residential areas on neighbourhood principle.[27] The Srikrishnanagar project had already failed to provide housing for LIG and EWS housing, which the Patna Improvement Trust aimed to compensate for in its new schemes. However, the Trust regretted its mistake of allocating land in Kidwaipuri and Shrikrishnanagar. The chairman of the Patna Improvement Trust noted, '[W]e will not repeat the same mistake. After all, big roads—some eighty-feet [wide]—were running through the area and it would have been ill-advised to locate Low Income houses all along such roads in this area.'[28] The complacency of its officials and ministers in the government made it possible for the Trust to make these departures from the intended plan. Instances of corruption and capturing existed in the ruling party and within ministers in office. The Aiyar Inquiry Commission noted that the Chief Minister K.B. Sahay gave immediate orders to stop land acquisition during the 1967 elections in Patna West Constituency which had been approved on 19 January 1961. He had hoped to appease the landowners in his constituency and secure their votes. This was in relation to acquisition of 407.85 acres of land as mentioned earlier for acquisition for the Srikrishnanagar Housing Scheme. The chief minister noted on 5 February 1967: 'The notifications for parts which have not actually been acquired may be cancelled. We shall consider the case again if the collector sends fresh requisition. We need not remind them.'

27 Bihar Town Planning and Improvement Trust Act, 1954, p. 16.

28 Report of the commission to inquire into the affairs of the Patna Improvement Trust, Patna Municipal Corporation and the Patna Water Board appointed by the Government of Bihar (published in 1969 by the Superintendent Secretariat Press, Bihar).

Some of the deviations (Sundaresan 2017) to the original plan were more systematic and planned. For example, the creation of the Aniket Housing Society[29] by changing the land-use agreement and violating the actual layout by IAS officials. Twenty-seven officials formed this Society in 1980. As per the original layout plan, the plot was demarcated for a shopping complex in the Sri Krishnapuri Cooperative Housing Society. The housing department first tampered with the map in 1962 and converted it for non-commercial land use and instead earmarked the local park for a shopping complex. In 1980 when the allocation was approved, the chairman of the Housing Board was one of the key founding members of Aniket Housing Society, and it was the first decision taken by the board once he was in office.

The Kankarbagh Housing Scheme was initiated in 1954—a total of 597.22 acres of land was acquired in which 237.22 acres was earmarked for public amenities such as roads and parks. The approval for this scheme was made with an intention for slum clearance in Lohanipur and Mahmudi Chak for which 640 single room tenements had to be constructed. The first layout plan for this project was made in June 1961, and by January 1968 it had been modified several times by the Patna Improvement Trust and Housing Department. This severely affected the sewerage, drainage and road network schemes. The tampering of the land-use plan[30] was done frequently by encroaching over the land allotted for roads and public parks. Such encroachments were deftly undertaken by the bureaucratic class who had the necessary network and associational access to power. In one such case, a MIG plot was settled by the Housing Board with a lady whose son was Additional Secretary in the Animal Husbandry Department. The relevant High Court judgement[31] notes,

> It is abundantly clearly that the re-layout, had been done in 1966 for providing eleven more MIG houses. The width of the road had

29 '"Land Loot" by IAS housing co-operative', *Searchlight*, Patna edition, 25 July 1982.

30 Today, Kankarbagh remains one of the most flooded localities in the city due to poor sewerage and drainage construction work done when the scheme began. It is not to be missed that geographically it lies in a *jalla* area, meaning a low-lying part of the city.

31 *Rajendra Sinha and Ors* Vs *State of Bihar*, 1988.

> been reduced from twenty feet to 8–10 feet. He [IAS officer] utilised his contacts and influence and succeeded in not only getting the adjacent strip of land settled but also getting portion of the public road included… [whereas] the Superintendent Engineer, housing board [said] there was no need for another road [so] the chief engineer who appears to have been opposing the proposal finally gave in [...] things were manoeuvred in such a way that large area was ultimately settled [...] on the basis of bogus, untenable and collusive opinions and reports of 'friendly' officers of the Board.

Interestingly the first judgement given by the Patna High Court endorsed this encroachment as 'it was settling of residual lands for useful purpose and saving it from wasting land was itself in the public interest'. This was a classic example of primordial allegiances of the bureaucracy for people within the state machinery to be able to not only capture land but being endorsed by the judiciary too.

Sanctioned Deviations

The most contentious housing scheme was the Boring Road Development Scheme I envisaged in 1956 by the Patna Improvement Trust. Its approval came in September 1963, after several revisions in its financial estimates and plans for service development. A total of 64.49 acres of land was notified for acquisition in Village Dujra. The initial hesitation by the Housing Department was due to financial constraints that delayed the official approval. Meanwhile, private acquisitions had already been made in the notified area. The Patna Improvement Trust believed that the Boring Road Development Scheme was a very useful scheme, which if executed properly, would bring about essential and far-reaching improvements in the newly built-up area of Patna which was otherwise turning into a slum. All along for the same area to be acquired by the Patna Improvement Trust, a housing society called Budha Grih Nirman had sent a requisition to the government for land allocation. The society comprised members who were in authority and wielded a lot of influence in the city. The society was duly allocated 25.2 acres and requested a further allocation of 32 acres in the vicinity. The Inquiry Commission created to look into matters of corruption against the Patna Improvement Trust in 1969 notes a particular incident. According to its report, the secretary and LSG had supported the objection of the Patna Improvement Trust claiming that they should solely be given the acquired area but even then the Society managed to get the aforesaid parcel of land. The allocation of another 32 acres of land in the years to come was settled in an equal complicit manner.

A Vidhan Sabha committee looking into this matter further noted that the Trust was fully aware of the fact that proper sanction to the scheme was not given by the government, and yet the land was allocated to the housing cooperative. It concluded that the said thirty-two acres of land were allotted to people in the most arbitrary manner, many of whom were not even members of the Society at the time of their allotment. The committee directly implicated the then chairman of Patna Improvement Trust Mr B.N. Basu for the said transaction.[32] The land allotted to the Society had been agreed to be released to the urban poor in a decision taken by the state Cabinet on 23 September 1975 but no documentary evidence in its support could be provided to the government. The Supreme Court noted,[33] '[N]on-tractability of the Government order in the Secretariat file must in the circumstances be attributed to the deliberate destruction of the relevant chapters by the interested parties.' The High Court further commented that acquisition proceedings had been initiated in 1961 under the instructions of the government. But for the intervention of an influential person, it is highly improbable that the government would have ordered a stay of the entire land acquisition.

Slum Improvement as an Afterthought

Housing for the urban poor, Scheduled Caste members and municipal workers among others was an integral part of the government's programme in India. The slum clearance and improvement schemes

32 The decision to transfer land by the Trust was taken on 11 January 1975. An agreement was made for it on the same day and the entire process of transfer and registration of the land was completed.

33 *Ajodhya Bhagat and Ors* Vs *The State of Bihar and Ors*, MANU/SC/0035/1974.

introduced in the Second Five-Year Plan was aimed at clearing slums and rehabilitating the evicted families due to land acquisition.

The Patna Master Plan underlined the presence of many large and small pockets of the slum—many of them present for centuries. Predominantly, these slum pockets were in the eastern part of the city. The land-use proposals in the master plan defined its purposes for land acquisition (*Patna Master Plan* 1962) in the following words: 'to curb the mis-use of land so that it will not injuriously affect the interest of the community and prevent slums or over-crowding'. It also said 'to guide the re-use of land for more appropriate purposes for example slum clearance'.

The lack of technical staff and support in the Patna Improvement Trust meant projects related to slum improvements were a financially non-profitable and secondary consideration. As had been discussed earlier, the continuous ambition of the Trust to acquire land for building formal housing in the name of improving slum-like neighbourhoods of Patna meant diversions of funds were frequent. Moreover, after the initial years when it received regular grants from the state government, its financial condition started deteriorating. Under the given circumstances, it was housing for the urban poor that suffered. Though the Patna Improvement Trust had managed to get the master plan approved in 1964, it failed miserably in getting detailed plans and estimates for particular schemes approved by the government. Several of these were for housing schemes meant for the urban poor. The predisposition of the Trust to concentrate on financially profitable or self-supporting schemes pulled them in the direction of housing colony 'development schemes' rather than slum 'improvement schemes'.

The Slum Improvement Scheme was duly approved by the Housing Board in the following slum pockets: Mandiri, Mahmudichak, Salimpur Ahra, West of Rajendarnagar, Sabzibagh, Lohanipur, Jakkanpur, Langartoli and Nawab Bahadur Road. Most of the improvement work remained unimplemented due to lack of funds. The Improvement Trust clearly stayed away from land acquisition for slum improvement and development work because it was non-remunerative and needed additional funds. The uncertainty of matching funds for central government projects and the delayed and sporadic grants by the state government made slum improvement schemes a non-starter from the beginning. For instance, the above projects had to be completed by 31 March 1966, whereas the funds were released in the first week of March 1966. Road and sewerage constructions were completed only in few of these slum pockets. Particularly for drainage and sewerage network projects as well as road widening programmes, land had to be acquired in each of the slum pockets but the work was abandoned due to lack of willingness by the Patna Improvement Trust.

The Patna Improvement Trust in later years failed miserably on financial fronts. The Trust was unable to recover its due of 6,00,000 rupees from the Patna Municipal Corporation and stopped receiving the annual grant of 1,00,000 rupees from the government from 1961. This worsened its conditions. By 1965, the character of state politics changed and accordingly groups seeking patronage leading to large-scale reportage of corruption as highlighted in the Aiyar Commission Report. The ambitious large-scale acquisition during the inception of Patna Improvement Trust and an immediate setting in of complicit practices of deviations from the original plan meant financial roadblocks within a decade. The state politics became a centre of coalition politics thereby increasing the number of patron seekers (Mishra 1980). It led to large-scale corruption both by Patna Improvement Trust officials and politicians. Diversion of funds mid-way from one component to another or from one contract to others led to large-scale financial misappropriation and failure by the Trust to even build planned neighbourhoods for the urban elite.

Conclusion

The central component for neighbourhood planning was land, for which the government acted both as an enabler and a broker. All allotments were completed by the 1970s—a particularly volatile period in the history of state politics in Bihar. While the urban middle class occupied central localities in the city, the urban poor strived at the peripheries of these neighbourhoods. The frequent practice of procedural negligence on behalf of Patna Improvement Trust, which was the nodal agency for planning and implementation in the city, due to indifference of the government and the Trust's own decision making in several cases delayed even the well-intentioned schemes. For examples, in several colony roads, drains and sewerage work was undertaken by the Trust in anticipation of sanction by the government, but it was not duly supported by the state government. The Patna Improvement Trust and Housing Board also lacked rules of accounts procedure due to which financial auditing was neither maintained nor undertaken. The Housing Board lacked clear rules and regulations for allocation of land and housing and functioned through ordinances. Thus, the statutory dependence of the Trust was so high in the state that keeping control over its decision making was easier for the ruling government and seeking favouritism for the politicians possible.

The production of urban Patna itself became s a spatial representation of its caste and class assertions. The political interference and patronage ended up making acquisition of land and its distribution a political tool in the city politics. Vidyarthi (2014) identifies that in the Indian context, though formal planning mechanism was informed by Western planning paradigms, in the local context it was formed more through the instrumentalities of co-option, displacement and assimilation. In a city like Patna, which was an extension of its rural-feudal background the neighbourhood became a site of its caste and parochial networks. The structural, function and association factors for its formation, therefore, needs to be questioned in the discursive history of the city.

References

Boyk, D.S. 2015. 'Provincial Urbanity: Intellectuals and Public Life in Patna, 1880–1930.' Doctoral dissertation, UC Berkeley.

Brown, R.M. 2005. 'Patna's Golghar and the Transformations of Colonial Discourse'. *Archives of Asian Art*, Vol. 55, pp. 53–63.

Chakravartty, A. 2013. 'Territorial Self-fashioning: Place-making in Late 19th and Early 20th Century Colonial India'. Unpublished Thesis. The Pennsylvania State University.

Damodaran, V. 1993. *Broken Promises: Popular Protest, Indian Nationalism and the Congress Party in Bihar, 1935–1946*. Delhi: Oxford University Press.

Das, A.N. 1992. *The Republic of Bihar*. New Delhi: Penguin Books.

Fatima, S. 2018. 'Performing Governance in Urban Patna'. In *Sustainable Urbanization in India*, edited by J. Mukherjee, pp. 95–108. Singapore: Springer.

Fernandes, L. 2004. 'The Politics of Forgetting: Class Politics, State Power and the Restructuring of Urban Space in India'. *Urban Studies*, Vol. 41, No. 12, pp. 2415–2430.

Frankel, F. 1990. 'Caste, Land and Dominance in Bihar: Breakdown of the Brahmannical Order'. In *Dominance and State Power in India: Decline of a Social Order*, Volume I, edited by M.S. Rao, pp. 46–132. Delhi: Oxford University Press.

Frödin, O.J. 2012. 'Dissecting the State: Towards a Relational Conceptualization of States and State Failure'. *Journal of International Development*, Vol. 24, No. 3, pp. 271–286.

Ghertner, D.A. 2011. 'Gentrifying the State, Gentrifying Participation: Elite Governance Programs in Delhi'. *International Journal of Urban and Regional Research*, Vol. 35, No. 3, pp. 504–532.

Glover, W.J. 2008. *Making Lahore Modern: Constructing and Imagining a Colonial City.* University of Minnesota Press.

Gururani, S. 2013. 'Flexible Planning: The Making of India's "Millennium City", Gurgaon'. In *Ecologies of Urbanism in India: Metropolitan Civility and Sustainability*, Vol. 1, edited by A.M. Rademacher, pp. 119–143. Hong Kong: Hong Kong University Press.

Harriss-White, B. 2015. *Middle India and Urban-Rural Development.* New Delhi: Springer India.

Harvey, D. 2010. 'The Right to the City: From Capital Surplus to Accumulation by Dispossession'. In *Accumulation by Dispossession: Transformative Cities in the New Global Order*, edited by Swapna Banejee-Guha, pp. 17–32. New Delhi: Sage Publications.

Jacobs, K. 2001. 'Historical Perspectives and Methodologies: Their Relevance for Housing Studies?' *Housing, Theory and Society*, Vol. 18, Nos 3–4, pp. 127–135.

Jain, S.K. 1989. *Caste and Politics in Bihar.* New Delhi: Commonwealth Publishers.

Jones, R.W. 1974. *Urban Politics in India: Area, Power, and Policy in a Penetrated System.* California: University of California Press.

Karna, M.N. 1981. 'Economic Backwardness of Bihar and Certain Relevant Aspects of Census Data'. In *Studies in Bihar's Economy and Society*, edited by P. Sinha, No. 1, p. 90. New Delhi: Concept Publishing Company.

Kennedy, L. and A. Sood. 2016. 'Greenfield Development as Tabula Rasa: Rescaling, Speculation and Governance on India's Urban Frontier'. *Economic and Political Weekly*, Vol. 51, No. 17, pp. 41–49.

Kishore, R. 2015. 'Urban "Failures": Municipal Governance, Planning and Power in Colonial Delhi, 1863–1910'. *The Indian Economic & Social History Review*, Vol. 52, No. 4, pp. 439–461.

Kohli, A. 1990. *Breakdown in a 'Backward' State: Bihar*. Delhi: Oxford University Press.

Kumar, D.S. 2009. *The Social, Political Processes and the Economic Development of Bihar.* Delhi: Manak Publications.

Kumar, N. 1970. *Bihar District Gazetteers: Patna.* Patna: Gazetteers Branch, Revenue Department.

Kumar, S. 2004. 'New Phase in Backward Caste Politics in Bihar'. In *Caste and Democratic Politics in India*, edited by G. Shah, pp. 235–268. Anthem Press.

Mann, M. 2007. 'Delhi's Belly: On the Management of Water, Sewage and Excreta in a Changing Urban Environment During the Nineteenth Century'. *Studies in History*, Vol. 23, No. 1, pp. 1–31.

Mishra, U. 1980. 'Bihar Politics (1967–1977)'. Doctoral dissertation, Aligarh Muslim University.

Munnings, J.F. 1919. 'The City Beautiful'. *Proceedings of the First New Zealand Town-Planning Conference and Exhibition*, pp. 159–165. Wellington, New Zealand: Government Printer.

Omalley, L.S. 1924. *Bihar and Orissa District Gazetteers Patna.* Patna: Concept Publishing Company.

Patna Master Plan. 1962. Patna: Patna Improvement Trust.

Perry, C.A. 1929. 'City Planning for Neighborhood Life'. *Soc. F.*, Vol. 8, p. 98.

Planning Commission. 1983. *Task Forces on Housing and Urban Development: Planning of Urban Development.* New Delhi: Government of India.

Prasad, R.C. 1976. 'Bihar: Social Polarisation and Political Instability'. In *State Politics in India: Meerut*, edited by I. Narain, pp. 51–67. Meerut: Meenakshi Prakashan.

Rao, N. 2013. 'Community, Urban Citizenship and Housing in Bombay, ca. 1919–1980'. *South Asia: Journal of South Asian Studies*, Vol. 36, No. 3, pp. 415–433.

Roberts, H.M. 2013. 'Architect of Empire: Joseph Fearis Munnings (1879–1937)'. Unpublished PhD thesis, University of Cantebury.

Scriver, P. 2015. *India: Modern Architectures in History.* London: Reaktion Books.

Shanker, U. 2001. *Population Pattern and Urban Development: A Case Study of Patna.* New Delhi: Rajesh Publications.

Shatkin, G. 2014. 'Contested Developments: Enduring Legacies and Emergent Political Actors in Contemporary Urban India'. In *Contesting the Indian City: Global Visions and the Politics of the Local*, pp. 39–64. Wiley Blackwell.

Sinha, A. 1977. 'Class War, Not Atrocities Against Harijans'. *Economic and Political Weekly*, Vol. 12, No. 50, pp. 2037–2040.

Sinha, M.M. 1980. *The Impact of Urbanization on Land Use in the Rural–Urban Fringe: A Case Study of Patna.* New Delhi: Concept Publishing Company.

Sivaramakrishnan, K.C. 1978. *Indian Urban Scene.* Simla: Indian Institute of Advanced Study.

Spodek, H. 2013. 'City Planning in India under British Rule'. *Economic and Political Weekly*, pp. 53–61.

Srinivas, S. 2004. *Landscapes of Urban Memory: The Sacred and the Civic in India's High-tech City.* Orient Blackswan.

Sundaresan, J. 2013. 'Urban Planning in Vernacular Governance Land-use Planning and Violations in Bangalore'. Doctoral dissertation, The London School of Economics and Political Science.

———. 2017. 'Who Is Corrupt and Where Lies Corruption? Thinking with Land-use Planning Violations in Bangalore'. In *The Illicit and Illegal in Regional and Urban Governance and Development*, edited by F.H. Chiodelli, pp. 256–274. New York: Routledge.

Timberg, T.A. 1982. 'Bihari Backwardness: Does Feudalism Frustrate?' *Asian Survey*, Vol. 22, No. 5, pp. 470–480.

Vidyarthi, S. 2014. 'Building a "World Class Heritage City"'. In *Contesting the Indian City*, edited by G. Shatkin, pp. 241–264. Delhi: Orient Blackswan.

Witsoe, J. 2006. *Social Justice and Stalled Development: Caste Empowerment and the Breakdown of Governance in Bihar: India in Transition—Economics and Politics of Change.* Philadelphia: University of Pennsylvania: Center for the Advanced Study of India.

Yadav, S.K. 1986. *Residential and Social Structure: A Study in Urban Social Geography*. Stosius Inc./Advent Books Division.

Afterword

'Neighbours' as Neighbourhoods

AbdouMaliq Simone

The neighbourhood has long captivated, baffled, unnerved and exhausted both analysts and residents alike. As an object of both affection and disdain, of endurance and capture, the breadth of its countervailing connotations, let alone spatial definitions, has propelled many to run for the 'exits', and even here, disputes linger as to when and where specific neighbourhoods are really left behind. As the adage goes, 'You can take the boy [or girl] out of the 'hood, but you can't take the 'hood out of the boy.' Far from neighbourhoods being necessarily 'settled' somewhere or fixed to specific territories of operation, questions as to what makes neighbourhoods themselves are far from settled. What this raises is the possibility that instead of being sedimented as a particular spatial scale or modality of affective or social belonging, it is a processual infrastructure through which critical and discrepant forces and exigencies are 'worked out' in provisional settlements whose spatial parameters, distinctions from and connections to multiple elsewhere are continuously revised, even when the boundaries of demarcation and the internal characteristics of space and inhabitants would appear to remain the same.

This, of course, is the proposition of the book. Sadan Jha and other colleagues show that neighbourhoods are not easily translatable into steady states and standardised forms. For they entail difficult mediations among the needs for proximity and distanciation, for social cohesion and individual specificity, for social order and innovation. There can be no optimal formulaic balances among divergent yet seemingly complementary needs and aspirations. In part, because neighbourhoods are much more than simply the human inhabitants themselves; they are rather a more overarching atmosphere of relationality that is composed of climate, built environments, cultural designs, territorial location, multiple interfaces and material matter of all kinds that constitute both resources, potentialities and waste. In continuous processes of reciprocal 'treatment', all of these elements act on each other, shaping both their natures and implications. Only in detailed examinations of the histories of this reciprocal shaping, the resources available, the exposures of internal practices to a wider realm of scrutiny and the allowable and potential dispositions of what such reciprocal shaping can produce are we able to discern in any instance that proximity means intimacy, distance estrangement or conformity to the intensity of social ties, to cite a few.

If we start with the assumption that everyone must be emplaced somewhere, even temporarily, then under what circumstances and structures do that emplacement take place? How did those emplaced come to the neighbourhood in question, in what numbers and in what conditions? What degrees of volition and compulsion were at work; what choices were available; to what extent did affordability, residential history, common ethnicity, religious or regional identity, occupation, political restriction or economic aspiration play in terms of the inhabitant's locational decisions? How enduring are particular placements for particular populations and persons? What kinds of territorial parameters enabled particular kinds of residence to feel as they were able to exert some measure of control and definition over their situation. One could simply keep going itemising the factors at play, but perhaps it suffices to simply conclude that neighbourhoods are the sociopolitical, infrastructural and material renderings of multiple covariances, of endeavours to reside and convert a residence into something much more than the factuality of 'being there'.

While much attention has been paid in urban sociology to the contested existence of 'neighbourhood effects', that the neighbourhood constitutes at least the semblance of a coherent entity and force capable of imbuing residents with specific capacities and life orientations, there is also the matter of 'affecting neighbourhoods', in other words, bringing about neighbourhoods as either explicit or tacit objectives of concerted action on the part of various actors. While neighbourhood effects have largely been measured in terms of attitudes towards educational attainment, parenting, occupational behaviours, practices of consumption and rates of crime, neighbourhoods are also 'planes of affect', intensities of affiliation, of ways of paying attention, of negotiating co-presence as a choreography of everyday movement and transaction, which cannot be framed by social compacts or norms, and that is less a matter of overt consensus than an implicit and continuous process of mutual adjustments and recalibration. Here, coherence is less a matter of ordered divisions of labour, segmentation of discrete households and physical locales, or economic and administrative functions, but rather the curation of volatility, of ways of exacerbating challenges or conundrums that elicit experiments with problem-solving, that, over time, elaborate a differentiated field of responsiveness, of different ways of doing things that come to fore at various times and circumstances. Here, stability is less adherence to presumptions held in common but a willingness and adeptness to elicit from both human and built environments unanticipated actions and possibilities, with the implicit agreement that failure will not reflect on deficiencies in the collective capacities of the neighbourhood.

Here, neighbourhood is a collective practice of trial and error, of working what is available beyond the apparent terms of use and value. It is a mode of production, not only for the sustenance of the conditions of everyday survival but to harness those efforts in ways that generate surplus value, without that value necessarily being instrumentalised, but rather experienced as an enhanced capacity to do things. This does not mean that neighbourhoods are not subject to debilitating conflicts, to wild displays of parasitism, of entrenched disparities in authority and access to livelihoods. It does not mean that neighbourhood did not enforce often stultifying discipline or were quick to exclude or marginalise differences, or immune from spreading vicious gossip. Certainly, many classic depictions of neighbourhoods will emphasise all of the ways that mutual support comes at the cost of incessant intrusiveness, that vulnerabilities are often preyed upon by unscrupulous brokers and local authorities, that outsiders are regarded with suspicion and hostility, and that useless intensely gendered discriminations are enforced across public and private spheres. These dimensions certainly render neighbourhoods' domains of capture and biopolitical control. Indeed, it is often difficult to make any definitive calculations as to how the benefits of various manifestations of social solidarity and security outweigh the costs of the loss of individual and household autonomy, even when these categorical distinctions are themselves often not clear or culturally generalisable.

But there is something about the notion of neighbourhoods being made up of 'neighbours' that in all instances converts the apparent realities—whatever their limitations—into a domain of potentialities that are embodied in all 'neighbourhood situations'. This may be a matter of how one looks at specific neighbourhoods, from what position and angle. For many neighbourhoods that might appear to be anachronisms: spaces of confinement, repositories of the marginal, enclaves of the rich who have little to do with each other or simply administrative designations. There are substrates of 'strange alliances'—convergences of actors and materials—that constitute a field of interchange and social production under the radar. There can also be tipping points, unanticipated events that prompt neighbourhoods to switch registers in how they operate. While these substrates and tipping points might point to a certain opacity of all neighbourhood life, what I want to emphasise here is that the affective dimension of neighbourhoods—the choreographies of sense and sentiment that etch out circuits of how inhabitant come and go in one another's lives with oscillating proportionalities of involvement, mutual regard and everyday collaboration—make up shifting modes of spatial unity that lends some measure of coherence to the totality of actions taking place.

As such, neighbourhoods represent a form of compromise between the ways in which an appreciable number of inhabitants experience the dimensions of such spatial unity, the administrative apparatuses that have been deployed to designate governable units, and the histories of mapping and popular representation that have been brought into play over the years to designate spaces as neighbourhoods. That said, it is important to reiterate that spaces designated as neighbourhoods perhaps do not exist as neighbourhoods simply by virtue of the dearth of inhabitant that could be properly designated, or self-reported, as neighbours. So that the practice and position of being a neighbour, as something that potentially exceeds any other social category without necessarily replacing it, seems crucial in terms of simultaneously affirming the affecting of neighbourhood and the possibility of neighbourhood effects.

This practice and position of 'being neighbour' then suggests a fundamental equality of value regardless of all other calibrations and statuses. That inherent in the functioning of neighbourhoods is the possibility of inhabitants acting beyond all designated roles, including that of the distinct individual personhood, and where the performance of such a role is such that each neighbour is simultaneously substitutable for any other and irreplaceable. That to be neighbour is a position of mutual encompassment, translation, open-endedness, sameness and singularity.

Here, neighbourhood becomes the platform or domain of being neighbour, and in this collective performance the basic precepts and renderings of where residents are both reconfirmed and defamiliarised. For, in order to reproduce the very grounds of stability and endurance, any entity has to readjust to the volatile worlds outside of itself even when the subsequent disposition seems to look the same as it was before. Unless they succumb to atrophy, all neighbourhoods must continuously remake their interfaces with external worlds; they must support the differentiation of inhabitants and their subsequent networks and affiliations with those outside worlds in ways that enable the continuous provisioning of new ways of doing things and the information required for adaptations. When neighbourhood seems to be stuck in time, when they seem to reiterate calcified practices seemingly out of joint with the larger surrounds or incapable of sustaining long-term households or integrating new ones, then they may cease to be neighbourhoods in their own right and may become appendages to larger or even smaller-scaled territorial organisations in which their apparent sedentariness functions as a foil for reorganisations of spatial economies occurring elsewhere.

Much of these observations are based on an engagement with very particular neighbourhoods over the past years, and in the most recent decade and a half, those of the urban core of Jakarta, Indonesia. Here, the process of being neighbour, more than a kind of concrete abstraction, becomes materialised in the very heterogeneity of built form. While this heterogeneity may represent the divergent income capacities, histories and networks of particular residents, it is also something that exceeds such stratification in the ways in which there is not only co-existence among discrepant forms but an encountering that lends each new dimensions, functions and possibilities.

Lane after lane is replete with mixtures of different materials, designs, formats and construction values that have been deployed to make homes, workshops, businesses, offices, mosques, churches and storage places. There are also highly divergent trajectories of development; some plots have retained their original structures over decades, while contiguous plots have witnessed multiple buildings come and go. Well laid-out grids marking standard plot size may be preserved without alteration. But then in the neighbourhood 'right next door', it is possible to find a frontage bordering the marked streets that mirror these grids, but with an interior behind that has completely taken on a life of its own, precipitated by a few random subdivision of anterior plots that then have been extended laterally in different directions, often housing a class of residents markedly poorer than those who continue to live 'in front'.

Residents play with the textures of the surface; they connect wires and cables across different sites and kinds of ownership and use; they fill-in vacancies and recesses with provisional structures and activities; they 'skip over' interruptions, blockages and cul-de-sacs to expand various projects. While the fabric can look chaotic, ill-managed and often on the verge of collapse and over-use—and indeed often is—there are also incessant recalibrations, adjustments and repair. In order to make discrepant uses and environments work together, there needs to be various negotiations and deals from which it is difficult to exclude inhabitants simply based on their background or identity. These things, too, must be put into play. In other words, they become potential resources for the continuous process of working things out, of managing the tensions and overloads.

In most Jakarta neighbourhoods there were mixtures of purchased, scavenged, recycled and hybridised material inputs, the division and consolidation of plots and structures, micro-incremental and unilateral renovation. In the local economy, there were moves toward intensive specialisation and upscale, multidimensional production; the proliferation of small diversified businesses owned by related families and social networks and the aggrandisement of economic activities under the corporate ownership of previously unrelated entrepreneurs.

Such processes may be largely endemic to the particular structural and historical conditions that precipitated specific trajectories of urban development, but they are nonetheless illustrative of the entangled processes of affecting neighbourhoods and neighbourhood effects as cyclical acts of self-constitution that parallel any top-down imposition of territorial arrangements. Whether this opportunity is taken up, whether the overarching conditions exist for such self-constitution to take place are, of course, critical considerations. That 'neighbourhoods lie in waiting', that they could materialise at any moment for some governmental regimes, is a threat that must be contained, or when the very dynamism of such neighbourhood effects becomes an object of extraction, which in turn compel residents into defensive manoeuvres or lead them to calculate that their interests are best served by not being 'neighbours'. For certainly neighbourhoods have been launching pads for more toxic political processes and have occasioned gentrification and acts debilitating 'renewal'.

After all, neighbourhoods do die or wither away into pale versions of former selves. This is not to say that neighbourhoods by definition must be incessantly dynamic and innovative. After all, the performance of being 'neighbour' could be performed in many different ways. The suggestion here is rather that what runs through all neighbourhoods is the possibility of a discernible, graspable way of inhabitants operating *in concert* that is actually or potentially available to be experienced. This operating in concert functions largely at the level of an affective atmosphere—a matter of witnessing, circumventing, encountering, relaying, cooperating, contesting—that exists parallel to the work of social institutions that informs those institutions, and also constitutes the rhythms of interchange among work, domestic life, leisure, trade and politics. What and how these dynamics are graspable may assume different spatial scales and may be possible in spaces of different sizes and histories. This is more (or less) than a matter of residents' acknowledgement that 'we are all in this together' or 'this is where I come from (or belong)'. Rather it is a more tacit sense that things and inhabitant are enjoined in a common yet ever-changing vernacular of interpreting the 'ins' and 'outs' of everyday life made salient at a unified scale, that whether such vernacular is part of an individual's discourse or not, his or her way of making sense of things, that its existence is at least acknowledged as a common currency, a currency for attaining a sense of having something in common. That no matter the tensions, disputes, inequities and manipulations, that the neighbourhood always exists *in beta*, as both a before and after of all of the accounts of its economic functions, social compositions and status within larger scalar formations.

Neighbourhoods are prototypes of a form of sociality that is yet to be fully resolved, that in its actual operations takes on certain dimensions and complexions, that demonstrates highly variegated proportions of belonging and estrangement, of collective coordination and individuation, yet these matters and demonstrations are only part of what is or could be the story of its existence. This sociality without resolution, without being settled once and for all, makes the neighbourhood a particular kind of settlement that can thus show up across varying spatial registers as a unity in the making. In emphasising this sense of 'in the making', what is important is that this conjoins neighbourhoods that seem 'made' and 'unmade', that neighbourhoods are always in some process of 'making' and it is within this process that neighbourhoods might be found.

About the Editors and Contributors

Editors

Sadan Jha is trained in the discipline of history and his research interests are in the fields of visuality and contemporary urban experience. His books include *Reverence, Resistance and the Politics of Seeing the Indian National Flag* (Cambridge University Press, 2016), *Devnagari Jagat ki Drishya Sanskriti* (Raza Foundation and Rajkamal Prakashan, 2018) and *Half Set Chay aur kuchh Yun Hi* (Raza Foundation and Vani). He has articles in *Economic and Political Weekly*, *Indian Economic and Social History Review*, *History and Sociology of South Asia*, *Journal of Human Values,* etc. He is an associate professor at the Centre for Social Studies, Surat.

Dev Nath Pathak teaches sociology at South Asian University (SAU), New Delhi, and has written on folklore, visual art and anthropology in South Asia. His latest monograph is titled *Living and Dying: Meanings in Maithili Folklore*. He co-edits the journal *Society and Culture in South Asia* (Sage Publications) and is an editorial member of *Journal of Human Values* (Sage Publications). He has several edited and co-edited books to his credit.

Amiya Kumar Das teaches sociology at Tezpur University, Assam. He has co-edited *Investigating Developmentalism: Notions of Development in the Social Sphere* (Palgrave Macmillan, 2019). His main research is broadly in the areas of sociology of governance, development sociology and sociology of health and illness. He also works as a coordinator of Centre for Public Policy and Governance, Tezpur University, and is involved in organic farming.

Contributors

Gauri Bharat is an associate professor, Faculty of Architecture, and program head of Architectural History and Theory at CEPT University, Ahmedabad. Her research interests include understanding how people engage with the built environments and the ways in which people produce, transform and inhabit them. Her latest monograph titled *In Forest, Field and Factory: Adivasi Habitations through Twentieth-Century India* (Sage Publications, 2019). She is also a recipient of the prestigious Graham Foundation Research Grant Award 2019 on 'Modernization Before the Modernists: The Rise of Concrete in Early Twentieth-Century India'.

Rashi Bhargava is an assistant professor in the Department of Sociology, Maitreyi College, University of Delhi. She completed her doctorate from Centre for the Study of Social Systems, School of Social Sciences, Jawaharlal Nehru University, New Delhi. Her research fields include politics and culture in North-East India, political sociology, sociology of gender and urban spaces, sociology of visual culture and disciplinary practices of sociology and social anthropology in South Asia.

Richa Chilana teaches in the Department of English, Maitreyi College, University of Delhi. She recently submitted her PhD thesis titled 'Negotiating the Veil: Purdah in Twentieth-Century Indian English Writing' at Centre for English Studies, Jawaharlal Nehru University, New Delhi. She has an avid interest in gender studies, Indian English writing, post-colonial literature and women's writing.

Abhijit Dasgupta is a teaching assistant and a doctoral student in sociology in the Department of Humanities and Social Sciences, Indian Institute of Technology Bombay (IIT-B). His area of interests includes anthropology of Christianity, sociology of neighbourhood studies and migration studies.

Sheema Fatima is an urban planner by training. Her interest area is urban politics and governance in small and medium towns of India. She is a faculty member of Kamala Raheja Vidyanidhi Institute for Architecture and Environmental Studies (KRIVIA), Mumbai. Her earlier work includes 'Performing Governance in Urban Patna' in Jenia Mukherjee's *Sustainable Urbanization in India*.

Yugank Goyal is an associate professor of economics at OP Jindal Global University, Haryana. He has a doctorate degree from Erasmus University, Rotterdam, and University of Hamburg. While his fields of inquiry and peer-reviewed publications lie at the intersection of regulation, institutional economics and informality, his real passion is in conceptualising institutions. Of late, he helped set-up a rural school in western UP.

Akanksha Kumar is an assistant professor in the Department of History, Janki Devi Memorial College, University of Delhi. She has completed her PhD from Centre for Historical Studies, Jawaharlal Nehru University, New Delhi. Her research interests are caste, partition violence and sociological patterns in the refugees of the partition of India in 1947.

Vijay Kumar is a PhD scholar of history at University of Delhi. His work focuses on Dalit history, labour history and popular culture in modern North India. He has published academic articles in reputed journals and has presented research papers on various aspects of Dalit society.

Sonal Mithal is a conservation architect, artist and educator with a doctoral degree from the University of Illinois at Urbana-Champaign. She is invested in post-humanist feminist inquiry to develop contemporary ecological and/or politically sensitive design thinking. She has created a series of research-based artwork, illustrating the palimpsestic nature of urban history.

Anakshi Pal is a doctoral student in sociology at South Asian University (SAU), New Delhi. Her research interests include sociology of death and dying, emotions and everyday life. She has previously worked as the editorial assistant for the journal *Society and Culture in South Asia*, co-published by the Department of Sociology (SAU) and Sage Publications.

Joyashree Sarma is a research scholar in the Department of Sociology, South Asian University (SAU), New Delhi. Her doctoral thesis examines the question of identity and belonging in the Indo-Bangladesh borderland of Assam. Her research interests are borders and borderland, identity politics, culture, ethnicity and media studies.

Harini Shah is a community architect working in rural and semi-urban spaces in India. Her design philosophy draws inspiration from the traditional wisdom of construction, local materials and vernacular crafts. She has developed her design philosophy that draws from history and contemporaneity of neighbourhoods. She even trains young architects in building such socially (not just climatically) responsive spaces.

AbdouMaliq Simone is a senior professorial fellow at the Urban Institute, University of Sheffield; a visiting professor of sociology at Goldsmiths College, University of London; a visiting professor at the African Centre for Cities, University of Cape Town; a research associate with the Rujak Center for Urban Studies, Jakarta; and a research fellow at Tarumanagara University, Jakarta. He is also associated with the Max Planck Institute for the Study of Religious and Ethnic Diversity.

Index

C